The World's
Most Evil Dictators

The World's Most Evil Dictators

Diane Law

This edition published by Parragon Books Ltd in 2006

Parragon
Queen Street House
4 Queen Street
Bath BA1 1HE, UK

Produced by Magpie Books,
an imprint of Constable & Robinson Ltd
www.constablerobinson.com

A copy of the British Library Cataloguing in Publication Data
is available from the British Library

ISBN-13: 978-1-4054-8826-6

Printed and bound in the EU

1 3 5 7 9 10 8 6 4 2

Contents

Introduction

Dictator, the very word conjures up images of a fearsome being, an absolutist or autocratic ruler who assumes sole power over the state or country of which he is in charge. We visualize human rights abuses, murder, torture, genocide, poverty, and mass graves. The dictator is virtually impossible to remove, all opposition is eliminated, and attempts at democratic elections are rigged. They are the epitome of evil, ruining their countries and, with them, the lives of their peoples. Perhaps, however, things are not so simple. At the start of their rule some dictators have seemed quite benign, even good for their countries. It usually takes a long time for international governments to realize the full truth of what is or has been taking place.

In ancient Rome, 'Dictator' was the title of a magistrate appointed by the Senate to rule the state in times of emergency. The dictator supposedly had absolute rule until the Senate decided that the time of crisis had passed. After such time the state returned to democratic government. As we shall see this was not necessarily always the case.

Modern dictators have also often come to power in times of crisis or emergency. Frequently they have seized power by coup. Some achieved office as head of government by legal means (election) and once in office gained additional extra-ordinary personal powers by inventing them. In particular, they create the power to make laws, without effective restraint by a legislative assembly. Latin American and African nations have undergone many dictatorships, usually by military leaders at

1

the head of a junta. A wide variety of leaders coming to power in a number of different kinds of regimes, such as military juntas, single-party states, and civilian governments under personal rule, have been described as dictators.

Almost all dictators have a compulsive need for enemies. They create lists of people they believe are against them and their regime and then begin a process of eliminating them. This continuously reinforces the 'state of emergency' within the country thereby keeping them in power and in control.

The association between the dictator and the military is a very common one, many dictators take great pains to emphasize their connections with the military and often wear military uniforms. Adolf Hitler in Germany served in the First World War. Mao Zedong was briefly in the army, although he hated it. Robert Mugabe of Zimbawe, Idi Amin in Uganda, Jean Bedel Bokassa in Central Africa, and Pinochet in Chile were all military commanders before taking power of their respective countries by coups. Genghis Khan created an army for Mongolia and the Roman Emperor Caligula was nicknamed 'Little boots' because he followed his father (an army general) into war as a child sitting up front on his father's horse.

There are dictators who have been noted as possibly suffering from some kind of mental instability. Adolf Hitler has been diagnosed as a sociopath and was receiving treatment for syphilis which causes symptoms of paranoia, and severe mood swings. Caligula is documented as having had some form of 'brain fever' (possibly encephalitis or meningitis), after which he was reportedly never mentally quite the same. Ivan the Terrible suffered severe mental illness towards the end of his life after killing his son. Then we come to Idi Amin who was actually insane and on a cocktail of anti-psychotic drugs.

Under Joseph Stalin, the concentration of power in the Communist Party in the Soviet Union developed into a personal dictatorship run solely by him for him. This creation of what is known as the 'personality cult' is another tactic employed by dictators to ensure they remain in power. Whether or not they actually believe it themselves, they create a nation state in which they are virtually deified. Among those who suffer from these delusions of grandeur, often rigging elections in their favour and having their images in every possible place, are Jean Bedel Bokassa, 'Papa Doc' Duvalier, Nicolae Ceauşescu, Robert Mugabe and Mao Zedong. They continuously project an image of themselves as adored by the people they govern, while eliminating all opposition.

Often there are outside factors involved when a dictator comes to power. The USA has covertly funded and aided regime changes in many parts of the world, most notably helping to put Saddam Hussein in power in Iraq and General Pinochet in control of Chile. In both of these cases it was the US's fear of communism that created dictatorships. In Africa, dictators took over after the colonizing European countries withdrew. Unfortunately it seems that many of these dictators ruled by learning from the autocratic power of white minority governments. Robert Mugabe spent ten years in prison because he opposed the white government which was run by Ian Smith. Once Mugabe was in charge, he outlawed all opposition. Of course, this was the system he had grown up with. The extra move from imprisonment to execution was to secure his position even further. Prior to colonization Africa had been a varied collection of tribes and regions and after the British and the French withdrew, those old tribal systems began to come back into play. They are still a source of trouble in Africa today.

Childhood is another factor which historians document as having some responsibility for the adult personality. Many dictators have had troubled or violent childhoods, perhaps enabling them to distance themselves from the reality of the brutality of their own rule. Hitler was often beaten as a child by his stepfather. Vlad Dracul was taken and held hostage by the Turks for nine years where he witnessed many executions and much torture. Ivan the Terrible was orphaned at three and often mistreated thereafter. Nicolae Ceauşescu had a severe stammer to the end of his life and was often mocked for it. Saddam Hussein had no father, a violent stepfather and eventually went to live with a politically influential uncle.

Whatever the reason these men ruled as they did, what is certain is that, collectively, they are responsible for the murder, either directly or indirectly, of tens of millions of innocent men, women and children. Likewise, they employed torture and imprisonment to remove all 'opposition'. In game theory and social choice theory, the notion of a dictator is formally defined as a person who can achieve any feasible social outcome he/she wishes. For the dictators in this book, that outcome was or is still a disaster for the countries over which they ruled.

Emperor Caligula

Ancient Rome was, in a sense, the beginning of the dictator. The title was invented by the Romans and designated an appointed leader in times of crisis. The *dictator* (meaning in Latin emergency commander) was granted special power by the free Roman people of the Republic, because it was recognized that hard times often demanded quick decisions, unimpeded by debates in the Senate. From around 500 BC Rome had several temporary dictators for various reasons. It was, however, not until Rome began to extend its territory into an empire, covering many countries, that it was decided that empires need emperors. From around 100 BC, the Roman Empire had spread throughout the Mediterranean. It is really forward of this date that records exist of the most famous (or infamous) emperors who at the time were some of the richest and most powerful people in the world. Since they usually also came from a military command background, they were often also the most bloodthirsty and the most cruel.

As the mighty Roman Empire expanded throughout Europe, Gaius Julius Caesar returned to Rome in 60 BC, victorious after having led his army as far north as Britain to create Roman settlements. Caesar was elected to consul the same year and formed the first Roman triumvirate government along with Pompey and Crassus. After Crassus was defeated and killed by Parthians around 50 BC, Caesar and Pompey extended what was already a competitive relationship for leadership into a civil war. Caesar began the war in 49 BC, by crossing the

Rubicon as a direct challenge to Pompey. Pompey, defeated by Caesar at Pharsalia in 48 BC, fled to Egypt where he was eventually murdered on the orders of Cleopatra in 47 BC. Gaius Julius Caesar returned to Rome the same year, after conquering Africa, and declared himself as the sole leader of the Roman Empire. In 45 BC he adopted his nephew Gaius Octavius as his heir. Gaius Julius Caesar was, however, overthrown and killed in 44 BC after which Rome created its second triumvirate government consisting of Mark Anthony, Marcus Aemilius Lepidus and Gaius Octavius, now renamed Gaius Julius Caesar Octavianus (Octavian). In 31 BC Octavian, after Mark Anthony challenged Octavian for leadership of the Roman Empire, defeated Mark Anthony and Cleopatra and Egypt became another Roman province. Mark Anthony and Cleopatra committed suicide. The following year, 30 BC, Octavian, now retitled Augustus, became the first Roman emperor. Tiberius, the second emperor of Rome, succeeded him in AD 37.

Roman emperors were not particularly interested in the virtues of restraint. Caligula's predecessor Tiberius, Rome's second emperor who cared for Caligula for most of his early life, went into semi-retirement on the island of Capri in AD 26. Once there, he established a colony of vice including wall-to-wall pornography, and round the clock, highly theatrical debauchery throughout the surrounding countryside. Boys whom Tiberius had selected as 'minnows', stocked his swimming pool ready for whatever act they were required to perform. Caligula spent five years on the island of Capri where Tiberius gave him personal tuition and attention among all this overtly sexual excess.

Caligula was born as Gaius Julius Caesar Germanicus on 31 August, AD 12, at the resort of Antium, the third of six surviving children born to Augustus's (the current ruling emperor) adopted grandson, Germanicus, and Augustus's granddaughter, Agrippina the Elder. Germanicus was son to Nero Claudius Drusus and Antonia Minor, and was also nephew to Claudius (the future emperor). Emperor Augustus had expanded the Roman Empire into a miracle of political and military engineering, extending from the French coast to Palestine and Syria, from Africa and Egypt to Spain and Belgium. There were over 6,000 miles of frontier. Caligula was, therefore, a prominent member of the Julio-Claudian dynasty and was revered as son of Germanicus, the most beloved general of the Roman Empire. He was also a great-grandson of Mark Anthony. As a boy of just two or three, he accompanied his father on military campaigns in the north of Germania and became the mascot of his father's army. His nickname Caligula, meaning 'Little (Soldier's) boot', was a reference to the small boots he wore as part of his costume.

When Tiberius became emperor, Caligula's father, Germanicus, was believed by many to have been Augustus's preferred successor, and the Senate was never happy with Tiberius's lack of co-operation. However, at the time of Augustus's death, Germanicum was too young to assume the office of Principate. As a result, Augustus had promoted Tiberius, with the caveat that Tiberus in turn adopt Germanicus and groom him for office when he was old enough. After a successful campaign in Germany and a triumph in Rome, Tiberius sent Germanicus east to distance him from Roman politics, where he died on 10 October, AD 19. It is claimed that agents of Tiberius, to prevent him from becoming emperor poisoned him. Relations between his mother and Tiberius deteriorated rapidly amid accusations of murder and conspiracy. Caligula's mother died in AD 25, again rumoured to have been killed by members of Tiberius's Senate. Caligula's brothers were publicly disgraced and exiled from Rome, where they eventually died, or were murdered. In general Emperor Tiberius was a very unpopular leader.

After the deaths of his parents, the adolescent Caligula and his sisters were sent to live first with his great-grandmother, and Tiberius's mother, Livia, in AD 27. Following Livia's falling-out with Tiberius and her death two years later, he was returned to his Julian relatives and sent to his grandmother Antonia. In AD 31, as Tiberius reintroduced the crime of treason and its accompanying penalty of execution, Caligula was remanded into his personal care on Capri. It is said that Tiberius was particularly fond of the young Caligula. Suetonius writes of Caligula's servile nature towards Tiberius, and his indifferent nature towards his dead mother and brothers. By his own account, Caligula mentioned years later that this servility was a sham in order to stay alive, and on more than one occasion he very nearly killed Tiberius when his anger overwhelmed him. An observer said of Caligula: 'Never was there a better servant or a worse master!' Caligula proved to have a flair for administration and won further favour with the ailing Tiberius by carrying out many of his duties for him. At night, Caligula would inflict torture on slaves and watch bloody gladiatorial games with glee. In AD 33, Tiberius gave Caligula the position of honorary quaestorship, the only form of public service Caligula would hold until his reign.

Caligula, therefore, as a child, knew very few people who died of natural causes and his life was very unstable. His mother and her parents, sisters and brothers were banished, murdered or condemned for treachery or promiscuity. His father was poisoned, his brothers publicly disgraced and his brother Drusus starved to death in prison. Without parents, the remaining children were shipped from one relative to another. It was around the age of seventeen that Caligula is rumoured to have started sleeping with his sisters. His sister Drusilla, at the time around fourteen, was supposedly his favourite and according to Suetonius, the famous Roman historian and biographer, their grandmother Antonia discovered them in bed together. His first wife, Julia Claudilla, died young.

Undoubtedly, the instability and dubious morality of his upbringing influenced his character. The Romans hoped he would be more influenced by his noble bloodline, since his father Germanicus and Emperor Augustus, his great-grandfather, had been so admired. Unfortunately, the result of his tumultuous childhood was that only the deranged part of his character survived.

Tiberius died in AD 37. In his final years, he had appointed an ambitious outsider named Macro to the position of captain of the guard. Marco was so keen to secure a future in the leadership for himself that he encouraged his wife to sleep with Caligula. It was Macro who helped Caligula to become the third emperor of Rome.

Tiberius fell seriously ill at Misenum on the Bay of Naples. On hearing how serious his illness was Macro rushed to join Caligula at Tiberius's deathbed and between them they removed the imperial signet ring from his finger. Long before Tiberius had actually died, agents had been sent out to the various corners of the Empire to proclaim Caligula as the new Emperor. Tiberius nearly ruined their plans by having a sudden but brief revival and demanding his ring back. Caligula and Macro subsequently smothered him with his own bedclothes until they were certain he was dead. Caligula was already Emperor when he read Tiberius's will which actually named Caligula as joint heir along with another relative Tiberius Gemellus. Backed by Macro, Caligula had Tiberius's will with regards to Tiberius Gemellus declared null and void on grounds of insanity to shut Tibelius Gemellus out of the picture, otherwise he did carry out Tiberius's wishes. Caligula accepted the powers of the Principate as conferred by the Senate, and entered Rome on 28 March amid a crowd that hailed him as 'our baby' and 'our star'.

As stated above, Tiberius had not been a popular emperor and the inclination of the Roman people was to celebrate his death by destroying his body. Caligula had to actually prevent them from throwing Tiberius's corpse into the River Tiber. In accordance with this, in his opening speech, Caligula promised co-operation and respect with the Senate, humbly casting himself as their junior. His appearance was not impressive and as an adult he had become argumentative and a haunted insomniac. Though he himself had been the killer at his end, he openly wept at Tiberius's funeral in a public display of humility and respect. Whatever madness and desires for revenge were in his mind at this time, he managed to keep them under control. He would come back to them some time later.

He made a pilgrimage to retrieve his mother's ashes from

exile and lay them beside Augustus. He had coins made with her image on them and renamed the month of September after his father Germanicus. The laws that the Senate had passed against the descendants of Germanicus were rescinded, the first time such a thing had ever happened in the history of the Roman Empire. He bestowed titles on all surviving members of his family, and had his sisters made honorary vestal virgins. They were even included in a new oath of imperial allegiance: 'I shall not hold myself or my children dearer than I do Gaius Caligula and his sisters.'

Caligula declared an end to the puritan days of Tiberius. In the first months, Caligula's reign was mild and his policies showed some political judgement. He abolished Triberius's treason trials and declared that he had destroyed all the files on suspects kept by Tiberius. Even then though, Caligula took much pleasure in attending punishments and executions and he preferred to have them prolonged. Long before his life on Capri, Tiberius had initially banned the Roman games in the Colosseum, because he regarded them as cruel and degrading. They were now restaged by Caligula in an even more spectacular fashion. The new Temple of the Divine Augustus was opened and dedicated to him with the sacrifice of four hundred bears and the same number of lions.

A few months into his reign in October AD 37, Caligula became very ill and nearly died. Ancient sources, like Roman biographers Suetonius and Cassius Dio, describe Caligula as having a 'brain fever'. The symptoms of Caligula's condition could be attributed to an attack of meningitis or encephalitis. During his illness, a prominent citizen, Publius Politus, tried to prove his love for Caligula by publicly vowing that he would willingly sacrifice his own life to ensure the Emperor's recovery. Another citizen, Atanius Secundus announced he would happily fight a gladiator for the same reason. Rome waited in horror, praying that their beloved Emperor would recover. He became better, but his reign took a sharp turn for the worse. After he recovered, Caligula happily granted the wishes of Publius and Atanius. Publius was dressed up in sacrificial clothing and dragged through the streets by slaves who then hurled him off the Tarpeian Rock and into the Tiber. Atanius, who had never even held a sword, got his wish and the short fight ended in his death. In May AD 37, his grandmother Antonia, who might have been a good influence, died. There were now few people to guide him and it was immediately clear since his 'recovery' that his brain had suffered some kind of permanent damage.

Caligula became extravagant and emotional. He threw money about in lavish style, giving each member of the imperial guard the equivalent of a year's income as a bonus. Initially, he was very much the gay, generous public figure that the people wanted, inclined to kind spontaneous gestures that made them warm to him. Early in his career, he awarded an ex-slave 800,000 sesterces because he had heard that she had refused to inform on her former employer, even under torture. The average income per year was around 1,000 sesterces so this effectively made her a millionaire. He was sending out a message to the Romans: loyalty was a quality to be rewarded but that he also, accordingly, regarded most of them as possibly disloyal. Accordingly, Suetonius reported, 'So much for the prince; now for the monster.'

Caligula was, by now, displaying some signs of insanity including severe paranoia and delusions of grandeur in which he was beginning to think of himself as a god. His paranoia resulted in much unnecessary bloodshed. Silanus, the father of Caligula's dead first wife, Julia Claudilla, suffered from seasickness and politely declined the offer of a boat trip with him. Caligula immediately decided that Silanus was hoping for a shipwreck and dispatched troops to murder him. In despair, Silanus slit his own wrists.

He also had Tiberius Gemellus, whom Tiberius had named joint heir with Caligula, murdered along with his entire family. Tiberius Gemellus had caught a cold and treated himself with some medicine that Caligula presumed to be an antidote to poison. He became furious, believing that Tiberius Gemellus didn't trust him and had both him and his family killed. Macro,

11

who had helped him to power, was killed because Caligula had been sleeping with Macro's wife. He had Macro accused of pimping and then had him executed.

During his illness, Caligula had made his sister Drusilla his heir. For more convenience he freed her from her legal marriage and attached her to a male lover of his, Marcus Lepidus, who through this became heir-designate, though he was later executed for treason.

It became a capital crime not to bequeath the Emperor everything. In AD 39 Caligula revived Tiberius's treason trials. People suspected of disloyalty were executed or driven to suicide. A supervisor of games and beast-fights was flogged with chains before Caligula for days on end, and was not put to death until Caligula was offended by the smell of the gangrene in his brain. On one occasion, when there weren't enough condemned criminals to fight the tigers and lions in the arena, Caligula ordered some spectators to be dragged from the benches into the arena instead, so he could still watch the ensuing sport.

Every pretty young woman whom he did not possess irresistibly attracted Caligula. He would carefully examine women of rank in Rome and whenever he felt so inclined, he would send for whoever pleased him best. He debauched them and left them like fruit he had tasted and thrown away. Afterwards, he would openly discuss his bedfellow in detail with anybody in his court who would listen. His first wife, Julia Claudilla, died young. In the first year of his reign, Caligula attended a wedding and famously accused the bridegroom of 'making love to my wife'. He subsequently ran off and married the bride, Livia Orestilla, himself. Then bored of his conquest, he divorced her after a few days. His rich third wife, Lollia Paulina, had also been the wife of another man. He soon tired of her too but when they divorced he forbade her ever to have sex with another man again. An invitation to Caligula's bed, whether you were male or female, could not be refused. It was also a risky business. He was fond of telling them 'you'll lose this beautiful head as soon as I say so'. He made the older

Milonia Caesonia his fourth wife, in AD 38, when she was already pregnant. The sensual and immoral Caesonia, a former courtesan, was an excellent match for him. Caesonia gave birth to a daughter, Julia Drusilla, whom Caligula considered his own child, because 'she was so savage even in childhood that she used to attack with her nails, the faces and eyes of the children who played with her'.

The court of the Emperor was about as immoral as one could get. As already noted, Caligula was having sexual relations with Marcus Aemilius Lepidus whom he had married to his favourite sister Drusilla. Lepidus also had affairs with Caligula's other sisters. Meanwhile, Caligula forced Drusilla to live with him as his wife, following the practice of the Egyptian pharaohs. Suetonius said that when Drusilla became pregnant, Caligula couldn't wait for the birth of their god-like child and disembowelled her to pluck the unborn baby from her womb. True or not, Drusilla died in childbirth and Caligula lost his mind a little more.

After Drusilla died, in the summer of AD 38. Caligula was too distraught to attend her funeral, at which she was awarded the highest honours ever bestowed on a woman. During a period of mourning he imposed on the city, Caligula made it a public offence to laugh in public or private. He disappeared from Rome for a while only to return unwashed with wild hair, demanding that his sister be made a goddess. One smart citizen was given eight million sesterces after claiming that he saw her ascend to heaven. The Senate, afraid of Caligula's increasing reputation for madness and violence, awarded her her own shrines and priestesses and placed her golden image in the Senate house. Caligula frightened the Senate by telling them that he had spoken to the ghost of Tiberius, who had told him: 'Show no affection for them and spare none of them. For they all hate you and pray for your death, and they will murder you if they can.'

The next year, AD 39, Caligula had Marcus Aemilius Lepidus murdered. In addition, he had his sisters Livilla and Agrippina the younger, Nero's mother, exiled to an island, and

13

confiscated their possessions. In the same year, he reinstated Tiberius's treason trials. Next, he produced the secret files of Tiberius that he claimed to have destroyed, he investigated the public trials of his family under Tiberius and discovered that the same senators who grovelled to him had also accused and passed sentence on his dead relatives. He arranged the killings as rich pieces of theatre for himself. Parents were forced to attend the execution of their children, and Caligula would sometimes invite them to dine with him afterwards. One senator, thrown to the lions, insisted on his innocence. He was rescued, only for his tongue to be cut out before he was thrown back. Caligula had the limbs and bowels of another stacked in front of him as he was mutilated. He favoured slow killings, ordering the executioner to 'strike so that he may feel he is dying'.

After his extravagant spending, the realization that he was running out of money gave added impetus to the endless treason trials. He increased his income by beheading the rich and confiscating their estates. When one victim was discovered to have been bankrupt, Caligula said, 'he might as well have lived'. The crimes they were accused of were of little consequence to him.

He had no concept of the value of money and the scale of his extravagance is hard to grasp. Tiberius, who had been miserly by nature, left after his death, nearly three billion sesterces in the state coffers, the equivalent of six years of state revenue. Caligula spent it in one year. He would spend ten million sesterces on a single dinner. The various kings deposed by Tiberius were restored, and their lost revenues restored to them. One received a hundred million sesterces, a quarter of the entire Empire's annual revenue.

Eventually, on a trip to Lyon in Gaul, he was informed that he had bankrupted the state. He promptly sold off his divine sister's possessions. This proved so lucrative that he had the entire contents of the palace shipped from Rome, and ran a series of auctions. At these he compelled the country's richest men to buy family souvenirs at vastly inflated prices, introducing each item with a tag such as 'this belonged to my mother', or 'Augustus received this from Anthony'. Back in Rome, he auctioned off various gladiators. One man fell asleep at an auction only to wake to find he had purchased thirteen gladiators costing him nine million sesterces.

His quest for extra money continued. On one occasion in Lyon when he was gambling, he ordered that the public census list of Gaul to be brought to him and selected a few wealthy men from the list of inhabitants. He ordered their deaths on the basis that he would inherit their estates. Jokingly, he pointed out to his gambling companions that they had been playing for a few denarii, whereas he had just earned a hundred and fifty million.

Eventually, the Senate became almost too terrified to meet. When it did, the senators spent all their time pathetically praising Caligula in the hope they would be spared. Caligula didn't care what they thought of him, in his own eyes he had become omnipotent. 'Let them hate me, so long as they fear me,' he said. By now it wasn't simply the senators or those he imagined were treasonous or those whose wealth he wanted that he killed. Anyone who disappointed him or irritated him faced torture and execution. He could do whatever he liked.

Invasion and conquest were other ways in which he decided to express his imperial powers. He went north to Germany trying to take on the Huns. He couldn't find any so sent his own German bodyguards across the Rhine, so that his other troops could chase after them and bring them back as enemy captives. He had any Germans in his army hide in bushes and trees so he could personally find them and force them to surrender. In moments of insecurity he would abandon the elaborate hide-and-seek and call the legions together to order them to hail him Emperor.

After Germany he turned his attentions on Britain. He assembled his entire forces along the French coast, looking out over the Channel. After an enormous wait, the troops were told to embark on ships but no sooner were they at sea than they were told to turn back again on the orders of Caligula, who retreated to a tower and demanded that a charge be sounded. Afterwards, the soldiers were told to gather up seashells in their clothing and helmets. Wagonloads of these, named by Caligula as the spoils of victory, were returned to Rome along with a few Gauls whom he dressed up and displayed as Germans and Britons.

Eventually, arbitrary murder and international conquest was not a sufficient test of his authority and as his gestures became grander, he demanded a confrontation with heaven. Caligula decided to proclaim his mastery of the sea by building a three-mile-long bridge of boats across the Bay of Naples. In a two-day festival, he crossed them on horseback, wearing the breastplate of Alexander the Great. Thus, he claimed that, like the god Neptune, he had ridden across the waters. He gave a speech in which he praised himself for building the bridge and his troops for their courage for walking on water. He declared that the calmness of the sea indicated that the gods themselves were now afraid of him and considered him at least their equal, if not their better.

As his delusions of grandeur increased, Caligula demanded that he be worshipped as a god. Caligula's self-indulgence in his supposed divinity became another large part of his insane behaviour. He was convinced that he was entitled to behave like a god. In conviction of his deity, he set up a special temple with a life-sized statue of himself in gold, which was dressed, each day, in clothing such as he wore himself. Becoming even more extravagant, he gave his horse Incitatus jewelled necklaces, a marble stable with furniture and a staff of servants to itself. He made it a priest of his temple and even proposed to make it a senator. He claimed fellowship with the gods as his equals, identifying himself in particular with Jupiter, but also with female gods like Juno, Diana or Venus. Caligula once asked the actor Apelles whether Jupiter or Caligula were greater. When Apelles hesitated, Caligula had him cut to pieces with a whip. Caligula watched, praising his voice as he pleaded for mercy, remarking on the tunefulness of his groans. He justified himself by saying: 'Remember that I have the power to do anything to anyone.'

Caligula built new quarters on the Capitoline Hill in order to be close to his 'brother', Jupiter, whom he challenged to a duel when thunder interrupted a pantomime he was watching. He even had a bridge constructed between his palace and Jupiter's temple. He forced his family and various senators to pay him ten million sesterces each for the privilege of becoming his priests. He had always loved dressing up, especially as a woman, but now he began dressing as the gods, taking on whichever deity he fancied. He couldn't decide which god he was, so he tried out each of the male ones and then appeared as Juno, Diana and Venus. Everybody had to prostrate himself or herself in his presence and the living had to grovel among the dead on the floors of his palace. He made it a crime to look down on him from above, and not to leave him everything in a will. To the Roman people, this was considered nothing less than blasphemy. He decided he could make love to the moon. A provincial governor, Lucius Vitellus, encountered Caligula during one of his 'conversations' with the divine planet. Caligula asked him if he too had seen the goddess. Vitellus saved his own life by replying that 'Only you gods, Master, can see each other.'

He had many Jews put to death, enraged at their refusal to worship him, and ordered his image to be placed in the temple at Jerusalem. This very nearly caused a provincial war and eventually, reluctantly, he backed down. His good friend Herod Agrippa persuaded him to abandon the idea.

Now he was a god he dined in splendour with his favourite horse, Incitatus, serving loaves of gold bread to his guests. Incitatus, with his marble stable, became his most trusted adviser. Caligula highly valued loyalty and announced that he intended to make the horse a consul of the Roman people, as a preparatory step to full senatorial rank and eventual rule over the Empire. He was clearly quite mad and even those who were forced to be afraid of him could see, in the end, that they had to do something to get rid of him for good.

His eventual assassins were senators, tribunes and prefects from the Imperial Guard, all close associates of Caligula. One tribune, Cassius Chaerea, had a particular grudge against Caligula. Cassius had to obtain a new password from Caligula every day, and Caligula had taken to choosing sexually explicit ones to mock him. According to Suetonius, Chaerea had experienced years of abuse by Caligula over his so-called effeminacy (he had a high, effeminate voice which Caligula constantly imitated), possibly due to a wound to his genitalia during his time in the army. Suetonius records that Caligula commonly gave watchwords such as 'Priapus' (erection) or 'Venus' (Roman slang for a eunuch) when Chaerea was on duty. Thus, Cassius had become a laughing stock. Another of the conspirators was Cornelius Sabinus, whose wife had been debauched and publicly humiliated by Caligula.

What is known about Caligula's assassination is that on 24 January, AD 41, the Praetorian Tribune Cassius Chaerea and other guardsmen accosted Caligula while he was addressing an acting troupe of young men during a series of games held for the Divine Augustus. Chaerea had a distinguished record as one of Germanicus's best officers and had known Caligula since infancy. Chaerea requested the watchword from the Emperor and, after Caligula's response, struck the first blow. The co-conspirators quickly moved in and stabbed the Emperor to death, according to Josephus's account, only a few feet away from his guard and entourage. By the time Caligula's German guard responded in a rage by attacking the co-conspirators and innocent civilians alike, the Emperor was already dead. It is believed that the final blow was to Caligula's genitalia, delivered by Chaerea. Chaerea and another aggrieved tribune, Cornelius Sabinus, also stabbed and killed Caligula's wife Caesonia and killed their infant daughter, Julia Drusilla, by smashing her head against a wall.

Caligula's behaviour, caused by conflicting emotions and thoughts, would possibly be diagnosed today as schizophrenia. The absolute power that Caligula enjoyed strengthened and developed the worst features of his character. His grandmother, Antonia, and his sister Drusilla, who could have had a calming and restraining influence on him, died during the first two years of his reign – his grandmother in AD 37 and his sister in AD 38. The near-extinction of his family and the subsequent fear for his own life during his adolescent years will surely have marked his personality. However, Caligula's madness was very likely to have been organically influenced, because it was said to have become apparent after his serious illness in October AD 37. Some historians believe the disease he suffered from was encephalitis. If true, this could very likely have been a contributory factor to the new and bizarre features of his behaviour. Encephalitis can cause a marked character change and give rise to impulsive, aggressive and intemperate activity, similar in its symptoms to those of schizophrenia.

According to Suetonius he 'often sent for men whom he had secretly killed, as though they were still alive, and would then remark off-handedly a few days later that they must have committed suicide'. Seemingly he often forgot what orders he had sent out, even those sentencing people to death. The lack of a full accounting of Caligula's reign, and the hyperbolic nature of the records that do remain, creates several problems for a fully corroborated historical account. Also, it must be noted that all historical writings regarding Caligula are authored by Romans of senatorial rank, a class of individuals whose power had been severely checked by the growth of the Principate. For many ancient critics and historians on Roman politics, sexual perversity was often offered as a reason for or as a result of poor government. Suetonius accuses Augustus, Tiberius, Caligula, and Nero all equally of sexually perverse behaviour. He is also highly critical of many of the administrative aspects of these emperors' rules. However, it has been recorded in other ancient sources that much of what we would consider sexual perversity in today's society would be considered relatively normal two thousand years ago. Perhaps it is difficult to gain a balanced view on the lives of the Romans from our position in the twenty-first century. Regardless of the validity of any of the surviving anecdotes, historians tend to agree that Caligula was extremely unqualified and unprepared to be Emperor. His upbringing had been unstable, his emotional needs mostly ignored.

Given Caligula's famous unpopularity as Emperor, it is difficult to separate fact from fiction. What we do know is that Suetonius wrote that Caligula's four-year reign of terror had been so severe that the Romans refused to believe that he was actually dead until they could view his body themselves.

Genghis Khan

Genghis Khan was undoubtedly the greatest conqueror of all time, his empire at its peak being at least four times that of Alexander the Great. These conquests were achieved by practising benevolence towards those who sided with him, and inspiring terror and annihilating those who opposed them.

Genghis Khan was seen as such a force of destruction, that Muslim writers from Persian nations whose cultured empire Genghis Khan destroyed seven centuries ago still refer to him as 'The Accursed'. Many of the cities he razed in China, the Middle East and the Caucasus have never recovered their former status. Some have never been rebuilt and their ruins remain in eerie desolate silence – the silence of a place where all living things have been slaughtered. Indeed, in many places all living things (including animals) were massacred on Genghis Khan's orders.

However, while his image in most of the world is that of a ruthless bloodthirsty conqueror, Genghis Khan is an iconic and admired figure in some parts of Mongolia and China. He is seen as the father of the Mongol nation (now Mongolia) and precursor to united China under his grandson Kublai Khan. He became known as the Mongol political and military leader or Khan (posthumously Khagan) who had united the Mongol tribes and founded the Mongol Empire (1206–1368), the largest contiguous empire in world history. Genghis forged a powerful army, based on meritocracy, to become one of the most successful military leaders in history.

The advance of the Mongol hordes is one of the most significant historical events of the last thousand years. Quite apart from the destruction they wreaked, they completely altered the distribution of people, wealth and disease within the known world. But the early home life of Genghis Khan is something of a mystery.

Genghis Khan was born sometime around 1162 on the banks of the Onon River, in the mountainous area of Burhan Haldun in Mongolia. His name at birth was simply Temüjin. Little is known about Temüjin's early life, and the few sources providing insight into this period do not agree on many basic facts. At the time of his birth, the Mongols were a collection of nomadic tribes, with occasional, but unreliable alliances. Among them, his father was a leader of a sizeable group of clans. They lived on the move, in tents, and had no conception of organized town life. In fact, they could see no virtue in society as understood by others, which partly explains their lack of remorse in destroying everything they overran. His father died when Temüjin was nine, poisoned by some Tartars. Temüjin's early life was spent in struggle with poverty. His father's death had broken up the clan alliance and many tribes refused to swear allegiance to the boy. According to Mongol legend, he began his rise to power with only two arrows to his name. His mother succeeded in holding some allies together and he also received some protection from a blood brother of his father. His mother's counsel saved him many times. Mongols were polygamous but women were also regarded as wise companions, who wielded considerable influence through their advice, which was frequently sought.

Legend stated that when Temüjin was born he clutched a blood clot or 'a stone the colour of coagulated blood' in his fist, a divine sign that he was destined to do great things. Before becoming a Khan, Temüjin united the many nomadic tribes of north-east and central Asia, which he had not eliminated, with a common social identity as 'Mongols'.

Temüjin married Börte of the Konkirat tribe around the age of sixteen; they had been betrothed as children by their parents as a customary way of forging a tribal alliance. She was later kidnapped in a raid by the Merkit tribe, and Temüjin rescued her with the help of his friend and future rival, Jamuqa, and his protector Ong Khan of the Kerait tribe. She remained his only Empress, although he followed tradition by taking several morganatic wives. Börte's first child, Jochi, was born roughly nine months after she was freed from the Merkit, leading to questions about the child's paternity. Temüjin became blood brother with Jamuqa, and thus the two made a vow to be faithful to each other for eternity. Becoming 'blood brothers', mixing drops of each other's blood, was common practice in Mongol tribes and was meant to create a lasting unbreakable bond.

He consolidated his empire through numerous conquests including the Khwarezmid Empire in Persia. Genghis Khan laid the foundations for an empire that was to leave an indelible mark on world history. Several centuries of Mongol rule across the Eurasian landmass, a period that some refer to as 'Pax Mongolica', radically altered the demography and geopolitics of these areas. The Mongol Empire ended up ruling, or at least briefly conquering, large parts of modern-day China, Mongolia, Russia, Ukraine, Korea, Azerbaijan, Armenia, Georgia, Iraq, Iran, Turkey, Kazakhstan, Kyrgyzstan, Uzbekistan, Pakistan, Tajikistan, Afghanistan, Turkmenistan, Moldova, Kuwait, Poland and Hungary.

It was not that he took any pleasure in the business. The Mongols were very systematic and pragmatic about the slaughter. They simply wished to secure themselves against any uprising behind them, as they advanced. The population always outnumbered their army, so they readjusted the odds. There was also the obvious psychological spin-off, in that the terror the news of these tactics inflicted on the next city understandably reduced the will of the defenders they would meet at the next city. Frequently they offered to surrender so they might be spared. Often, the Mongols would agree and then kill them anyway. To them, this was just good military sense.

Once they had taken a city, either by siege or subterfuge, there followed a fairly standard form of behaviour. First, they plundered everything in a very democratic fashion and drove the population outside the city walls, where they would be assembled and men and women divided. If any of the men had useful skills, they might be enslaved and returned to Mongolia. Other young men would sometimes be taken for military purposes. These men became used as unarmed cannon fodder in their assaults, the Mongols would head several thousand of them in front of their own army as they swept down on their enemy. The remainder would be killed, generally decapitated, and their heads stacked in neat pyramids. The women, almost without exception, were raped. A few might be taken for slaves or concubines, and then the rest were also killed. If an example were to be made of a particular city, then no one would be spared for any purpose. The inhabitants might be driven out through a gate and decapitated as they walked through it, in a sort of ghastly conveyor belt of death. Sometimes each Mongol soldier was designated a number of executions to perform, which on occasion could be as high as five hundred men. These mass executions could take days to perform, even with the famous stamina of the Mongol troops. This was particularly true if the order was given that no living thing was to escape. All livestock, goats and sheep, even cats and dogs, were executed and babies in the womb were run through with swords. This was all performed in a much practised, highly disciplined fashion. At the end of the siege, the city would be set on fire or flooded if conditions permitted. The cities were left barren, often barely inhabitable. If the siege left them starving, whole populations sometimes resorted to cannibalism.

Temüjin began his slow ascent to power by offering himself as a vassal to his father's blood brother Toghrul, who was Khan of the Kerait and better known by the Chinese title Ong Khan (or 'Wang Khan'), which the Jurchan Empire granted him in 1197. This relationship was first reinforced when the Merkits captured Börte, it was to Toghrul that Temüjin turned for support. In response, Toghrul offered his vassal 20,000 of his Kerait warriors and suggested that he also involve his childhood friend Jamuqa, who had himself become Khan of his own tribe, the Jajirats. Although the campaign was successful and led to the recapture of Börte and utter defeat of the Merkits, it also paved the way for the split between the childhood friends, Temüjin and Jamuqa.

Toghrul's son, Senggum, was jealous of Temüjin's growing power and he allegedly planned to assassinate Temüjin. Toghrul gave in to his son and adopted an obstinate attitude towards collaboration with Temüjin. Temüjin learned of Senggum's intentions and eventually defeated him and his loyalists. One of the later ruptures between Toghrul and Temüjin was Toghrul's refusal to give his daughter in marriage to Jochi, the eldest son of Temüjin, which signified disrespect in the Mongol culture. This act probably led to the split between both factions and was a prelude to war. Toghrul allied himself with Jamuqa, Temüjin's blood brother, and when the confrontation took place, the internal divisions between Toghrul and Jamuqa, as well as the desertion of many clans to the cause of Temüjin, led to Toghrul's defeat. This paved the way for the fall and extinction of the Kerait tribe.

Next, Temüjin decided that his new direct threat was from the Naimans, with whom Jamuqa and his followers took refuge. The Naimans did not surrender, although enough sectors again voluntarily sided with Temüjin. In 1201, a Khuriltai elected Jamuqa as Gur Khan, universal ruler, a title used by the rulers of the Kara-Khitan Khanate. Jamuqa's assumption of this title was the final breach with Temüjin, and Jamuqa, his blood brother who had sworn allegiance to Temüjin for ever, formed a coalition of tribes to oppose him. Before the conflict, however, several generals abandoned Jamuqa, including Subutai, well-known younger brother of Jelme, one of Temüjin's future generals. After several battles, Jamuqa was finally captured in 1206 after several shepherds kidnapped him and turned him over to Temüjin.

According to *The Secret History of the Mongols*, Temüjin generously offered his friendship again to Jamuqa and asked him to turn to his side. Jamuqa refused and asked for a noble death, that is, without spilling blood, which was granted (his back was broken). The rest of the Merkit clan that sided with the Naimans were defeated by Subutai (or Subedei), a member of Temüjin's personal guard who would later become one of the greatest commanders in the service of Genghis Khan. The Naimans' defeat left Genghis Khan as the sole ruler of the Mongol plains. All these confederations were united and became known as the Mongols.

By 1206, Temüjin had managed to unite the Merkits, Naimans, Mongols, Uyghurs, Keraits, Tatars and disparate other smaller tribes under his rule through his charisma, dedication and strong will. It was a monumental feat for the 'Mongols' who had a long history of internecine dispute, economic hardship, and pressure from Chinese dynasties and empires. At a Kurultai, a council of Mongol chiefs, Temüjin was acknowledged as 'Khan' of the consolidated tribes and took the title Genghis Khan, meaning 'Perfect Warrior'.

Genghis Khan had amassed considerable military expertise after all those years of warring. Early explorers noted that there was remarkable discipline among his troops. Discipline was the main feature of the Mongol world that developed under Genghis Khan. Although frequent drunkenness on the obligatory fermented mare's milk was a traditional and substantial part of life, there was little serious quarrelling or crime among the Mongols themselves, once the warring tribes had been united. They reserved murder for their enemies. Loyalty was highly prized, with oaths sealed by the drinking of blood and the ceremonial slaughter of horses. The vast and impeccably co-ordinated military operations that Genghis Khan was intending to undertake depended upon skills that were perfected in the huge hunting expeditions the clans would make. The Mongols ate mainly meat. They were happy to chew on anything be it rabbit, rat or wolf. They had a particular fondness for horsemeat but seeing as their army was horse-riding cavalry, their way of life depended on the tough stocky horses, so they only ate them in dire circumstances. The meat from these horses was apparently so tough that it could be inedible unless softened up a bit. The Mongols would stick the meat under a saddle and ride until the meat was tender from the weight of their thighs. For the Mongols and their various superstitious ways, one of which was that since they revered the spirit of water, it was considered sacrilege to wash clothes, cooking utensils or bodies in water. Their personal hygiene was non-existent, so this meat must have been pretty awful when they did eventually get around to eating it.

The hunts could take one to three months. The entire Mongol army was sometimes deployed. The whole army, even at its greatest strength and including various auxiliaries, slaves and reserves, was probably never greater than 120,000. It is unlikely that the total population of the region was more than around 500,000. On a great hunt, the army would cordon off an area occupying thousands of miles. Then, slowly but surely, they would begin to herd every living creature, over hill and through forest, towards a central killing ground no bigger than nine square miles. Lions, wolves, bears, deer, yak, asses and hares were driven together in their hundreds and thousands, killing, mating, panicking, eating and sleeping. No killing whatsoever was allowed until Genghis Khan arrived at the scene with his entourage and wives and took up a good position from which to overlook the entertainment. After he gave permission for the hunting to begin, the chase, slaughter, and feeding and general festivities would go on for days.

The Mongol Empire created by Genghis Khan in 1206 was bordered on the west by the Western Xia Dynasty and to the east and south was the Jurchan Dynasty also known as the Jin Dynasty. The first object for this new military force was for Genghis Kahn to organize his people and his state to prepare for war with Western Xia, or Xi Xia. This was closest to the Mongol border. He also knew that the Jurchan Dynasty had a young ruler who would not come to the aid of Tanguts of Xi Xia. Indeed, this is exactly what happened.

From 1206 to 1211, Genghis Khan marched on through the

neighbouring Tangut territory towards China, about which he accumulated as much military intelligence as he could.

Eventually, Genghis Khan led his army against Western Xia and conquered it, despite initial difficulties in capturing its well-defended cities. By 1209, the Tangut Emperor acknowledged Genghis as overlord.

The Jurchan or Jin Dynasty of China considered themselves the masters of the Mongolian steppes. The Jurchan had also grown uncomfortable with the newly unified Mongols. It may be that some of their trade routes ran through Mongol territory, and they might have feared the Mongols might eventually restrict the supply of goods coming from the Silk Road. On the other hand, Genghis Khan also was eager to take revenge against the Jurchen for their long subjugation of the Mongols. For example, the Jurchen were known to stir up conflicts between Mongol tribes and had even executed some Mongol Khans.

In 1211, Genghis set about bringing the Nüzhen (the founders of the Jurchan Dynasty) completely under his dominion. The commander of Jurchan's army made a tactical mistake in not attacking the Mongols at the first opportunity. Instead, the Jurchan commander sent a messenger, Ming-Tan, to the Mongol side, who, probably for fear of his life, promptly defected and told the Mongols that the Jurchan army was waiting on the other side of the pass. At this engagement, fought at Badger Pass, the Mongols massacred thousands of Jurchan troops. When the Taoist sage Ch'ang Ch'un was travelling through this pass to meet Genghis Khan he was stunned to see the bones of so many people scattered on the ground. On his way back he stayed close to this pass for three days and prayed for the departed souls. The Mongol army crossed the Great Wall of China in 1213, and in 1215 Genghis besieged, captured, and sacked the Jurchan capital of Yanjing (later known as Beijing). This forced the Jurchan Emperor Xuanzong to move his capital south to Kaifeng.

In 1214, Genghis Khan said to the Jurchen Emperor: 'By the decree of heaven you are now as weak as I am strong. But I am willing to retire from my conquests . . . as a condition of my doing so it will be necessary for you to distribute largesse to my officers and men to appease their fierce hostility.'

The Emperor appeased them with 3,000 horses, two loyal princesses, five hundred young men and girls, a herd of white camels and as much swag as they could carry. Genghis Khan went back to Mongolia, leaving an army to mop up. However, the Jurchen were not completely subdued, since their leader merely moved south and the war with China went on long after Genghis Khan's death.

Back in Mongolia, Genghis Khan came up against his old enemy Kushlek, the Naiman clan's Khan. Kushlek had ingratiated himself with his hosts, the Khitian Tartars, and then, in an act of treachery, enlisted the help of the Persian neighbours to then usurp the existing ruler who was forced to abdicate in favour of his former guest, Kushlek. By this time the Mongol army was exhausted from ten years of continuous campaigning in China against the Tangut and the Rurzhen. The operation against China was highly successful, with a string of victories encouraging desertion to the Mongolians. The terror that went in advance of them persuaded garrisons to surrender without a fight. Kushlek would remain a thorn in Genghis's side, and had to be defeated. The army, split into three prongs, moved with phenomenal speed. Genghis sent only 20,000 soldiers against Kushlek, under a brilliant young general, Jebe, known as 'The Arrow'.

Genghis Khan expected unwavering loyalty from his generals, and granted them a great deal of autonomy in making command decisions. Muqali, a trusted general, was given command of the Mongol forces against the Jurchen Dynasty while Genghis Khan was fighting in Central Asia. At the same time, Subutai and Jebe were allowed to pursue the Great Raid into the Caucausus and Kievan Rus, an idea they had presented to the Khagan on their own initiative.

Mongol agents, leaving the Naiman forces open for Jebe to overrun the country, incited an internal revolt against Kushlek; Kushlek's forces were defeated west of Kashgar. Kushlek fled, but was hunted down by Jebe and executed. As Kushlek counted as nobility and it was forbidden to shed the blood of nobles, Genghis had him suffocated under a pile of carpets. Genghis Khan annexed the Persian kingdom of Kara-Khitan for the Mongol Empire. A curious consequence of this was that, for a brief time, Genghis Khan became something of an Islamic hero. Kushlek had treated the Muslims of his hijacked realm badly, but Genghis Khan and his Mongol hordes were tolerant in matters of religion. When not under orders to massacre, the Mongols could be very easygoing, preferring parties to pogroms. However, his position as saviour of the Muslim world did not last long.

Genghis's territories now extended up to the border with the Khwarizm Empire of eastern Iran/Iraq. Genghis was keen to establish trade links with other nations; trade was also another means of diplomatic dialogue with these nations. After an encounter with merchants from the Khwarizm Empire, he sent a Mongol delegation back to the Khwarizm ruler, Shah Mohammed, with a message of intended peace couched in evocative terms: 'We have . . . dispatched to your country, a group of merchants in order that they may acquire the wondrous wares of those regions; and that henceforth the abscess of evil thoughts may be lanced by the improvement of relations. And agreement between us and the pus of sedition and rebellion be removed . . .'

If the delegation bearing this message had reached Mohammed, who was keen on peace and trade, the Mongol advance might have stopped right there, instead the Mongol army would eventually come to the very doors of Europe. The result of this was that several million more people would die. Unfortunately, what followed the delegation being sent with their message was probably one of the more significant mistakes in all history.

At the border town of Otrar, the governor was a rather stupid, suspicious and greedy man named Inaljuk. He didn't bother to check the official position with Mohammed before massacring the delegation on the grounds that they were spies, and seized their goods. Inaljuk was apparently ignorant of any proposed dialogue between Mohammed and the Mongols.

Genghis Khan was furious. He demanded apology and recompense. Mohammed was too proud to concede and sent the Mongol envoys back minus their beards. What began as a punitive expedition by the Mongols soon turned into an enormous, vicious invasion that took them through Khwarizm into Armenia and Russia, capturing almost the entire Middle East.

The Mongols attacked with four armies under the command of Genghis Khan and his various sons. Mohammed faced them with an army of 400,000 and quickly lost 160,000 of these in a spectacular battle. The Mongols' ability to co-ordinate vast, tactical troop movements on several simultaneous fronts and proceed according to minutely devised plans was simply too sophisticated for the Muslim forces. They favoured open, pitched battle grounds.

In addition, the Mongols had by now picked up a whole new range of siege machinery in their Chinese wars, which they now put to good use as city after city fell to them. They adopted new ideas, techniques and tools from the people they conquered, particularly in employing Muslim and Chinese siege engines and engineers to aid the Mongol cavalry in capturing cities. Otra fell, then Khojent, Tashkent and Nur. Bokhara, 'the City of Science', was utterly destroyed, and Merv, one of the legendary jewels of Muslim civilization and home of the '1001 Nights of Arabia', was burned to the ground. Merv surrendered after making an unwise bargain with the Mongols and 700,000 people were killed. Hundreds of cities were obliterated in the Mongol advance. The populous centre of Herat was initially spared.

Mohammed died of pleurisy; it was said that he much regretted his earlier pride. His son, the gallant Jelaliddin, took up battle against Genghis Khan, who pursued him relentlessly, while developing a healthy admiration for his courage. In the end the battle was fruitless. After bitter fighting, the Persian forces were defeated and Jelaliddin only escaped by jumping twenty feet into a river on his horse, which impressed Genghis considerably. Jelaliddin escaped to Delhi, out of the Mongols' reach, and Genghis had to console himself with subsequently ravaging the Asian provinces of Peshawar and Lahore.

In the meantime, one or two cities that had initially co-operated to avoid destruction, rebelled. Herat was one of these, and it is here that 1,600,000 are recorded as having been killed in methodical executions lasting a week. At Nishapur, where one of his favourite commanders was killed, Genghis Khan decreed: 'That the town be laid waste, that the site be ploughed upon and that in the exaction of vengeance not even cats or dogs should be left alive . . .'

By 1222, the Mongols, conquerors of China and the Middle East, had advanced through Astrakhan to the Don River, where the Russians stood, dismayed at this strange, stinking, invincible army.

The mobility, toughness and discipline of the Mongol army were a new phenomenon in the world at that time. The Mongols were strong, stocky troops, and the entire army was mounted. Each man had at least one spare horse, and often three or four of the squat strong horses from the Mongolian steppes which they used. The soldiers wore fur caps with protective ear pieces for casual wear, and a leather and metal helmet for battle. On their horses they carried a great array of tools and weapons; two bows and several quivers of arrows, a lance with a hook on it for pulling people off horses, an axe, a lasso, a sharpening stone, a kettle and a few emergency rations. These consisted mainly of around ten pounds of curdled milk dried in the sun. When required, about half a pound was dissolved with water to make foul smelling, cheesy syrup. Although, given the complete lack of hygiene of the Mongols, they probably didn't notice the smell. The men quite literally lived on their horses, and could happily sleep in the saddle. The horse also enabled them to cross seemingly impassable rivers, as they would float across on a bundle of possessions, holding on to the tails of their mount. The Mongol cavalryman could go for several days without a cooked meal, and if necessary would open up a vein in the neck of his horse and suck some of the blood, afterwards closing up the wound. His proficiency with bow and arrow was such that he could hit a man at a range of 200 to 400 metres.

The massacres and rumours of massacres played their part in the psychology of inducing terror, which was an important part of Genghis Khan's Mongolian war plan. In this, although their army was often smaller than the opposing forces, they deliberately built up the illusion of a vast 'horde' of an army. The extra horses certainly helped with this. They would often even mount dummies on their spare horses initially to give the impression that their army was three or four times the size it actually was. During the night, each soldier lit several torches; when seen from the walls of a besieged city, all these misleading pinpricks of flame served as demoralizing evidence of the approaching army's numbers.

As previously noted, they had another secret weapon, their total lack of hygiene. The Mongolian hordes are said to have stank to high heaven; their approach could be smelled miles way, as they advanced in terrifying, completely controlled silence. In the actual attack, the stench of the unwashed Mongol hordes and their horses was both so potent and alien that defenders sometimes became paralyzed with nausea.

Again, in Russia, the Mongols sent envoys, and the Russians made the fatal mistake of killing them, thus once again precipitating a conflict. It was this stinking army the Russians then faced. The Mongols rampaged through Bulgaria, and even penetrated as far north as Novogrod, after which they returned, stuffed with goods, to Mongolia. The basis of the nation's economy seems to have been the loot from their expeditions.

It is not entirely clear what Genghis Khan's personality was truly like, but his character was undoubtedly moulded by the many hardships he faced when he was young, and while unifying the Mongol nation. Genghis appeared to fully embrace the Mongol people's nomadic way of life, and did not try to change their customs or beliefs. As he aged, he seemed to become increasingly aware of the consequences of numerous victories and expansion of the Mongol Empire, including the possibility that succeeding generations might choose to live a sedentary lifestyle. According to quotations attributed to him in his later years, he urged future leaders to follow the Yassa and to refrain from surrounding themselves with wealth and pleasure. He was known to share his wealth with his people and awarded subjects who participated in campaigns handsomely.

The Yassa was a document written for the Mongol people, thought to be extremely comprehensive and very specific, although no copies of it survive, even in part. The main purpose of the document was probably to eliminate social and economic disputes that existed among the Mongols and future allied people. It was like a day-to-day set of rules for people under Mongol control that was enforced strictly with very stiff punishments (often execution) for violators. The word Yassa translates into 'order' or 'decree'. The Yassa was written on scrolls and bound into volumes that could only be seen by the Khan or his closest advisers, but the rules in the content were widely known and were followed.

Genghis Khan valued and practised meritocracy extensively in his rule without regard to the person's ethnicity and background. There is plenty of evidence that the Mongol Empire was ruled in a hands-on fashion by able commanders and governors, such as Subutai (Tuvan), Muhammad Khan (who was of Arab descent), and many Chinese governors in conquered China who came from a number of different ethnic backgrounds. He was quoted as saying: 'Those who were adept and brave fellows I have made military commanders. Those who were quick and nimble I have made herders of horses. Those who were not adept I have given a small whip and sent to be shepherds . . .'

He seemed to value honesty and loyalty highly from his subjects. Genghis Khan put some trust in his generals, such as Muqali, Jebe and Subudei, and gave them free rein in battles. He allowed them to make decisions on their own when they embarked on their own campaigns, very far from the Mongol Empire capital, Karakorum. An example of Genghis Khan's perception of loyalty is written in *The Secret History of the Mongols*: one of his main military generals, Jebe, had been his enemy and had shot Genghis Khan's horse. When Jebe was captured, he admitted that he had shot the horse and said that he would fight for Genghis if he spared his life or would die if that's what he wished. The man who became known as Genghis Khan spared Jebe's life and made him part of his team, and he became one of his most powerful, successful and loyal generals.

Yet, accounts of his life are marked by a series of betrayals and conspiracies. These include rifts with his early allies such as Jamuqa (who also wanted to be a ruler of Mongol tribes), betrayal by Wang Khan (his and his father's ally) and problems with the most important Shaman who was trying to drive a wedge between Genghis Khan and his brother Qasar who was serving Genghis Khan loyally.

Towards the latter part of his life, Genghis Khan became interested in the ancient Buddhist and Tao religions. The Taoist monk Ch'ang Ch'un, who rejected invitations from Sung and Jurchen leaders, travelled more than 5,000 kilometres to meet Genghis Khan close to the Afghanistan border. He was renowned for his knowledge of Taoist alchemy, which pursued the elixir of life. Genghis Khan, mistaking the pursuit of the philosophical idea as an indication of the elixir's actual existence, became convinced that this man might know where he could find the philosopher's stone that would confer immortality on him. With this, he intended to subjugate the heavenly powers to his will. When asked where the means to immortality lay, the monk replied, 'There are many means of prolonging life, but no medicine of immortality.' The monk's negative answer disheartened Genghis Khan, who nevertheless thanked him courteously for his honesty, and consulted with him about Taoist philosophy for several days. After the monk's departure they maintained contact until Genghis Khan's death in 1227. Perhaps a rare insight into Genghis Khan's perspective of himself was recorded in a letter to this Taoist monk. The letter was presumably not written by Genghis Khan himself, as tradition states that he was illiterate, but rather through a Chinese person and recorded as Khan's in the Chinese histories. A passage from the letter states: 'Heaven has abandoned China owing to its haughtiness and extravagant luxury. But I, living in the northern wilderness, have not inordinate passions. I hate luxury and exercise moderation. I have only one coat and one food. I eat the same food and am dressed in the same tatters as my humble herdsmen. I consider the people my children, and take an interest in talented men as if they were my brothers. We always agree in our principles, and we are always united by mutual affection. At military exercises I am always in front, and in time of battle am never behind. In the space of seven years I have succeeded in accomplishing a great work, and uniting the whole world in one empire.'

He passed a decree exempting all followers of Taoist religion from paying any taxes. This made the Taoist religion very powerful at the expense of the Buddhists. Genghis Khan was by and large tolerant of the multiple religions he encountered during the conquests as long as the people were obedient. However, all of his campaigns caused wanton and deliberate destruction of places of worship. Religious groups were persecuted only if they resisted or opposed his empire.

Minhaj al-Siraj Juzjani, a local chronicler, left a description of Genghis Khan, written when the Khan was in his later years: 'Genghis Khan . . . was a man of tall stature, of vigorous build, robust in body, the hair on his face scanty and turned white, with cat's eyes, possessed of dedicated energy, discernment, genius, and understanding, awe-striking, a butcher, just, resolute, an overthrower of enemies, intrepid, sanguinary, and cruel.'

Genghis Khan was also supposed to have endorsed the pleasures of murder, theft and rape by saying: 'The greatest pleasure of a man, is to vanquish your enemies and chase them before you. To rob them of their wealth and see those dear to them bathed in tears. To ride their horses and clasp to your bosom their wives and daughters.'

During his last campaign with the Tangut Empire, in southern China, he derived from the conjunction of the planets that evil awaited him, and turned homewards. At the Si-Kiang River in Kansuh he fell ill and died on 18 August, 1227. The reason for his death is uncertain. Many assume he fell off his horse, due to old age and physical fatigue; some contemporary observers cited prophecies from his opponents. The Galician-Volhynian Chronicle alleges the Tanguts killed him. There are persistent folktales that a Tangut princess, to avenge her people and prevent her rape, castrated him with a knife hidden inside her clothing and that he never recovered.

Genghis Khan asked to be buried without markings. After he died, his body was returned to Mongolia. Presumably he was taken to his birthplace in Hentiy Province, where many assume he is buried somewhere close to the Onon River. According to legend, the funeral escort killed anyone and anything that came across their path, to conceal where he was finally buried. The Genghis Khan Mausoleum is his memorial, but not his burial site. On 6 October 2004, 'Genghis Khan's Palace' was allegedly discovered, and that may make it possible to find his burial site, but it is doubtful. Folklore says that a river was diverted over his grave to make it impossible to find (the same manner of burial of Sumerian King Gilgamesh of Uruk). Other tales state that his grave was stampeded over by many horses, and trees were then planted over it, and the permafrost also did its bit in hiding the burial site. The Mongolian emperors have no burial mounds. The final resting site of the 'Conqueror of the World' remains undiscovered to this day.

Genghis Khan left behind an army of more than 129,000 men; 28,000 were given to his various brothers and his sons, and Tolui, his youngest son, inherited more than 100,000 men. This force contained the bulk of the elite Mongolian cavalry. This was done because, by tradition, the youngest son inherits his father's property. Jochi, Chagatai, Ogedei and Kulan's son Gelejian received armies of 4,000 men each. His mother and the descendants of his three brothers received 3,000 men each.

There was no enormous Emperor's fortune to be inherited. For Genghis Khan, his army had been his fortune, his beginning and his future and his legacy.

Ivan the Terrible

It is often said that there are few stories in all history that compare with that of Ivan IV Vasilyevich and the sheer numbers of murders he ordered. He is known in English as Ivan the Terrible, although in his native Russia he was named Ivan 'Grozny', which translates into English as Ivan the Fearsome. He was the human embodiment of two contradictory forces in his society at the time. He was a devout Christian, as Russia was at the time devoutly Christian, a legacy left behind by Rome. However, there was also a pre-Christian darker mythological pagan side to the culture – a dark and terrible worship of destruction.

Late in his life, Ivan confessed that throughout his life he had secretly worshipped Cronus, the ancient pagan father of the gods. According to folklore, Cronus is Time itself, and devours his own children. In a letter to aristocrats who he believed had poisoned his much loved wife, Anastasia, he wrote, 'If you had not taken her from me, there would have been no sacrifices to Cronus.' Towards the end of his life he continuously drew this self-portrait of himself as a dark God-of-Wrath, consuming his subjects in revenge and anger.

Ivan IV Vasilyevich was born on 25 August 1530. Ivan (or Ioann, as his name is written in Church Slavonic) was a long-awaited son of Vasili III, the Grand Prince of Moscow from 1505 to 1533. In 1533, an inconspicuous mark had appeared on the thigh of Vasili III; it eventually turned into a boil which swelled until he was barely able to walk. Worried about his health, Vasili III, moved to secure the throne for his little son. He set up a regency council to rule during Ivan's childhood, and obliged the Boyars, Russia's aristocrats, to swear allegiance to his son. The boil became a huge abscess that eventually burst. The pus apparently 'filled a basin', and a core one-and-a-half inches wide came out. It seemed that Vasili III was to recover, but only briefly. The wound became infected with gangrene and on 3 December 1533 he died of blood poisoning.

Upon his father's death, Ivan IV Vasilyevich formally came to the throne at the age of three. His title was the Grand Duke of Muscovy and the pre-appointed regency council took over. Soon after, his mother Elena Glinskaya made a bid for the throne and was successful. The regency council disintegrated as its members were gradually imprisoned and exiled. According to historical accounts from the time she was not a bad ruler, but she was also not a good mother. She died when Ivan was only eight, apparently poisoned by enemies from within the Kremlin. Ivan was then left orphaned and utterly alone in the world.

The young Ivan inherited a country equivalent to France, Spain, Britain and Italy in size. In spite of its enormity, it hardly appeared on a map. Explorers expected to find China battened onto the eastern side of Europe. The huge plains and wastes of Russia had only ten to twelve million inhabitants in total. Most were peasants, many in conditions of serfdom that was little more than slavery. The peasants were further crushed by taxes. The Russians of the time were a tough and stocky race with a passion for alcohol and celebration. They also had a reputation for sodomy that apparently amazed foreign visitors who reported that they do it 'not only with boys but with men and horses'. Husbands habitually beat their wives, a popular saying at the time was 'if a woman not be beaten with the whip once a week, she will not be good . . .' Torture was legal and women convicted of killing their husbands were buried alive. Counterfeiters had molten lead poured down their throats. Merely spoken evidence was necessary for conviction, but as it was a religious society, witnesses had to kiss the cross before speaking. In short, Russia was a contradiction of pious religion and physical cruelty.

The Russian Orthodox Church saw itself as the last bastion of true Christianity. All other Churches and faiths were heretical. Foreigners, especially those who were Catholic or Jewish, were regarded with suspicion and all movements of the population were restricted. Foreign travel without permission was punishable by death in case the people learned things about foreign lands that might damage the rule of the Church. The Church was a vast, wealthy and powerful organization, with a messianic mission as successor to the Christian empires of Rome and Constantinople. A monk had once prophesied to Ivan's father: '. . . the ruler of the present Orthodox Empire is on Earth the sole Emperor of the Christians . . . two Romes have fallen, but the third stands and a fourth there shall not be . . .'.

According to Ivan's fabricated family tree he was directly descended from the Roman Emperor Augustus. The symbolic importance of his social position placed a huge and suffocating burden on the young Ivan. Although acclaimed publicly as a virtual god, he was privately abused and ignored by his ministers. In his own words, his childhood was spent in shadows and fear. He wrote in later life that no one gave him '. . . any loving care . . . everything I experienced was unbefitting my tender years . . .' He was either dressed up in the stifling uniform of a prince or treated like a beggar. This insecure early childhood full of fear and uncertainty, absolutely lacking in love, created a darkened character, nursing distrust and revenge that he was to store up for the future.

After the death of his mother, the Boyars, and their governing body, the Duma, who had sworn to Ivan's father that they would protect and support his young child, fought bitterly over power they now considered theirs. His mother was replaced as regent by Boyars from the Shuisky family. According to his own letters, Ivan customarily felt neglected and offended by the mighty Boyars from the Shuisky and

41

Belsky families. In one letter, he painfully recalls an episode when one drunken Boyar put his dirty boots on Ivan's bed. These traumatic experiences undoubtedly contributed to his hatred of the Boyars and to his mental instability. Ivan, now aged twelve and already developing a savage and morbid temperament, had taken to throwing cats and dogs off the Kremlin battlements and out of the windows 'to observe their pain and convulsions'.

Ivan's violent behaviour continued. At the age of fourteen, he gathered together a teenage gang and roamed the streets of Moscow, exorcizing his anger and frustration by mugging innocent pedestrians. Lacking any close mentor, he increasingly confided in the Metropolitan Makary, the leader of the Orthodox Church, and Ivan Vorontsov, a member of the old Moscow gentry. After Prince Andrey Shuisky, a member of the dominant Boyar family, broke in on a meeting of the three and tried to kill Vorontsov in front of him, he eventually asserted his position and had Shuisky thrown to the dogs.

At sixteen he told the Duma that he intended to take the title of Tsar, the first ruler of Russia to do so. He also announced his intention to marry. Tsar was a title equivalent to emperor, or Caesar. It also resembled the Tartar title of Khan meaning 'A king that giveth not tribute to any man'. His mother had Tartar ancestors; in Ivan, the blood of both Christian Russian aristocrats and their bitter enemies, the pagan Mongol emperors, flowed together. The Duma was impressed with the adult nature of his speech. His budding cruelty was matched by his sharp intelligence. Accordingly, in January 1547, he was crowned Tsar and Autocrat of All Russia, with Monomakh's Cap, at the Cathedral of the Dormition.

He married Anastasia Romanova-Zakharyina-Yurueva on 3 February 1547. She was untitled but from a loyal Boyar family. The older aristocracy regarded her with snobbery, thinking she was a upstart commoner. She gave birth to a total of six children: Anna, Maria, Dmitri, Ivan, Evodokia and Feodor. Her descendants, the Romanovas, were still ruling Russia three hundred and fifty years later when the Bolshevik

Revolution wiped them out. After their wedding, Ivan made the first of many penitential pilgrimages, walking over forty miles through the bitter Russian winter.

He returned home to a country in a troubled state. The Tartars took advantage of bitter infighting among the Duma to invade Russia's borders, burning monasteries, raping and dismembering nuns and monks. The aristocratic Glinsky family had now become the lords of misrule. Much of the population joined in with the arson to express their despair. In June 1547, a fire gutted the heart of Moscow, killing thousands. The angry mob turned on Ivan who came to his senses and realized that he had to begin to govern. In order to help him do this, he surrounded himself with a 'Chosen Council', the Zemsky Sobor, or 'council of nobles'.

Priestly figures often exerted great influence within the Russian court and in his youth Ivan turned to a monk named Sylvester, who enchanted him with stories of ghosts and miracles. Ivan later described him as 'scaring me with bogies'. Equally significantly, Ivan was also influenced by the theories of a pamphleteer called Peresvetov. This man was a well-travelled mercenary, who referred in his writing to the occult wisdom in a book called the *Secreta Secretorium*. Ivan had this book in his palace library, it supposedly contained the secret advice given by Aristotle to Alexander the Great. The Turkish Emperor Mehmet had learned a philosophy of terror from it, and swept away all who opposed his reforms. The book told rulers to inspire awe in their subjects, to be remote and distrustful and to test the loyalty of nobles by seeing 'what each will suffer on your account'. According to this book, those who wished to be absolute rulers should not be afraid of shedding blood; it was the only reputation worth having.

The early part of Ivan's reign was one of relatively peaceful reforms and modernization. Ivan desperately needed to have land that he could reward people for their loyalty with. Thirty per cent of all arable land in Russia was owned by the Church which was opposed to any reforms which might affect their vast wealth. The Church took badly to Ivan's attempts to make it liable for tax or to make it set up poor houses. He therefore turned to the aristocracy. He cursed the Boyars for their treatment of him as a child. His reforms very quickly ran up against their interests. He revised the law code (known as the *sudebnik*), which established the investigative nature of legal proceedings, provided different kinds of punishment, such as death penalty, flagellation, etc., and also sought to protect the feudal land ownership in favour of the princes and the aristocracy. Ivan initially proposed reforms in taxation and the system of justice to benefit the peasants. There had been a fee for peasants who wanted to leave their feudal lord and he proposed to abolish this. He also established a universal day (26 November) across the Russian state for peasants who wanted to switch places with their masters for the day. He then confirmed the position of the Church with the Council of the Hundred Chapters, which unified the rituals and ecclesiastical regulations of the entire country.

Between the 1540s and 1550s, he created a standing army (the *streltsy*), initially recruited from free trade people and the rural population. *Streltsy* had identical uniforms, training, and weapons (harquebuses, muskets, poleaxes, sabres, and sometimes pikes). They were subdivided into electives. The *streltsy* of Moscow guarded the Kremlin, performed general guard duty, and participated in military operations. The municipal *streltsy* performed garrison and border duty and carried out orders of the local administration. Now that he had an army, his next mission was to wage war.

In 1552, at the age of twenty-two, his army took the fortified Tartar city of Kazan and massacred the highest-ranking Tartar nobility. For Russia, this was an historic victory over her old enemies. With Kazan annexed, the conquest of Tartary and Siberia transformed Russia into a multiethnic and multi-confessional state. It was after this that the Russian people gave him the name 'Grozny' or Fearsome, to indicate the awesome stature he had acquired. He had St Basil's Cathedral constructed in Moscow to commemorate the seizure of Kazan. Legend has it that he was so impressed with the structure that he had the architects blinded, so that they could never design anything as beautiful again.

After his victory in Kazan, Ivan fell ill. His fever was not thought to be of entirely natural causes since his reforms had been so unpopular with the Boyars. As he lay on what many thought of as his deathbed, he asked the Boyars to swear allegiance to his infant son, Dimitry, just as his own father had done before him. This time, however, they said they would not serve 'a babe', and set about organizing a rebellion. Once he realized how little he could trust his supposed allies, Ivan's rallied his strength, manipulated his loyal forces from his deathbed and succeeded in crushing the rebellion. The Boyars now had a fearsome enemy. In the ten years that followed, Russia became the region's greatest power, but would later be forever locked in an endless and futile battle to conquer the Baltic.

In the 1550s, English merchants, looking for China, found their way to Russia. An erratic relationship began between the two monarchs, Ivan and Elizabeth I. The English merchants saw Ivan at the height of his reign, enthroned in splendour, encrusted with jewels and crossing himself before each of his frequent mouthfuls of food and drink. One said of him, 'He setteth his whole delight upon two things. First to serve God, as undoubtedly he is very devout in his religion, and the second, how to subdue his enemies.'

After his illness, Ivan suffered a dramatic change in personality. His worsening mental state is linked, historically, to the near-fatal illness in 1533 and also the death of his first wife, Anastasia Romanovna on 7 August 1560. His son Dimitry had drowned as an infant in a tragic accident when his nurse dropped him in a river and Anastasia had helped him through this tragedy. When she was no longer around to give him her support, life in Russia began to change. Ivan introduced laws restricting the mobility of the peasants, which would eventually lead back to serfdom.

Despite initially being renowned for his conquests and initiating reforms which improved the peasants' lot Ivan was becoming increasingly cynical. He began drinking heavily and having decided that no one was trustworthy, he surrounded himself with sycophants, from whom he expected nothing but shallowness. He developed an addiction to masked balls and theatrical executions. He became promiscuous with both sexes and any criticism of him was punishable by death. Dmitry Obolensky, a prince, reproached the son of one of Ivan's generals for his homosexual relationship with Ivan. Dmitry was invited down into Ivan's cellars to select a favourite vintage of wine and was then hacked to death among the casks.

The ongoing stalemate in the Baltic wars made Ivan frustrated and furious. He began to see the failure to capture the Baltic as a plot to undermine his rule. He killed one of his princes with a mace and accused his prize general, Kurbsky, of treason. Kurbsky deserted his regiment and denounced Ivan for 'torturing his subjects with red-hot pincers and needles driven under the nails . . .' Ivan compelled the messenger who brought Kurbsky's letter to read it aloud while Ivan drove the iron point of his staff through the messenger's foot into the floor. This was the first of many bizarre letters the two sent each other. Ivan wrote long angry letters to Kurbsky, who remained in exile. Kurbsky became an unwilling confidant as Ivan revealed an exceptional literary talent, casting himself as a man who resented the position fate had thrust upon him. It seemed that all his life he wallowed in self-pity.

Increasingly, his personality became driven and obsessive, eating up the world around him. While she was still alive, his wife Anastasia restrained his full potential for cruelty and bitterness. Anastasia had a calming effect on Ivan, and for thirteen years he had made solid reforms, expanded Russia and chose good advisers. But her death drove Ivan back towards insanity. His impatience became anger, and suspicion deepened into paranoia. Casual cruelty grew into a need for daily sadism. Convinced that the nobles had poisoned her, Ivan, in a wave of tortures and executions, killed many of the Boyars, high priests and citizens. Examination of the bone remains of Anastasia in the late twentieth century by archaeologists and forensics experts have been able to provide evidence that could actually sustain her husband's claim. Ivan began to distance himself from his former advisers. According to one of his contemporaries, he 'lived in great danger and fear of treason which he daily discovered, and spent much time in the examination, torture and execution of his subjects . . .'

Amid growing dissent in Russia, Ivan began to toy with the idea of abdication. At the end of 1564, hundreds of sleighs began to move tons of treasure and icons from the palace and treasury to Sloboda, a hunting lodge sixty miles from Moscow. This became transformed into a heavily fortified camp. Ivan told nobody what he was up to and they watched his actions, mystified. Without designating any heir, he eventually slipped out of Moscow and left the nation leaderless.

He sent a letter to the Boyars which was read out by a messenger on 3 January 1565. In it he bitterly accused the Church and government of corruption, treason and responsibility for all his personal troubles, past and present. The tone of the letter wallowed in melodramatic self-pity: 'Wherefore the Tsar and Grand Prince not wishing to endure these many acts of treachery, has abandoned the Tsardom with a heavy heart and now travels wheresoever God may lead him.'

The peasants feared the loss of their champion. An uprising was on the cards and all around Russia's borders the foreign leaders began thinking about invasion. The Duma humbled itself and sent the Archbishop of Novgorod to plead with Ivan for his return. They promised him that if he returned, he could 'punish traitors at his own discretion'. Ivan refused the offer, he wanted more than that.

He eventually returned to Moscow in February 1565, still only thirty-five years old, he had now lost most of his hair and his eyes were 'strangely glazed'. After four weeks of negotiation, he had been granted absolute power over the life and property of any disobedient subject. A part of the nation was to be set aside for him, existing only to further his will, staffed and run by his hand-picked personnel. He called this region of Muscovy the *Oprichnina* (meaning widow's portion – perhaps reflecting his continuing self-pity). The *Oprichnina* initially consisted of twenty towns and their surroundings. Ivan expanded it to include over a third of the entire empire. His intention was to undermine and destroy the hereditary aristocracy he so feared and blamed for his childhood misery and the obstruction of his authority. The rest of Russia was left to the former administration, with Ivan presiding over everything.

The members of the *Oprichnina* were called the *Oprichniki*. They became agents of the security police, dressed all in black, the symbol of death, and attached emblems of a broom and a dog's head to their saddles. The broom signified the rider's mission to sweep Russia clean of treason and corruption while the dog signified the watchfulness of the *Oprichniki* in service to Ivan. The main objectives of the *Oprichnina* were to end the threat of treason and to eliminate the political influence of the landed aristocracy. A mass transfer of the population ensured the destruction of the landed aristocracy. The territories that belonged to the *Oprichnina*, including the streets in Moscow and other urban centres, were cleared of property owners and were settled with the *Oprichniki*. The displaced Boyars and former princes were given estates in service tenure elsewhere, most likely in distant border regions. This practice was not foreign and was used by Basil II, Ivan III, and Basil III, but the extent to which Ivan carried it out was never seen before. Ivan transported old hereditary landowners from one district to another, cutting their connections, and ending their influences. The *Oprichnina* was a form of self-government. The crown made a monopoly of all the trade through the *Oprichnina*, and newly conquered lands were annexed to the *Oprichnina*.

Ivan now possessed power that the pharaohs would have envied. The staff he employed to run his personal empire had to swear complete and unquestioning obedience to Ivan in all things. An oath was created by him: 'He that loveth father or mother more than me is not worthy of me; and he that loveth son or daughter more is not worthy of me . . .'

Ivan's revenge began almost immediately. No specific

charges were needed for the deaths that followed, though sometimes a generally vague accusation would be made that someone had done, plotted, or simply thought something evil. He showed no gratitude for past services; the hero of Kazan, Prince Gorbaty, along with his adolescent son were executed, as well as countless other nobles. One named, Dmitri Sheyev, apparently 'sang all day from memory the canon to our Lord Jesus Christ' as he was slowly impaled on a stake. An English merchant, visiting Moscow in 1566, wrote: 'This Emperor of Moscovia hath used lately great cruelty towards his nobility and gentlemen, by putting to death, whipping and banishing above 400 . . . one worried with bears, of another he cut off his nose, tongue, his ears and his lips, the third he set upon a pole . . .'

When Ivan discovered a real plot a year later in 1567, the carnage extended beyond the immediate suspects and their families. The *Oprichniki* rode around Moscow for days armed with axes, chopping down anyone they chose to. One Boyar found hiding in a monastery was roasted alive in a large pan. Moscow became a dangerous place to be. The English ambassador, negotiating between Ivan and Elizabeth I, wrote anxiously to the Queen: 'Of late the Tsar hath beheaded no small number of his nobility . . . causing their heads to be lain in the streets to see who dares to mourn them . . . I intend to see him so soon as I can . . . the sooner to be out of his country where heads go so fast to the pot.'

Even though he had annexed a whole suburb of Moscow for his personal use, Ivan spent most of his time at his fortress in Sloboda, indulging equally in religion and depravity, his favourite pleasures. One brought out a craving for the other. There were several church services a day, starting at 3 a.m., and after each service he would head for the dungeons to gratify the desire for torture that worship aroused in him. He was described as being 'never so happy', as when he was in the dungeons. 'Blood often splashes in his face, but he does not mind.'

He began organizing large-scale executions. He had several hundred beggars drowned in a lake and fed many friars to wild animals or sewed them up in bearskins and threw them to the dogs. There are also reports that many times Ivan would beat himself, pounding his own forehead on the ground until it turned black with bruises and ran with blood.

Russia's disastrous wars in the Baltic laid an enormous burden of taxation on the people. Ivan, who had managed to maintain a trading agreement with England, asked Elizabeth I for help with weapons and a possible alliance and refuge should he have cause to flee. The Queen did offer Ivan refuge but would not be drawn into his wars, which offended him. Although she did supply him with some weapons, she obstructed his efforts to marry into the English royal family.

After Anastasia's death he had made a political marriage to a Tartar princess, Maria, who had a reputation for cruelty. She was poisoned by a fish supper in 1569 and Prince Staritsky, who ran what was left of Russia, was convicted on the words of the cook. Ivan compelled Staritsky to drink poison and then murdered his entire family, including his mother. He also murdered the cook, the cook's family, the fishmonger who had sold the fish and the fisherman who had caught it. Two years later, his third wife, Marfa, also died of poisoning. He married a total of seven times, sometimes divorcing his wife after just a week. He also claimed to have deflowered a thousand Russian virgins.

It was a year later that Ivan staged his most spectacular massacres, at Novgorod and Pskov. Novgorod was on the border of warring Lithuania, and a prime target for Ivan's paranoia. He was told that these cities were plotting against him and sent an army of 15,000 *Oprichniki* into action but with great secrecy. In order to maintain surprise they were ordered to kill anyone who came into their path. On 2 January 1571, they reached the outskirts of Novgorod. The *Oprichniki* sealed up all exits and refuges. It was here that, based on unproven accusations of treason, Ivan had the *Oprichniki* massacre and torture all 60,000 citizens of Novgorod. The occupants, irrespective of age or sex, were hanged, flayed, beheaded or thrown off the bridge. Ivan had a chute built into the Volkhov

River and slid any still breathing torture victims down into the shallows where the *Oprichniki* waded in boots, hacking and stabbing. Observers reported that so many bodies littered the Volkhov River, which bisects the city, that it overflowed its banks and the water turned red. Ivan then moved on to Pskov where the population suffered a similar fate. The killings only stopped when a man told Ivan that he foresaw Ivan's death if the killing continued. Ivan was susceptible to prophecies and ordered the killing to stop. That same year, there were mass public executions in Moscow. Contradictory as ever, after each bout of executions, the Tsar ordered monks to pray for the souls of those who were killed.

In the winter of 1571, Russia suffered a terrible famine. Peasants resorted to cannibalism to stave off starvation, often eating Ivan's victims. A plague followed the famine and killed off thousands more. The final blow came in the summer of 1572 when the Tartars invaded from the south and swept into Moscow. They set fire to Moscow, and then surrounded and cut down anyone trying to escape the flames. Half the population was killed, around half a million people.

By now, the English believed Russia to be a dangerous and cruel place and called the catastrophes the 'just punishment of God on such a wicked nation'. They also observed that with his own cruelties, 'the Tsar hath but few people left'.

The Tartars were eventually defeated at the battle of Molodi on 3 August 1572, after which the *Oprichnina* was slowly re-integrated back into the state and the *Oprichniki* disbanded, or perhaps disintegrated through sheer exhaustion. There was little left in Russia worth fighting over.

Ivan survived for another decade, presiding over the collapse of the Russian Empire he had once taken to such heights. His cruelty remained but the scale diminished. His attempt to create a new class based on loyalty had failed, he was feared and hated but could not command loyalty without purchasing it. Russia was demoralized and poor, plunged into pagan gloom. While the rest of Europe basked in the Renaissance, Russia was still ruled by the shadow of Cronus. Out of the 34,000 settlements recorded at the end of Ivan's reign, 83 per cent were deserted. In November 1581 Ivan upbraided his daughter-in-law, who was pregnant, about her clothes. Her husband, Ivan's son Ivanovitch, intervened, and Ivan, in a fit of rage, drove the spike on his iron-tipped staff into his son's head. The wound festered and Ivanovitch died a few days later. Ivan's murder of his son brought about the extinction of the Rurik Dynasty and the Time of Troubles.

After his death, Ivan became distraught with remorse. He quite literally went insane with grief, tearing his hair out and crying for nights without end. He began to dispense his horded wealth to the monasteries, ordering that they pray for his son every day. He also drew up a list of the victims of his terror whom he wished the clergy to pray for, displaying an amazing memory for names. From Novgorod alone he listed 1,500 men and their wives and families. The countless unknown were to be acknowledged by the constant sad refrain: 'as to their names, O Lord, you know them . . .' For the next two years until his death, Ivan would never sleep properly again and his screams of anguish could be heard from outside the palace.

In 1583 he started suffering acutely from a condition rather like arthritis, which resulted in the rapid deterioration of his joints. His vertebrae fused solid and he was bent nearly double. He virtually began to rot on his feet. In the words of one English merchant: 'The Emperor began to swell grievously in his coddles, with which he had much offended above fifty years, boasting of virgins and the like . . .'

As his body putrefied internally, Ivan sat, playing chess and doting on his treasure, regretting that he would have to leave it. Sixty witches were imported from Lapland to predict the exact date of his death. After consulting with each other they came up with 18 March.

Ivan's health improved. He even entertained guests whom he took on tours of his treasury, where he lectured them on the occult properties of his jewels. On 18 March, Ivan rose up healthy and cheerful. The witches remained confident. Later Ivan leapt out of a relaxing bath and began making preparations for a game of chess. He suddenly fell over and died. When Ivan's tomb was opened during renovations in the 1960s, his remains were examined and discovered to contain very high amounts of mercury, indicating a high probability that he was poisoned. Modern suspicion falls on his advisers Belsky and Boris Godunov (who became tsar in 1598). Three days earlier, Ivan had allegedly attempted to rape Irina, Godunov's sister and Fyodor's wife. Her cries attracted Godunov and Belsky to the noise, whereupon Ivan let Irina go, but Belski and Godunov considered themselves marked for death. The tradition says that they either poisoned or strangled Ivan in fear for their own lives. The mercury found in Ivan's remains may also be related to treatment for syphilis, which it is speculated that Ivan had.

Upon Ivan's death, the ravaged kingdom was left to his sickly and childless son Fyodor, who was unfit to govern. There followed civil wars and destruction at the hands of the Polish and Tartar armies; the glory days of the Russian Empire were long over.

Stalin

In 1912 Ioseb Dzhugashvilli celebrated being promoted to the Central Committee of the Social Democratic Party by changing his name to Joseph Stalin, taking the Russian word 'stal', meaning steel, to create his new name. It was a name that would eventually be known throughout the world as belonging to one of the most notorious and ruthless dictators of the twentieth century.

Local records show that Ioseb Dzhugashvilli was born in December 1878 in Gori, Georgia, a small town in the Caucasus region on the eastern end of the Black Sea. The 'official' date given by Soviet records shows his birthday as December 1879, one year later, but no one knows why this discrepancy exists. His father was a cobbler, one of the lowest ranking trades of the artisan class, and his family was poor. Determined that her son should have a better life, his mother had ambitions for him to become a priest, an esteemed profession that would take the family out of poverty. So, after finishing his school education in a church school in 1894, Dzhugashvilli was admitted to Tiflis Theological Seminary to begin his training for the priesthood. By all accounts he was never really cut out to be a priest but he did excel at memorizing biblical texts, showing a formidable capacity for memory which he would later put to use in his ruthless political career. It was in this academic environment that he began to learn of the intellectualized political movements calling for social change. He was reading the works of Karl Marx and Darwin as much as he was reading the Bible.

At the end of the nineteenth century Russia was undergoing a period of unrest. The Tsar, Nicholas II, a direct descendant of the Tsar known as Ivan the Terrible from the Romanovna family 350 years earlier, was very unpopular. Peasants were rioting for more land, students and intellectuals were getting involved in debate and demonstrations looking for a new and more liberal society. Until this time the Russian Empire had been governed by Tsars who had ruled with a firm hand, resisting any 'modernizing' of the empire and quashing calls to hold elections for a government-led democracy. Political activism was closely watched by the Tsar's secret police, so when Dzhugashvilli joined the Marxist-inspired Social Democrat Party in 1899 he was automatically placed under their observation. By the time he was twenty-one his behaviour had got him expelled from the Tiflis Seminary whereupon he devoted himself to full-time political activism. By this time he had become an atheist and had found himself repulsed by the tedious rules of school administration, the bourgeoisie and everything else that he thought represented Tsarist Russia.

It was around this time that Vladimir Lenin was promoting his ideas of the kind of revolutionary party he wanted to create. Key to his plan was the nature of the people he thought should form the members of such a party or as he called it the 'Centre'. In his view they should be dedicated to 'the cause' and submit to the Centre at the expense of all other personal or social goals. To Lenin, 'the cause' was the abolition of Tsarism and the promotion of a socialist revolution. Nothing should come between this and the people who were to fight for it. Many recruits to the party were professional workers such as doctors, lawyers and academics but most were drop-outs from school or university who had been expelled because of their political activity. Ioseb Dzhugashvilli became a very efficient teacher of Marxist ideas to the illiterate workers. If nothing else his time at the seminary had given him the ability to break down complex ideas for consumption by the general public. This ability to connect with the workers was something that in later life would help in his rise to power and gain him a reputation as a speaker who used a simple and direct style understandable by all.

Initially, Dzhugashvilli's role was that of agitator. He was given the job of visiting the industrial areas of the Caucasus secretly inciting strikes and sometimes rioting. Some of these occasions resulted in bloodshed and invariably shocked some of his party members while gaining him a reputation for revolutionary devotion in others. He was never directly involved in any violence himself and throughout his life never would be. He was simply the one who lit the touch-paper and then watched from the sidelines as his small flame became an inferno.

By now, his name and mugshot photograph were well known to the secret police. In 1902 he was arrested in the Black Sea port of Batum and imprisoned. Eighteen months later he was exiled to Novaya Uda in eastern Siberia where conditions were bitter cold with little shelter or food. Two years later, in January 1904, he escaped from the harsh Siberian exile and made his way back to Tiflis. To avoid detection he gave himself a new name, Koba, that he took from his favourite novel *The Parricide* by Kazbegi. Although the Social Democratic Party disapproved of religion he married his first wife Yekaterina Svanidze, the sister of a fellow revolutionary, in a religious ceremony in Tiflis, Georgia, in 1904. The couple had a son, Yakov, in 1907 but within a year Yekaterina suffered from either tuberculosis or typhus (records remain vague) and died. A friend at the funeral remembered Koba pointing to Yekaterina's coffin and saying that with her had died his last warm feelings for all human beings. It was to prove an ominously prescient remark.

Soviet Russia rewrote Stalin's history between 1903 and 1913 claiming him to be one of the foremost activists, central to the revolution in its pre-Great War phase. In fact he was active but mainly on the fringes. His activities got him arrested six more times and each time he was either sent to prison or exiled to one of the labour camps in northern Russia where the harsh Siberian winters with little food or shelter caused many deaths. His subsequent escapes from all except his final exile in August 1913, where he was sent to Turukhansk on the Arctic Circle, serving four years, made many of his opponents and some of his comrades suspicious that he was a spy for the secret police. These suspicions would dog him for the rest of his political career.

In 1903, Tsar Nicholas II had offered some minor reforms as a bid to placate the rising tide of disaffection. These reforms caused the Social Democrat Party to split down the middle. On the one side were the Mensheviks who were arguing for Russia to aim for a bloodless evolution into a parliamentary democracy with a constitutionally controlled monarchy (such as was the case in Britain). The other group called themselves the Bolsheviks who followed the teaching of Karl Marx much more closely. They insisted on a bloody revolution in which the 'State Apparatus' (the Tsarist regime) would be abolished and in its place should be a country run collectively by its workers. Dzhugashvilli favoured the Bolshevik view and turned his attention to their cause. Many of the Mensheviks were members of the Jewish Socialist Party some of whose activists had had earlier run-ins with Dzhugashvilli and which may have paved the way for his later 'ethnic cleansing' activities.

After the split in the Social Democrat Party the Mensheviks took control of the party newspaper *Iskra*. Lenin set up his own paper *Vpered* ('Forward') and set about making his own organization not just another faction of the Social Democratic Party but *the* party itself. In 1906 he created a secret Bolshevik Centre that would operate purely in his interests regardless of any remaining links with the Mensheviks. Despite the untrustworthy evidence of Stalin's early political activity, factual evidence exists to show that by December 1905 he was sufficiently important to be invited to St Petersburg where he met Lenin himself. Documents from around that time show that he found Lenin to be far too informal. Tellingly, the increasingly prominent 'Koba', thought that such a great man should be more forbearing and much less approachable than he found the quietly spoken Lenin to be.

In 1912 Dzhugashvilli got his first big break on the political career ladder. Vladimir Lenin promoted him to the Central Committee and he found himself finally a part of the 'Centre'.

As already explained, Ioseb Dzhugashvilli celebrated this by renaming himself Joseph Stalin. This name change while clearly emulating the surname 'Lenin' also seemed to distance him from his Caucasian origins, although he was never to lose the strong Georgian accent which he had all his life. Stalin then spent a brief period of time as editor of a new Bolshevik paper called *Pravda* but in 1913 he was arrested again and sentenced to life exile in Siberia. This time he remained in the harsh hinterlands out of all political action until in 1917 the system that had put him there fell apart.

A minor democratic parliament called a Duma had been allowed to form by Tsar Nicholas II in 1906. However, when elections returned liberalizing majorities in 1907 the Tsar promptly refused them any authority and subsequently dissolved them. He had to have final control over who was elected and what they did. Because of his tendencies to take away any promises made, the people no longer trusted him and the seed of mass discontent was fatefully sown.

The tide against the tsarist regime finally turned fully in 1914. The Russian Empire entered the 1914 Great War fighting on the side of the French and the British against the Germans and the Austro-Hungarians. Tsar Nicholas II in his typically dithering and incompetent leadership managed the war situation disastrously. There were huge losses on the battlefield and terrible food shortages at home. In St Petersburg in March 1917 food riots began in the streets with starving protestors demanding some action be taken. Nicholas ordered the capital's garrison to fire on the demonstrators but the garrison refused and instead, perhaps sensing what was to follow, joined the protestors instead. Nicholas II abdicated on 15 March. He and his family went into hiding but were all executed secretly by the Bolsheviks a year later because it was believed that pro-tsarist militants were about to mount a coup to reinstate them.

Stalin returned to St Petersburg on 25 March 1917, meeting up with Lenin who by then had also been in exile. A hastily put together government was managing the country almost as badly as the tsarist regime. Against this setting the Bolsheviks were drumming up support among the urban workers of the city. On 24 October, the Bolsheviks, with strong support from the workers, brought about a coup d'état with very minimal bloodshed. The new Marxist government made peace with the Germans almost at once and set about rebuilding the broken down Russian economy.

In the immediate aftermath of the 1917 October revolution Joseph Stalin, who had played a central role in organizing the revolution, felt himself to be usurped by Lenin's right-hand man Leon Trotsky. Trotsky as head of the Bolshevik (Red) army in the 1918–1920 civil war against the anti-Bolshevik (White) army had won huge party support for his brilliant handling of the matter. He was also, like Lenin and unlike Stalin, a middle-class intellectual, the sort of person Stalin instinctively distrusted. Stalin, with his background of village poverty, was almost certainly deeply jealous of the intelligent and charismatic Trotsky. Later Stalin-era Soviet historical rewritings put Stalin second only to Lenin in importance in the party with Trotsky playing a minor role but closer to the truth was that this role was played by Trotsky. As was characteristic of Stalin he kept his feelings to himself and put the matter to one side until such time came when he could act to bring his opponent down. During this time he exercised his bureaucratic abilities to make himself indispensable to the structure of the ruling party which now called itself Soviet rather than Bolshevik. There were many party leaders at the time that thought of Stalin as a simple unintelligent workhorse for the party's organizational needs. They had badly misunderstood his quiet determination and his mental capacity, including his phenomenal memory for those who had betrayed or tried to undermine him. Most eventually paid for their misjudgements with their lives.

Under Lenin's leadership Stalin was made Commissar of Nationalities in the hope of taking the borderland nations under Soviet control. Some people in these states thought that they should become independent communist states but this was a vain hope. Stalin announced that only those minority states considered 'proletariat' enough would be granted independence. Even with this glimmer of hope it was eventually decided by the Petrograd Soviet in 1920 that Central Asian cotton and Caucasian oil were too important to the state to allow economic independence. By 1922 due to his organizational strengths and the odd favour Stalin had convinced enough people of his abilities to have been made Secretary General to the Soviet Central Committee. This placed him at the heart of the entire governmental system and because of the power he held in other departments now virtually nothing could be enacted without his approval.

Much of Stalin's rise to central party power was due to the fact that Lenin himself was by this time very ill. After being shot in the neck during an assassination attempt in 1918, doctors advised Lenin that to remove the bullet would be too dangerous to his life. But by 1921 the bullet was obviously killing him anyway so they took the risk of removing it. He subsequently suffered bouts of paralysis temporarily down one side of his body. As his condition worsened it became clear that he did not have long to live. During his last few months Lenin devoted his time to writing attacks on both Leon Trotsky's desire to spread communism throughout the capitalist west through his 1905 ideas for 'permanent revolution' and also Stalin's inward-looking centralism. He described Stalin, after becoming General Secretary, as having 'enormous power' in his hands and wrote that he was not sure Stalin had the knowledge of how to use such power with 'sufficient caution'. Lenin eerily predicted that such a centralization of command would lead to an autocratic single-voiced government ruling like the tsars they had fought so hard to replace.

After a series of strokes Lenin finally died in 1924. He was pseudo-deified by the party leadership. His corpse was embalmed and laid out as a spectacle for the Soviet masses to worship as their saviour. Though in his final years he had called for the ousting of Stalin, his views were quietly 'ignored'. Stalin had become too powerful a man to risk angering. During this time Trotsky was convalescing in Georgia. Lenin's death deeply undermined him as Stalin made sure he was misinformed about the date of the funeral and Trotsky's non-attendance made him unpopular with the party senior ranks. Two of the party bosses Grigory Zinoveiev and Lev Kamenev formed a triumvirate leadership with Stalin thus ousting Trotsky permanently from the Central Committee. This partnership, however, didn't last long. As soon as he felt he could Stalin sacked the other two and then formed another leadership with right-wing senior party members Nikolay Bukharin and Aleksey Rykov. Again Stalin later dumped these two as well and by 1928 Stalin had sole control of the whole party.

From 1928, with Joseph Stalin at the helm, the people of Russia were to discover the harshness of the regime under which many of them had initially enthusiastically chosen to live. Lenin had made it clear that there would be no hiding place in Russia for the bourgeoisie: they must work or perish. Stalin put this into practice by ensuring that every citizen was conscripted into one party-approved organization or another. The organizations would dole out the due allocation of food, money, living space and any other minor benefits the state could afford. Among the rank and file of the new Soviet Party the general demeanour was to accept central authority, support the leaders to avoid inner party conflicts and concentrate on the practical matter of putting the new system into place, i.e. to toe the party line. Trotsky was deported from Russia in 1929 and went on to live in Mexico where he continued to write.

Now firmly in control, Stalin abandoned any pretence of still putting Lenin's theories into practice. His major goal was absolute centralization of power and the state control of every aspect of people's lives. Using the excuse of 'modernization' Stalin put in place programmes that totally changed and destroyed the framework of Russian life. Most of the population of the USSR at that time were peasant farmers (*muzhiks*) who owned their scraps of land and lived in small communities that had had the same cultural life for hundreds of years. Stalin ordered the liquidation of these farms and even some of the communities. In their place he wanted huge collective farms all directly under central government control. After the revolution the labour camps in Siberia to which Stalin had once been sent were closed down. Stalin now reopened them knowing of their harsh conditions but determined to make them even worse by drastically reducing food supplies. The peasants that refused to hand over their assets and land were called *kulaks* by the party and either executed on the spot or deported along with their entire families to these vast slave labour camps. A new word entered the language, *dekulakization*, referring to the treatment of anyone, not just well-off peasants, who resisted the new policy. Most were sent to the labour camps now called *Glavnoye Upravleniye Lagere* ('Gulags') and people sent there were worked and starved to death. Probably the worst of the labour camps was at Kolyma. Located in north-eastern Siberia, temperatures dropped to -90 degrees during the winter. Fed little or nothing at all about 30 per cent of the prisoners in Kolyma died each year. People sent to the Gulags included peasants who were accused of 'individualistic tendencies' and those who opposed the establishment of collective farms. Large numbers of Ukrainians, Kazakhs, Uzbeks, Kirghiz, Mordovians and Caucasians fell into this category. Around nine million men, women and children were ripped from their homes and cast into oblivion, starvation and death. Countless others had their houses, tools and valuables confiscated and were deported to remote areas of northern Russia and Siberia. Stalin even once confessed to Winston Churchill that ten million people had been affected, but lied to him that they had been 'wiped out by their labourers', when in fact it had been by the NKVD, as the secret police were then called, or armed groups of party activists.

In 1932, Stalin relaunched his drive against the *kulaks* with renewed energy due to a growing crisis. The Ukraine and the

Volga regions with a population of around 30 million people were struck by famine. The cause was Stalin's insistence that almost all of the grain grown on the new collective farms should be exported to fuel Russia's economy. It was important to Stalin that the USSR was seen as successful abroad and the Ukraine was once seen as the 'breadbasket' of the Russian Empire. As a consequence millions starved to death on land which they had once owned, farmed and made a living from. In August 1932 Stalin passed a law to deal with those who through desperation stole even a handful of grain. They were condemned as 'enemies of the people' and the sentence was death or ten years in the camps where they would almost certainly die.

At the same time that most of the USSR was on basic food rations or starving Stalin came up with a 'five-year plan' at the end of the 1920s to modernize Soviet industry. His plan was to bring the workers into the machine age and away from small-scale peasant farming. Workers who had pre-revolutionary industrial skills were greatly rewarded as long as their social background fitted the 'proletariat' bill. Many were given the task of training the new recruits of an expanding workforce. His demand for rapid industrial advancement turned the industrial arena into a crazy world of impossible output targets and huge physical and mental stress on the workforce. The accident rate and the level of damage to machinery were at an unprecedented high and there were the beginnings of the rumblings of discontent in the workplace.

By 1930 Stalin had set off on a course of what was to become a climate of fear and intimidation chosen by him to restore order. He began in 1930 by rounding up the country's leading economists and accusing them of plotting to restore capitalism in the USSR with the help of outside forces. Show trials were staged and all resulted in execution. Next he ordered Molotov, his chief confidant, to publish lists of the 'wreckers of food supply' (mostly Ukrainian peasants starving and desperate for food) and again staged trials and had them summarily executed too. There followed an intense period of trials intended to show that failures in industrial and agricultural targets were the result of 'enemies of the people' rather than the party's unrealistic expectations. Ordinary workers, men and women in the street, began to realize they were not safe from such accusations themselves. It was a time to keep your head down and follow the party line with the ever-present threat of severe punishment for people who did not. Simply showing interest in things deemed forbidden, such as religion or foreign travel, was enough for lengthy Gulag imprisonment or execution. Throughout the 1920s and 1930s Stalin obsessed over and built up the secret police developed over the decades with various titles, the Cheka, the GPU, the OGPU, NKVD and, most famously, the KGB, to carry out his bidding. The secret police worked ruthlessly and tirelessly to get people to inform on friends, neighbours and family. A love of 'Mother Russia' was reinforced by every newsreel, film and newspaper. Comrade Stalin himself was near deified by his PR machine. By the mid-1930s Stalin's former rivals began to 'disappear'. In 1934 Sergey Kirov was shot dead by an unknown assassin. Leon Trotsky, writing now in Mexico, was branded an 'arch traitor' for allegedly constructing an international plot to destroy Stalin himself. His former allies Zinoviev and Kamenev were dragged out of their enforced political obscurity, charged with treason offences, put on trial and then shot dead. Many other prominent party officials were given the same treatment. Gradually it became clear that Stalin was by now systematically killing off all those who had been part of the regime before he himself came to gain absolute power. All those he had ever had any reason to resent were destroyed. Throughout the 1930s Stalin and many other newer party officials (those who had supported Stalin in his singular leadership), made allegations against other party members. Because of this way of dealing with political 'infighting' it is likely that many loyal Stalinists were put to death as well as members of the old guard. The political purges of the 1930s resulted in thousands of deaths, but because the Soviet authorities kept scant records, there is no way of knowing the exact numbers.

In 1936 Stalin had introduced a new constitution, proclaiming the USSR as a democracy with full civil rights for all citizens. In reality every kind of initiative depended on party approval and the party was embedded in every aspect of Soviet life.

Those who were close to Stalin and observed his private life have said that his private life and his working life were one and the same thing. He smoked heavily but was not much of a drinker. He worked late into the night and preferred to rise late in the morning. He took little or no exercise and liked to watch one or two films a week, usually late at night, and go to the Bolshoi ballet. Once he became General Secretary he moved into a small apartment in the Kremlin. Later, he gradually moved into larger and grander apartments inside the Kremlin. He also owned a small dacha outside Moscow, first at Zubalovo and later at Kuntsevo where he spent his last days. In 1918 he married his second wife Nadezhda Alliluyeva. Stalin had known her since she was two years old, she came from Tiflis and worked as his secretary in the People's Commissariat for Nationalities. She was twenty-two years his junior. Their first child, a son Vasili, was born in 1922 and their second child, a daughter Svetlana, was born in 1926. It was not by any accounts a very close family. Stalin was simply obsessed by his work and political life and frequently dismissive towards his wife. In 1932, during a party held to celebrate the anniversary of the revolution, Stalin was rude and insulting to Nadezhda. Clearly furious she locked herself inside a room at the Kremlin and shot herself using a small pistol that had been a gift from her uncle. Ironically it had been the same uncle that had introduced her to Stalin in the first place. The public explanation for the death was given as a severe bout of appendicitis. Following this death of his second wife Stalin lost interest in family matters entirely and devoted himself to his work. He remained alone for the rest of his life with only the company of his housekeeper Valentina Istomina.

After the political purges in the 1930s an increasingly paranoid Stalin looked for possible threats to his leadership from other sources. He turned his attention to the Red Army, about the only organization that could take on his carefully constructed secret police and win. In the years between 1937 and 1939 from field marshal to lieutenant, almost every officer was accused of treason and either shot or sent to die slowly in the Gulags. Disastrously, Stalin had been so busy sorting out his assumed 'enemies' at home he hadn't been paying attention to what was happening politically on the international stage. In Germany, Hitler and the Nazis had come to power and were using many of Stalin's totalitarian techniques to establish themselves as a major world power, such as love of the 'Fatherland' and the ruthless crushing of any assumed internal political opponent. By 1939 German armies stood ready to invade the rest of Europe and inevitably the USSR. In Hitler's *Mein Kampf* he wrote that his intentions were to take Russia as the breadbasket of the Greater German Reich. Hitler declared the USSR to be the source of a Jewish conspiracy to take over the world. Stalin produced his own propaganda attacking Nazism as the enemy of the working class. Pacts and alliances were being made throughout Europe. Hitler feared a Soviet-Western alliance that would oppose him on two fronts. Stalin feared a Nazi-Western pact making it easier for Hitler to attack the USSR before he could reorganize his now leaderless army. Playing for time Stalin made a pact with Hitler with the conquered and divided Poland as the prize. Meanwhile Stalin was busy training commanding officers for his huge army and Hitler was building up his own forces until they were large enough to conquer the USSR.

Hitler won the race and invaded the USSR on 22 June 1941. Stalin reacted in his usual ruthless and angry style by rounding up the commanding officers on the western front and having them all arrested and shot. The men of the once again leader-less Red Army were killed in their thousands as the German army advanced as far as the outskirts of Moscow. They were eventually forced to retreat by winter and Stalin's Siberian snow troops, who were better prepared for the harsh weather than the Germans. Now that Stalin had Hitler as the undisputed enemy of the Soviets he no longer needed Leon Trotsky in the position of arch enemy, an element of keeping Stalin at the helm by fomenting a continued state of crisis to involve all citizens on his side. He had Trotsky assassinated in Mexico by a specially appointed NKVD squad in 1940. They killed him by plunging an ice pick into his head as he sat at his desk writing. The defeat of the German army cost the USSR dearly in terms of lives. Some 8.6 million Red Army soldiers were killed and nearly 17 million Soviet civilians. One casualty was Stalin's son Yakov. The Germans had captured him during the war and offered to return him to Stalin in exchange for captured German prisoners. But Stalin refused and his son died in a Nazi prison camp. The families of captured Soviet soldiers were routinely rounded up and sent to the Gulags as a warning to other soldiers fighting at the front. Stalin declared all Soviet POWs outside the law and their families were deprived of state support, which meant that in Russia they would have had nothing at all because making a private income was forbidden. Not even his daughter-in-law or grandchildren were to be saved from imprisonment in the Gulags after Yakov became a prisoner of war. He had already dealt with most of his first wife's family, the Svanidze, in the purges of 1937–1938. The few Soviet soldiers who returned from Nazi prison camps after the war had the same treatment meted out to them and their families.

After the Second World War the USA and the USSR were seen as the two main world superpowers. Their ideologies differed greatly and, with the benefit of hindsight, it seems obvious that they would eventually become enemies. Stalin would be blamed for the post-war hostility, what would become known as the Cold War. It is true that Stalin had no intention of giving up the Eastern European states, such as Poland and Hungary, that the Red Army had captured from the Germans. However, documents from the US Freedom of Information Act in the 1970s show that it was what Stalin saw as a betrayal by the Western powers that soured relations between the USSR and the USA. President Roosevelt and British Prime Minister Churchill promised Stalin at the Yalta

Conference in 1945 that defeated Germany would be permanently held under Allied military control so that the threat of a
'Fourth Reich' could never arise. Shortly after this Roosevelt
died and his replacement President Truman reneged on this
agreement (with the support of Churchill) and politically
rebuilt West Germany – at that time under US, French and
British control – aiming for its full independence as soon as
possible. Infuriated by this, Stalin instigated bullying tactics
such as the Berlin Blockade causing the Western politicians to
characterize him as a warmonger.

The reality of what was going on on the Russian side of the
'Iron Curtain', as it came to be called, was very different.
Russia had been economically sapped by the war on Germany
and was having enough trouble holding onto the territories it
had gained. Stalin in his final years was less sadistic than he
had been in his early days but the purges continued, the show
trials of anyone who showed 'signs' of being a traitor to the
state continued and no one was allowed to leave the mighty
proletariat state of the USSR. The new Stalinism was to deride
everything foreign (and more especially Western capitalism) as
decadent and subversive.

The nineteenth party congress in October 1952 was preceded
by the execution of thirteen of the fourteen members of the Anti-
Fascist Jewish committee. Stalin was now intent on unmasking
the 'Zionist conspiracy' as he saw it. In January 1953 Stalin
ordered the arrest of a number of leading Soviet Jewish doctors.
Now seventy-four years old he was again showing signs of his
old paranoia. The doctors were charged with poisoning a number
of leading party members with drugs and also killing them on the
operating table, implying that those in power had ordered their
deaths to gain power themselves. Stalin made it clear that a
'Jewish conspiracy' of major proportions had been planned to
take over control of the party. It seemed that Stalin had again
become distrustful of the senior party members surrounding him
and was preparing a new round of executions. He died suddenly
on 5 March 1953. It has been suggested (although never proven)
that his own Kremlin doctors poisoned him. Normally his staff at

the dacha expected him to call for tea at around 10 a.m. but on 2 March no order was placed. The staff had strict orders never to enter his room until asked to do so. There have been reports that a light came on around 6 p.m. but still no call was made for staff to enter. Finally at 10 p.m. one of the guards entered the room using the excuse that the mail had arrived and reported that he found Stalin lying helplessly on the floor in a pool of urine. It was not until 9 a.m. on 3 March that a team of Russian doctors was allowed into the room. His son and daughter were called and described what they saw as horrendous, that his death agony had been dreadful to watch. His son Vasily drunkenly shouted that his father was being murdered. Doctors struggled for days to overcome the inevitable until eventually at 9.50 a.m. on 5 March they announced his death. It seemed that the fear that he had instilled at all levels of Soviet society had played a role in his own death, as those around him were too fearful to help him when they might have done.

Joseph Stalin, by moving quickly on his political rivals and becoming party master by 1930, had then turned on his peasants forcing them by brutal means to accept his concept of efficient collective agriculture. He removed all threat of opposition in the party by removing its intellectual leadership and replacing it with functionaries whose loyalty was to him alone. He did the same with the Red Army, removing the experienced generals and officers and replacing them with soldiers slavishly loyal to him.

Stalin's mummified body was placed next to Lenin's in the mausoleum, sharing the catafalque until 1961 when an old Bolshevik woman said to the twenty-first party congress that Lenin often spoke to her in her dreams and that he had told her he hated having Stalin laid next to him. Stalin was promptly removed that night. Within a month of his death the Jewish doctors were released as the evidence that had led to their arrest was deemed invalid for having been extracted by illegal means. Stalin's henchman Beria was arrested in 1953 and after prolonged interrogation and a trial, he was executed in December. Stalin's successors feared Beria as the man who may have had the most incriminating information on them and so moved quickly to take him out of action in the old tried and tested way.

Almost all Soviet documents from the Stalinist era were destroyed so there is little information on exactly how many murders, executions and exiles were ordered. The sum total often stated is around 30 to 40 million men, women and children.

Adolf Hitler

Who was Adolf Hitler? Was he a madly driven, tortured artist, slowly losing his mind through a syphilitic infection that prevented any normal sexual life or relationship? Or was he a cold, calculating misanthrope and racist murderer obsessed with war and power, indifferent to human suffering? Perhaps he possessed elements of some or all of these attributes. What we do know about him is that between 1933 and 1944 he was responsible for ordering a staggering estimated eighteen million deaths of men, women and children.

Adolf Hitler was born on 20 April 1889 in Braunau, Austria. The region was then part of the Austro-Hungarian Empire. He was the son of customs official Alois Hitler, who by all accounts was a notorious womanizer. Alois's wedding to Adolf's mother was his third marriage and she was his second cousin – he was old enough to be her father. His first wife had left him after discovering he was having an affair with their maid. The maid became his second wife but died within a few years of their marriage. His third marriage was to Klara, his second cousin, who had been sent to live in his care. She was already pregnant when they married but the son subsequently born died within a few days of his birth. Hitler was the fourth of five children from this marriage but only his sister Paula and Adolf himself survived. Hitler had a half-sister, Angela Raubal, whose child, Geli Raubal, became very close to him later in his life.

Documents suggest that Alois was frequently drunk and

behaved violently both towards his wife and their children, Hitler's childhood was not a happy one. Hitler's life changed at the age of fourteen when Alois died in 1903. Since his sister had mental health problems and was cared for mainly in institutions, his mother, liberated from her oppressive and violent marriage, began to spoil her only surviving son, indulging his every whim. Hitler's school reports described him variously as 'arrogant, argumentative, evasive, sly and lazy'. He was deemed to be fairly intelligent but with an unusually obsessive interest in war games and North American Indians. He was also noted as being a bit of a loner.

With a tendency towards self-dramatization and the assumed position of a tortured outcast, Hitler decided his vocation was art and announced that his intention was to try for the Vienna Academy of Arts. However, characteristic of his noted laziness, he repeatedly put off taking the entrance exam and instead fantasized and talked of his wonderful, undiscovered talent. As his mother continued to indulge him he began to project himself as a bit of a dandy, posing around Linz and drawing up grand plans to completely redesign the city. He dressed himself up like a wealthy student, often succeeding in making people believe that he was the real thing, a misconception that he did nothing to set right. He often talked about his talent as being so prodigious that he didn't know on which of the arts he should bestow his great ability: music, literature, architecture or painting.

There are no reports in Vienna of Hitler having any relationships at this point, though some historical theorists maintain that he contracted syphilis from a Jewish prostitute, which was the beginning of his pathological hatred of all things Jewish. This illness would explain his seeming inability to have a normal sex life and his possible madness later in life. It is also well known that Hitler's favourite philosopher Friedrich Nietzsche eventually died of syphilis and Hitler could have found a common bond in his suffering through his writings. However, anti-Semitic pamphlets were freely available everywhere in Vienna at this time and it is probably more likely that he picked up his anti-Semitism from reading these leaflets in the many bars and cafés he frequented. At the end of the nineteenth century, Vienna had a large and prosperous Jewish population which was very dominant in its artistic and cultural life. Many people were jealous of the intellectual and material accomplishments of the Jews and anti-Semitism was already beginning to raise its ugly head within the political mutterings of the non-Jewish population. Apparently, Hitler read these racist pamphlets avidly and had a large collection at home along with a collection of pornography, mythology and books on the occult. It was around this time that Hitler's mother died of cancer. Throughout his life, Hitler would make much of the fact that the doctor who couldn't save her was Jewish. Many painful and useless chemical treatments were used on his mother under the theory that poison should be used to drive out a greater poison. These chemicals were often chlorine-based, as were the chemicals eventually used to murder millions of Jews in the Nazi concentration camps.

In 1898, Hitler tried again to enter the Vienna Academy of Arts but was refused permission to take the examination. Mortified by this he vanished from his lodgings and entered the Viennese underworld. By 1909, Hitler was destitute and living on the streets, surviving on soup kitchen handouts and staying in shelters for the homeless. Between 1910 and 1913 he lived in a charitable Home for Men. He became an established resident in the home but never made any close friendships. Instead he began lecturing to a captive audience in the reading room. Many of these 'speeches' show that he had no time for democracy, these were not discussions or debates. Hitler despised the debates of parliamentary democracy, he merely talked and talked. During this time he made a living selling postcards of Vienna that he copied from photographs.

In 1913, Hitler moved to Munich intending to apply to the Munich Art Academy. He never achieved this but loved living in the German heartland free of the 'Babylon of races', as he saw Vienna, and he was captivated by the city of Munich. He called himself a 'painter and writer' and returned to his favourite role as an eccentric artist who lived an isolated life. He was also arrested because he had 'forgotten' to enrol for military service but was eventually excused on the grounds of his 'physical weakness'.

A year later, in 1914, the Great War erupted, and Germany and Austria declared war on Russia and Serbia. Because of this, internal political differences and social unrest were put aside and instead a unified sense of patriotism took over. Hitler volunteered for the army and was accepted, much to his delight. After training he was sent to the front as a runner, carrying messages between regiments. Typically, he kept himself to himself and remained at a remove from his fellow soldiers, many of whom quickly lost their enthusiasm for war. These soldiers Hitler branded traitors – he was living out his childhood fantasies of war games and became a 'super-patriot'. His devotion to duty never wavered and he was awarded the Iron Cross after the end of the war. By all accounts he enjoyed the war, including the horror and human destruction of the trenches, in later life recounting all he had seen with relish. He has been quoted as saying 'war is for man what childbirth is for women', seemingly never realizing the difference between life and death that these two events convey.

When news of the Armistice and Germany's surrender came, Hitler was lying in hospital suffering from the after-effects of a gas attack. Through the Treaty of Versailles Germany was now required to make huge payments to its former enemies as compensation for the war waged on them. In addition, 13 per cent of the empire's territory was taken away, including Hungary and Poland. For right-wing nationalists, including Hitler, those who had signed the treaty were seen as traitors to the German fatherland.

He went to a meeting of the German Workers Party on 12 September 1919. Encouraged by the founder of the party, Anton Drexler (1884–1942), who had been impressed by his ability to give rousing speeches, he joined the party as the member responsible for recruitment and propaganda. On 16 October 1919, he made his first public speech and felt a new career in politics was launched. 'I talked for about thirty minutes, and what I had always felt deep down in my heart was . . . here proved true; I could make a good speech.' However, some of the old guard, including Drexler and Karl Harrer – the original national chairman of the party, began to accuse the young rabblerouser of delusions of grandeur. Hitler's new party had simple explanations for Germany's ills – namely the money paid to enemy countries and the wealth deficit to the German people due to the fact that many professions and family businesses were owned by Jews or by nationals of countries in which Germans were in the minority.

Hitler was initially unimpressed by the easy-going democratic spirit that seemed to motivate party discussions; he became determined to reorganize the party along military lines. He was rightly convinced that by thinking small, the party would be condemned to political insignificance. In his efforts to make the party more militaristic, Hitler began recruiting people with military backgrounds. Of course they had to be more loyal to him than to the conservative old guard. He then began his plans to stage mass rallies. The first of these was to be on 24 February 1920.

He was undeniably a very accomplished public speaker, engaging the audience as co-actors. Even when the response was hostile heckling, Hitler seemed more energized than ever. The aim was not so much to tell the truth than to appear credible and to convert the masses to a definitive position in following his leadership and ideas. On 8 August 1920 Hitler had the name of the German Workers Party changed to the 'National Socialist German Workers Party' – the 'Nazis'. He was appointed Führer in 1921. However, the Nazis did not come to power through speeches alone. There was often an extreme system of violence to back up the propaganda. The Nazis also formed a paramilitary wing called the SA or 'Brownshirts' organized by Hermann Göring. These were made up of disillusioned ex-soldiers whose orders were to carry out whatever intimidation and brutality was necessary against political rivals – in particular, the communists, whom

Hitler thought were part of a Jewish conspiracy because of recent events in Russia.

On 8 and 9 November 1923 Hitler staged what is now known as the Beerhall Putsch. The plan was to march on Munich and stage a coup, overpowering the Bavarian authorities and proclaiming a new national government headed by Erich Ludendorff, Hitler and those loyal to the cause of overthrowing the Reich government. The plot was wildly over-optimistic if not idealistic and sure to fail. Shortly before 8 p.m. Adolf Hitler drove up to the Bürgerbräu keller with three colleagues and was met by Putzi Hanfstaengl, who was supposed to act as Nazi liaison with the foreign press. They had some difficulty getting through the police cordon blocking the entrance to foreign visitors and were then joined by several other Nazis in the lobby, including Göring, Göring then burst into the meeting room followed by twenty-five SA troops brandishing pistols, all followed by Adolf Hitler and his entourage. Hitler and his entourage then climbed onto the speaker's platform whereupon he shouted out his famous announcement: 'The national revolution has broken out in the whole of Germany. This hall is occupied by six hundred armed men, and no one may leave it. Reichswehr and State police are marching under our banner from their barracks; a national German and Bavarian government is being formed; the government of Knilling and the Reich government are deposed.'

Hitler then shoved Gustav von Kahr (the then State Commissar), General Otto Hermann von Lassow (German General Staff Officer) and Colonel Hans von Seisser (Head of the Bavarian State Police) into a side room and, brandishing a pistol, held them hostage. The three hostages eventually came out of the side room and reluctantly pledged support for the new Reich government.

Meanwhile, elsewhere in the city of Munich, out-of-control SA thugs were enacting a reign of terror directed at all political opponents and Jews. Hitler's Strossrupp unit broke into the socialist *Münchener Post* and ransacked the press room and editorial offices. This was apparently stopped by a 'police official' wearing a swastika arm band, who suggested some of the equipment might be useful for the future regime. Hitler's mistake that night was to leave the beerhall to take care of unsuccessful efforts by his party to take over several military barracks. By leaving his post he had unwittingly relinquished control to Kahr, Lassow and Seisser. Left behind, Ludendorff allowed them to leave after they had promised, on their word of honour as German officers, that they would abide by the terms of the agreement reached earlier that evening. Already that evening, Hitler's trust in German officers had been put to the test precisely because the plan to capture various barracks had failed because the Reichswehr officers in charge had refused to hand over power to civilians without specific orders from their superior officers. By morning it had become clear that the Reichswehr units, though sympathetic to the coup, were not going to defect after all. Hitler had said to his followers: 'If it comes off, all's well, if not we'll hang ourselves.' As we know, none of them did because the fight for power was not yet over.

The police killed sixteen of his party activists and Hitler himself was arrested at the country home of Putzi Hanfstaengle and ended up in prison for high treason. He had every reason to expect the death penalty, but he was, of course, spared. On 4 April, he was sentenced to five years in the minimum security prison fortress of Lansberg, apparently living there in considerable comfort with as many visitors as he pleased and half a pint of wine or half a litre of beer a day. Morale at Landsberg was high and it was a hotbed of political discussion. It quickly became a hotbed of party activity. Cells were decorated with swastikas. At mealtimes Nazis would gather in the common room like a family and listen to the words of their Führer seated at the top table. In any case Hitler served only nine months, during which time he wrote the now infamous *Mein Kampf*, no doubt thrashing out his ideas to his captive Nazi Party audience. Consequently, he came out of prison a hero on 20 December 1924. *Mein Kampf* was first published on 18 July 1925, by Franz Eher Publications in Munich.

The conditions in Germany at the time were ideal for the

Nazis. Since the Great War, Germany had been a poor, humiliated and politically turbulent country. There was no real sense of a strong leadership in the government. The Kaiser had abdicated due to force from the people and the military and Germany's government post-1919 was cobbled together from endlessly arguing groups of coalition parties, which frequently fell apart, needing to be replaced. As for the economy, in 1923 a thousand billion marks had the same spending power as one solitary mark had had in 1914. On top of this, Germany still had to pay vast sums of money to its Great War enemies. In Italy, too, fascists were on the rise, led by Mussolini.

After leaving prison in 1924, Hitler himself had become the Nazi Party and, far from being lonely and down and out as in his earlier days, he was now a celebrity. This time, however, he acknowledged the failure of attempting to seize power in Germany by force and decided to go about it legally. He wanted to be elected to power and from now on the mission of the party was to work within the democratic system, using the methods of democracy to destroy democracy. He visualized the new party as a state within a state, almost like a shadow government ready to undermine the present government and subsequently take its place. Thus, a new order NSDAP was reborn in February 1925. There were still many years to go before the Nazis would finally come to power, but by 1932, the Nazis were the largest single party, with over fourteen million votes. However, they were unable to win an outright majority over the ruling conservative and nationalist coalition. Hitler forced election after election, continually destabilizing the governing authorities by soaking up some of their support until they were at last forced to deal with him.

Hitler's skill as an orator and actor made him famous in the huge, staged Nazi rallies of the 1930s. He ingratiated himself with his listeners with his ability to speak to the hearts and minds of the people. His attitude to the crowd was not to persuade, but to appeal to their feelings, to do what God refused to do – to liberate them from reason and responsibility, a crude but effective interpretation of Nietzsche's writings.

Even though he spoke well, most of his speeches were never-theless incoherent in parts. He alternately beat and then praised the crowd in a barely concealed sado-masochistic relationship. At this time these speeches to the public were the closest human relationship he had. From the early 1930s onwards there was growing racial violence. Signs were put up telling people to stop buying from Jews, and Hitler's Brownshirts were carrying out murders under Hitler's orders. One of the original founding Nazis, Otto Strasser who later deserted Hitler said: 'Hitler responds to the vibrations of the human heart with the delicacy of a seismograph or perhaps of a wireless set . . . enabling him to act as a loudspeaker proclaiming the most secret desires, the least admissible instincts, the suffering and personal grievances of a whole nation . . . he sniffs the air . . . he gropes . . . he feels his way . . . senses the atmosphere. Suddenly he bursts forth. His words go like an arrow to their target . . . telling it what it most wants to hear . . .'

Combined with the spectacle of the Nuremberg rallies, the Germans fell under his spell, enraptured by charisma and carefully chosen rhetoric. What appeared as outbursts of passion were actually extremely calculating. He frequently put forward questions to which there could be only the answer 'yes' or 'no' and often spoke without a break for two or more hours. In the most important elections in the 1930s he would often make several speeches a night, travelling around the country by aeroplane in a similar way to how leaders of political parties do now during elections. In the Reichstag elections on 14 September 1930, the Nazis gained a spectacular break-through, gaining 6,409,600 votes and seating 107 deputies in the new 577-member Reichstag. Hitler was, however, defeated by President Hindenburg in two presidential elections on 13 March and 10 April 1932. Finally, on 30 January 1933, Hindenberg finally appointed Hitler as Chancellor in a coalition government. The many politicians who had done deals with the Nazis in order to keep power themselves were now forced to join them. Bizarrely, however, at this time it seems that no one took Hitler seriously. Von Papen, the Vice-Chancellor, reportedly said of

Hitler that he was 'no danger at all . . . we hired him for our act'. Even the British didn't believe the Nazis were a threat, few countries overseas could understand how the German nation could take him seriously.

Hitler stage-managed a fire at the seat of government, the German Reichstag, on 27 February 1933, blaming the communists and so allowing himself to declare a state of emergency, suspending civil liberties and allowing police to place suspects in 'protective custody'. By threatening to use his legal powers to dissolve the government thus throwing the country into chaos again he created an Enabling Act which gave him dictatorial powers whereupon he banned all other political parties and the formation of new ones on 14 July 1933. Finally, the Nazis had triumphed. Hitler established the Reich Chamber of Culture headed by Joseph Goebbels and set out the Nazi manifesto, which was essentially an agenda to restore German pride. The country had been in a severe economic crisis and the Nazis basically decided to tear up the Treaty of Versailles and refused to continue to pay reparations to the victorious allies; they would rearm Germany; they would reclaim Germany's lands lost in the settlement following the First World War; and they would solve the 'Jewish problem' and in that way take care of the communists as well. As a result of all this, Germany withdrew from the League of Nations on 14 October 1933. A hybrid organization called the SS, originally subject to the SA, was formed, initially as an elite bodyguard to protect the Führer, though it subsequently evolved into a party police force. It gained independence on 20 July 1933 under the leadership of Heinrich Himmler. The economic cost to Germany of all this restructuring was vast and Hitler knew that he would eventually have to take action to secure more lands for his new Germany to generate the wealth necessary to build the nation of his dreams.

As the country prepared for war, Hitler began to suffer physical problems in addition to his mental illness. His symptoms were what would now be called irritable bowel syndrome but at the time there was no such diagnosis. He had long been vegetarian – after Geli, his niece and the object of his infatuation, died he never touched meat again, claiming that it was like eating corpses. It makes one wonder how physically involved in her death he had been for him to find raw, or even cooked, meat so unpalatable. To try to address these new symptoms he began seeing a doctor called Theo Morrel. By the end of his life Hitler was taking up to thirty different drugs and vitamins each day. Theo Morrel had become his almost constant companion. Morrel had invented a substance called 'Mtuaflor' which was made from the cultured faeces of a Bulgarian peasant from the 'best Aryan stock'. Around this time Morrel was also giving Hitler painkilling injections for his colon pains which contained amphetamines to which, some medical commentators think, Hitler became addicted because they 'perked him up'.

So, in the mid-1930s, Germany rearmed, driven by a policy of huge deficit spending, abandoning the Versailles treaty, withdrawing from the League of Nations and building *autobahns*, motorways, that could carry its troops to war. By 1938, it was now or never. The country was again in deep financial crisis. Hitler's grand plan of another war had to be implemented.

Almost immediately, Austria became part of Germany without a fight. Hitler could now call himself German by birth. The Rhineland, which had been occupied by the French since the end of the Great War was infiltrated by Nazi soldiers. Next he attacked Czechoslovakia and then Poland under the pretext that he was merely protecting German minorities living within those countries' borders. The British Prime Minister, Neville Chamberlain, went to meet Hitler and came back with an agreement which, according to Chamberlain, would bring 'peace in our time'. This document was, of course, worthless. Hitler also signed a non-aggression treaty with Stalin, supposedly in order to share Poland between them, but Hitler knew that he must eventually gain land from the Russian communists. On 31 August 1939, the Germans launched a 'Blitzkrieg' (literally 'lightning war', an all-out attack) on Poland. Although the Polish army was a million strong, the Germans swept them away within hours.

On 3 September 1939, in accordance with their pact with Poland, Britain and France declared war against Germany. In the spring of the following year, Germany invaded France. The German army's advance was so rapid that Hitler felt at one point that his tanks were too far ahead of the rest of his army. However, after months of training and building up the German army, the Germans had a huge advantage over the French, and just about everyone else, in the form of military hardware. Dive-bombers (fitted with Wagnerian sirens on Hitler's direct orders) cleared a path for the advance of the tanks and behind them came the ground troops. Within six weeks the French had surrendered and the remnants of the British army were gathered on the beach at Dunkirk. Goering felt sure that the German army would inflict a massive defeat on the British army, but with the help of a flotilla of small boats and calm seas the British effected a miraculous evacuation.

By this time, Hitler's forces were in Norway, Africa and Greece. Italy, under Mussolini, was an ally and Spain was neutral, but friendly. Hitler was almost insanely convinced of his military genius and of his army's invincibility. On 13 August 1940, Goering's air force began to bomb Britain. By 17 September the raids had been ended because of unsustainable losses of German planes and aircrews. Seventy-one aircraft had been shot down in one day and Nazi Germany could certainly not continue to sustain such losses indefinitely. Germany badly needed oil and other raw materials, and so Hitler decided that the Third Reich must conquer Russia.

Hitler had other plans for Russia too. He wanted to subjugate the Slavs, whom he saw as an inferior race, to the German race. He saw everything outside Germany as a wasteland inhabited by subhumans who should be enslaved. Perhaps the most evil of the Nazi's policies, sometimes attributed to the SS leader Heinrich Himmler, the so-called 'Final Solution' was initiated in 1941. With meticulous skill and single-minded dedication Himmler assembled the SS, police and concentrations camps to develop and expand a state that would be 'racially pure'. It was Poland that was to become an enormous human abattoir. Of an estimated eighteen million victims of Nazi brutality in Europe, eleven million died on Polish soil. Of that number, five million were Jews.

We are familiar now with most of the names of these places where men, women and children, young and old, were systematically killed through being gassed, starved, tortured and worked to death by their German captors. Although mass shootings had been going on throughout and, indeed, before the war, the SS leadership decided that execution by poison gas in annihilation camps was the most efficient method of murdering the Jews and other 'undesirables' (homosexuals, communists and other detractors). Belzec was the first death camp to be set up in 1941 and became operational in 1942. A second death camp at Sobibor in eastern Poland opened the same month, followed by one at Treblinka, a fourth at Majdanek, and the most notorious at Auschwitz. These camps could execute up to fifteen thousand people a day. At Auschwitz, a new and more effective chemical agent, Zyklon-B, was introduced. It was believed that this could achieve a better death rate than other camps which continued to use the diesel method (similar to putting a hose pipe from a car exhaust through into a car with closed windows). Zyklon-B took the form of bluish pellets which were contained in a small canister. The operator, wearing a mask, had to drop the pellets into the gas chamber through a hole, whereupon they became a deadly gas that could kill people in twenty to thirty minutes.

Höss and Himmler had created at Auschwitz an extermination camp that could house 150,000 prisoners. It started out as a camp for political prisoners, mostly Polish, but was rapidly extended into a work camp and then as a site for Hitler's other 'major inferiority groups', Jews, Gypsies and 'Asiactic inferiors'. By 1942, Auschwitz had been divided between three sites with a second at Birkenau and another at Monowitz.

The invasion of Russia, 'Operation Barbarossa' began. Three separate armies forced their way into Russia and Hitler sent the extermination squads, the 'Einsatzgruppen', to liquidate the Jewish-Bolshevik ruling class. Over 300,000 civilians were killed within six months. Of 5,700,000 Russian prisoners taken, barely one million survived. The Nazis continued their policy of racist genocide.

Of Hitler's private life at this time, much remains a mystery. Of the seven women known to have had relationships of some sort with Hitler, six met an untimely death. All of these were attributed to suicide but there remains suspicion over their inquest verdicts. There are some theorists who believe that these women were killed because they had learned enough about Hitler's peculiar sexual needs that he felt it would damage his reputation if they revealed them. Among these 'suicides' was the well-known actress Renate Mueller whom Hitler invited back to his home one evening. She confided to her director that Hitler had become excited and animated while describing to her the process of Gestapo (the special duty police squad). He had then fallen to the floor demanding that she beat him. She eventually gave in to his pleas to be kicked, whereupon the more she kicked him, the more excited he became. Shortly after revealing this tale, she mysteriously 'flew' out of the window of a Berlin hotel. (It was now 1937 and the Nazis were firmly in power. Hitler had become the dictatorial ruler, he could not allow his private 'needs' to become public knowledge.)

Before this there was Geli Raubal, the daughter of his half-sister. After Hitler returned from prison he asked Geli and her daughter to come and work as his housekeepers. By this time Geli was in her late teens and had become quite a beauty and Hitler's interest went beyond that of a benevolent uncle. He began escorting her around town on his arm. She was the blonde, youthful embodiment of his Aryan dream. Hitler set Geli up in a Munich apartment with her mother and paid for her to have singing lessons hoping for her to become an opera singer, because of his love for Wagner. His attentions to this young lady did not go unnoticed by other party members who complained that he was too diverted from politics by giving such constant attention to his niece.

Hitler consolidated his relationship with Geli in 1929 by buying a luxurious home in Munich for himself and Geli and sending her mother to live in his weekend house. He and Geli had separate bedrooms but they were on the same floor. Hitler became very possessive and jealous around her. She had apparently confessed to friends that she wanted to escape from him because of his obsessive need to control her. She died suddenly on 18 September 1931, after having apparently 'shot herself in the chest' after an argument with Hitler. Again her death was reported as a suicide, although there remains controversy about it to this day. It is generally thought that she was murdered either on Hitler's orders or by Nazis worried about her influence on him. A journalist, Fritz Gerlich, suggested he had conclusive evidence linking Hitler to the murder, but he was killed before he could reveal any evidence and all his documents were burned with him. Geli had, shortly before her death, told people of the nature of Hitler's sexual requirements: that she was obliged to urinate on him. Such revelations could have been damaging to his power.

It is thought that Hitler's affair with Eva Braun started while Geli was living in his apartment. Their relationship was noted as seemingly very unaffectionate in public and he continued to flirt with other women. He preferred small blonde women, like his mother, and is on record as having said that a woman should be a '. . . cute, cuddly, naïve little thing – tender, sweet and stupid'.

For Hitler and his long dreamed of war, the tide began to turn a year later in November 1942. Rommel was defeated in Africa at El Alamein. The USA had joined the war and the Allies were bombing Germany. Crucially, in Russia, the German advance had ground to a halt in the carnage of the Eastern Front. Increasingly, Hitler began to distance and isolate himself from the war he had created. He refused to listen to reports of bomb damage to Germany or of the military situation of his army. He continued to send his armies into hopeless battle and almost certain death. In 1943, the Allies declared that they would not seek a peace settlement, only 'unconditional surrender'. In June

1944 the Allies landed in France. Within ten days, 600,000 troops were ashore and, by the end of the month, nearly a million. Still, Hitler would not accept the implications of this assault on the Reich. A number of high-ranking army officers realized that to save Germany, Hitler had to die. They came up with a plot to put a bomb in a briefcase under a table in the conference room on 20 July. Miraculously, Hitler survived, apparently protected by the thick leg of the table from serious harm. Those thought to be involved in the bomb plot were sought out by Himmler and the Gestapo. Field Marshal von Witzleben, Generals Hoepner, von Hase and Stieff, together with four others, were hanged by piano wires from meat hooks, which meant a slow death by throttling. Hitler enthusiastically made a film of the execution and would happily watch it again and again.

The failure of the bomb plot simply made the deranged Führer even more convinced that he was the right person to be in charge as heaven itself had spared him. However, on 25 August 1944, Paris was liberated and on 11 September a US patrol crossed the German border. Hitler moved into his bunker permanently, living on expensive delicacies and cakes while the rest of the citizens of Germany starved. On 30 September when Allied forces entered the bunker, they found the burned bodies of Hitler and his wife Eva Braun. She had taken a cyanide capsule and Hitler had a gunshot wound to the head. He had not survived to be called to trial for the millions dead, both through genocide and war. Arrogant to the end, he had made sure that he would never be answerable for his countless crimes against humanity.

Mao Zedong

In China, it is common for many people to regard Mao as a revolutionary hero in the first half of his life but to hold that he was corrupt after gaining power. The legacy of Chairman Mao Zedong is still one which, even today, produces the largest amount of controversy among historians of the period, one argument being about how many tens of millions died, either on his orders or because of his policies.

Mao Zedong was a Chinese Marxist theorist, soldier, poet, and statesman who led China's communist revolution after decades of foreign occupation and civil war in the twentieth century. Following the Communist Party of China's military victory over the Kuomintang, the right-wing nationalists, in the Chinese Civil War, Mao announced the establishment of the People's Republic of China on 1 October 1949, in the culturally significant Tiananmen Square in Beijing.

Mao Zedong was born on 26 December 1893 in a village called Shaoshan in Xiangtan county, Hunan Province. He was the eldest child of a moderate family. His family spoke Xiang, rather than Mandarin. His ancestors had migrated from Jiangxi province during the Ming Dynasty, married indigenous women, and had settled there as farmers for generations.

During the 1911 revolution, Mao served for months in a local regiment in Hunan. He was unhappy with life in the military and eventually left the army and returned to school in Changsha. He graduated from the First Provincial Normal School of Hunan in 1918, then travelled with Professor Yang

Changji, his high school teacher, his future father-in-law, to Beijing during the May Fourth Movement in 1919.

Professor Yang held a faculty position at National Peking University. Because of Yang's recommendation, Mao got a job as an assistant librarian at the university with Li Dazhao who was then curator of the library. At the same time, Mao registered as a part-time student at Beijing University and attended many lectures and seminars by some famous Chinese intellectuals, such as Chen Duxiu, Hu Shi and Qian Xuantong. It was during this time that he married Yang Kaihui, Professor Yang Changji's daughter, who was a fellow student of his. He already had an arranged marriage organized by his father in his home village, Shaoshan. However, Mao never acknowledged this marriage.

It was in Beijing in 1920, before he was married to Yang Kaihui, that Mao was introduced to Marxism. 'There were three books that left great impressions on my mind,' Mao recollected. 'They helped build up my solid faith in Marxism.' Among the three important books was the *Manifesto of the Communist Party*.

Mao turned down an opportunity to study in France because of poverty. Later he claimed that it was because he firmly believed that China's problems could be studied and resolved only within China. Distinctly different from his contemporaries, Mao went in the opposite direction, studying the peasant majority of China's population where he began his life as a professional revolutionary.

Nevertheless, becoming a Marxist was a gradual process for Mao. During 1920 in Hunan, Mao contributed several essays to the newspapers advocating the autonomy of Hunan Province. He firmly believed that provincial autonomy was a prelude to the success of local prosperity, which, in turn, would add to the existence of a stronger and more prosperous China in the world.

In 1920, Mao developed his theory of violent revolution, which he adopted from his readings of the experiences of the Russian revolution, and which could probably be attributed to his early reading experience of *Outlaws of the Marsh*, one of the four masterpieces of Chinese ancient literature.

Mao's theory of violent revolution sought to subvert the alliance of imperialism and feudalism in China. As a rather strategic communist, Mao had not ignored those Chinese nationalists, who he thought to be both economically and politically vulnerable. Mao concluded that the violent revolution that he favoured could by no means be steered by the nationalists. And that the proletariat should conduct such a violent revolution with the help from the Chinese nationalists, and certainly under the supervision of a communist party.

In the 1920s, Mao helped to conduct many labour struggles based on his study, propagation and organization of the contemporary labour movements. However, the government subdued these struggles and Mao fled Changsha after he was labelled a radical activist. Later, Mao recollected the failures over which he pondered seriously and carefully. Mao finally realized that Chinese labour workers were not able to lead the revolution because they made up only a relatively small proportion of China's population, and that unarmed labour struggles could not resolve the problems.

Mao began to depend on Chinese peasants who later became staunch supporters of his theory of violent revolution, which eventually distinguished Mao from all his predecessors and contemporaries. Mao had a natural relationship with the farmers and peasants at home, since he was from a farming family himself, and he developed his reputation among them. Most importantly, he introduced them to Marxism, although certainly with his own adjustments and modifications.

On 23 July 1921, Mao, at the age of twenty-seven, attended the first session of the National Congress of the Communist Party of China in Shanghai. Two years later, he was elected one of the five commissars of the Central Committee of the Communist Party of China (CPC) during the third session of the congress.

Mao stayed for a while in Shanghai, an important city that the CPC emphasized for the revolution. However, the party had encountered major difficulties in organizing labour union movements, and relations with its nationalist ally, the Kuomintang, had become poor. Mao was so disillusioned with the revolutionary movement that he moved back to his home village of Shaoshan. Mao rekindled his interest in the revolution, after having been informed of the 1925 uprisings in Shanghai and Guangzhou. He then went to Guangdong, the base of the Kuomintang, with a return of his political ambitions. During his stay there, Mao took part in the preparations for the second session of the National Congress of Kuomintang.

In 1927, Mao conducted the famous Autumn Harvest Uprising in Changsha, Hunan, as Commander-in-Chief. The Revolutionary Army of Workers and Peasants, led by Mao, was defeated and scattered after some fierce battles. Afterwards the exhausted troops were forced to leave Hunan for Sanwan, Jiangxi, where Mao reorganized the scattered soldiers, rearranging them from a military division into a smaller regiment. Mao ordered that each company must have a party branch office with a commissar as its leader who would give political instructions based upon superior mandates. This military rearrangement in Sanwan, Jiangxi, initiated the CPC's absolute control over its military force and has been considered to have the most fundamental and profound impact upon the Chinese revolution. Later on, they moved to the Jinggang Mountains in Jiangxi.

In the Jinggang Mountains, Mao persuaded two local insurgent leaders to pledge their allegiance to him. Mao reunited his army with that of Zhu De. Thus he created the Workers and Peasants' Red Army of China, which became known as the Red Army.

From 1931 to 1934, Mao helped establish the Soviet Republic of China, in the Jinggang Mountains, and was elected chairman of this small republic among the mountainous areas in Jiangxi. Here, Mao was married to He Zizhen. His wife Yang Kaihui was sacrificed for the revolution, she had been arrested and executed in 1930, just three years after their departure.

Mao had built a modest but effective army and undertook experiments in rural reform and government. He provided refuge for communists fleeing the rightist purges in the cities. Mao's methods are normally referred to as guerrilla warfare; but he himself made a distinction between guerrilla warfare (*youji zhan*): 'The enemy advances, we retreat. The enemy camps, we harass,' and mobile warfare (*yundong zhan*): 'The enemy tires, we attack. The enemy retreats, we pursue.'

Mao's guerrilla warfare and mobile warfare was based upon the fact of the poor armament and military training of the Red Army which consisted mainly of impoverished peasants, who, however, were all encouraged by revolutionary passions and aspiring after a communist utopia.

Around 1930, there had been more than ten regions, usually entitled 'Soviet Areas', under control of the CPC. By now, the numbers of Red Army soldiers ran to a hundred thousand. The prosperity of 'Soviet Areas' startled and worried Chiang Kai-shek, chairman of the Kuomintang nationalists, who launched five waves of besieging campaigns against the 'Central Soviet Area'. More than one million Kuomintang soldiers were involved in these five campaigns, four of which were defeated by the Red Army led by Mao.

Chiang Kai-shek, who had earlier assumed nominal control of China due in part to the Northern Expedition, was determined to eliminate the communists. By October 1934, he had them surrounded, prompting them to engage in the 'Long March', a retreat from Jiangxi in the south-east to Shaanxi in the north-west of China. It was during this 9,600-kilometre (5,965-mile), year-long journey, that Mao emerged as the top communist leader, aided by the Zunyi Conference. At this conference, Mao entered the Standing Committee of the Politburo of the Communist Party of China.

From his base in Yan'an, Mao led the communist resistance against the Japanese in the Second Sino-Japanese War (1937–1945). Mao further consolidated power over the Communist Party in 1942 by launching the Cheng Feng, or 'Rectification' campaign against rival CPC members such as

Wang Ming, Wang Shiwei, and Ding Ling, who were expelled and executed. In the 1940s, in Yan'an, Mao divorced He Zizhen and married the actress Lan Ping, who would become known as Jiang Qing.

In 1938 Mao wrote *On Protracted War During the Sino-Japanese War in 1938*. His strategies were opposed by both Chiang Kai-shek and the United States. The US regarded Chiang as an important ally, able to help shorten the war by engaging the Japanese occupiers in China. Chiang, in contrast, sought to build the Republic of China (ROC) army for the conflict with Mao's communist forces which was sure to come after the end of the Second World War. This fact was not well understood in the USA, and precious lend-lease armaments continued to be allocated to the Kuomintang nationalist forces. In turn, Mao spent part of the war (whether it was most or only a little is disputed) fighting the Kuomintang for control of certain parts of China. Both the communists and nationalists have been criticized for fighting among themselves rather than allying against the Japanese Imperial Army.

In 1944, the Americans sent a special diplomatic envoy called the Dixie Mission, to the Communist Party of China. According to Edwin Moise's *Modern China: A History* (the second edition): 'Most of the Americans were favourably impressed. The CPC seemed less corrupt, more unified, and more vigorous in its resistance to Japan than the Guomindang. United States fliers shot down over North China . . . confirmed to their superiors that the CPC was both strong and popular over a broad area.' In the end, however, the contacts which the USA developed with the CPC led to very little.

Then again, modern commentators have refuted such claims. Among others, Willy Lam stated that during the war with Japan: 'The great majority of casualties sustained by Chinese soldiers were borne by KMT, not Communist divisions. Mao and other guerrilla leaders decided at the time to conserve their strength for the "larger struggle" of taking over all of China once the Japanese Imperial Army was decimated by the US-led Allied Forces.'

In 1946, after the end of the Second World War, the US continued to support Chiang Kai-shek, now openly against the communist Red Army, in the civil war for control of China. The US support was part of its effort to contain and defeat 'world communism'. Likewise, the Soviet Union gave quasi-covert support to Mao, acting as a concerned neighbour rather than as a military ally, to avoid open conflict with the US. The USSR gave large supplies of arms to the Communist Party of China, although newer Chinese records indicate the Soviet 'supplies' were not as large as previously believed, and consistently fell short of the promised amount of aid.

On 21 January 1949, Kuomintang forces suffered massive losses against Mao's Red Army. In the early morning of 10 December 1949, Red Army troops laid siege to Chengdu, the last KMT-occupied city in mainland China, and Chiang Kai-shek evacuated from the mainland to Taiwan (Formosa) that same day. China had finally become communist.

The People's Republic of China (PRC) was established on 1 October 1949, when Mao made a speech in Tiananmen Square. It was the culmination of over two decades of civil and international war. From 1954 to 1959, Mao was the chairman of the PRC. During this period, Mao was called Chairman Mao or the Great Leader Chairman Mao. The Communist Party assumed control of all media in the country and used it to promote the image of Mao and the party. The nationalists under General Chiang Kai-Shek were vilified, as were ultra-capitalist countries such as the United States of America and Japan. The Chinese people were exhorted to devote themselves to build and strengthen their country. In his speech declaring the foundation of the PRC, Mao announced: 'The Chinese people have stood up!'

Immediately, almost every Chinese citizen was issued with a book called *Quotations From Chairman Mao Tse-Tung* which was regarded as a source of infallible truth in discussions or arguments at schools or in the workplace. Mao took up residence in Zhongnanhai, a compound next to the Forbidden City in Beijing, where he ordered the construction of an indoor swimming pool. Mao often did his work either in bed or by the side of the pool, preferring not to wear formal clothes unless absolutely necessary, according to Dr Li Zhisui, his personal physician. (Li's book, *The Private Life of Chairman Mao*, is regarded as controversial especially by those sympathetic to Mao.)

The Maoist era also attempted to improve women's rights. Indeed, Mao once famously remarked that 'Women hold up half the heavens.' A popular slogan during the Cultural Revolution was, 'Break the chains, unleash the fury of women as a mighty force for revolution!' The CPC abolished prostitution, a phenomenon that was to return after Deng Xiaoping and post-Maoist CPC leaders increased liberalization of the economy.

Following the consolidation of power, Mao launched a phase of rapid collectivization, lasting until around 1958. The CPC introduced price controls as well as the simplification of the Chinese system of written characters aimed at increasing literacy. Land was taken from landlords and wealthier peasants and given to poorer peasants. Large-scale industrialization projects were also undertaken.

Mao pursued the ideal of a strong and prosperous China, endeavouring to build a modern, industrialized nation. However, the disastrous results of Mao's most significant socio-political programmes – including the Anti-Rightist Campaign, the Great Leap Forward, and the Cultural Revolution – crippled China's development, leading to economic hardship, social turmoil and widespread starvation. Ultimately, this would lead to the deaths of tens of millions of Chinese people.

During the 1950s Mao created the Hundred Flowers movement, which was supposed to grant everybody, and all organizations, freedom of speech. However, after a few months of arguments opposing its policies, Mao's government reversed its policy and persecuted those who had made criticisms, and even those who were merely alleged to have made criticisms; immediately around 500,000 people were condemned to death.

The party called this new law, the Anti-Rightist Movement. Authors such as Jung Chang have alleged that the Hundred Flowers movement was merely a ruse to root out 'dangerous' thinking. Others such as Dr Li Zhisui have suggested that Mao had initially seen the policy as a way of weakening those within his party who opposed him, but was surprised by the extent of the criticism and the fact that it began to be directed at his own leadership. It was only then that he used it as a method of identifying and subsequently persecuting those critical of his regime. The Hundred Flowers movement led to the condemnation, silencing, and death of many intellectuals, also linked to Mao's Anti-Rightist movement, with death tolls through execution and murder possibly in the millions.

In January 1958, Mao launched the second 'five year plan' known as the Great Leap Forward. This was a plan intended as a Chinese alternative model for economic growth similar to that of the Soviet Union, which focused mainly on industry. Under Mao's economic programme, the relatively small agricultural collectives which had been formed to date were rapidly merged into far larger people's communes, and many of the peasants ordered to work on massive infrastructure projects. Industry began to be expanded, starting with the small-scale production of iron and steel. All private food production was banned; all livestock and farm implements were brought under collective ownership. As in the Soviet Union nothing could be privately owned.

Under the Great Leap Forward, Mao and other party leaders ordered a variety of unproven and unscientific new agricultural techniques to be implemented by the new communes. Combined with the diversion of some labour to steel production and other infrastructure projects, the reduced personal incentives under a commune system led to an approximately 15 per cent drop in grain production in 1959, followed by further 10 per cent reduction in 1960 with still no recovery in 1961. In an effort to win favour with their superiors and avoid being purged and possibly executed, each layer in the party hierarchy exaggerated the amount of grain produced under them. Based on this fabricated success, party cadres were ordered to requisition a disproportionately high amount of the true harvest for state use, primarily in the cities and urban areas, but also for export. The result, which was compounded in some areas by drought and in others by floods, was that the rural peasants were left with nothing to eat and many millions starved to death in what is thought to be the largest famine in human history. This famine caused the deaths of tens of millions of Chinese peasants between 1959 and 1962. Many children who became emaciated and malnourished during these years of hardship, died shortly after the Great Leap Forward came to an end in 1962.

The extent of Mao's knowledge as to the severity of the situation has been disputed. According to some, most notably Dr Li Zhisui, Mao was not aware of anything more than a mild food and general supply shortage until late 1959.

Jung Chang and Jon Halliday, in *Mao: the Unknown Story*, provide ample documentary evidence that Mao knew of the vast suffering and claimed that he was dismissive of it, blaming bad weather or other officials for the famine: 'Although slaughter was not his purpose with the Leap, he [Mao] was more than ready for myriad deaths to result, and hinted to his top echelon that they should not be too shocked if they happened.'

Whether Mao was aware of it or not, the Great Leap Forward led to millions of deaths in China. Mao lost esteem among many of the top party cadres and was eventually forced to abandon the policy in 1962, also losing some political power to more moderate leaders. However, he was able to use his support base – he was still popular to a certain extent within the party – to mitigate the damage caused by the failure of the programme, implying that he was only partly to blame. As a result, he was able to remain secretary of the Communist Party.

The Great Leap Forward was a disaster for China. Although the steel quotas were officially reached, almost all of it made in the countryside was useless lumps of iron, as it had been made from assorted scrap metal in home-made furnaces with no reliable source of fuel such as coal. According to Zhang Rongmei, a geometry teacher in rural Shanghai during the Great Leap Forward: 'We took all the furniture, pots, and pans we had in our house, and all our neighbours did likewise. We put everything in a big fire and melted down all the metal. Moreover, most of the dams, canals and other infrastructure projects, which millions of peasants and prisoners had been forced to toil on and in many cases die for, proved useless as they had been built without the input of trained engineers, whom Mao had rejected on ideological grounds.'

There is a great deal of controversy over the number of deaths by starvation during the Great Leap Forward. Until the mid-1980s, when the Chinese government finally published official census figures, little was known about the scale of the disaster in the Chinese countryside. The handful of Western observers allowed access during this period had been restricted to model villages, where they were deceived into believing that the Great Leap Forward had been a great success. There was also an assumption that the flow of individual reports of starvation that had been reaching the West, primarily through Hong Kong and Taiwan, must be localized or exaggerated as China was continuing to claim record harvests and was a net exporter of grain throughout the period. Censuses were carried out in China in 1953, 1964 and 1982. The first attempt to analyze this data in order to estimate the number of famine deaths was carried out by American demographer Dr Judith Banister and published in 1984. Given the lengthy gaps between the censuses and doubts over the reliability of the data, an accurate figure is difficult to ascertain. Nevertheless, Banister concluded that the official data implied that around 15 million excess deaths occurred in China during 1958–61 and that, based on her modelling of Chinese demographics during the period, and taking account of assumed under-reporting during the famine years, the figure was around 30 million. Various other sources have put the figure between 20 and 43 million.

On the international front the Sino-Soviet split was starting.

This resulted in Khrushchev withdrawing all Soviet technical experts and aid from the country. Most of the problems regarding communist unity resulted from the death of Stalin and his replacement by Khrushchev. Stalin had established himself as the successor of 'correct' Marxist thought well before Mao controlled the Communist Party of China, and therefore Mao never challenged the suitability of any Stalinist doctrine (at least while Stalin was alive). Upon the death of Stalin, Mao believed (perhaps because of seniority) that the leadership of the 'correct' Marxist doctrine would fall to him. The resulting tension between Khrushchev (at the head of a politically/militarily superior government), and Mao (believing he had a superior understanding of Marxist ideology) eroded the previous patron-client relationship between the USSR and CPC.

Partly surrounded by hostile American military bases (reaching from South Korea, to mainland Japan, Okinawa, and Taiwan), China was now confronted with a new Soviet threat from the north and west. Both the internal crisis and the external threat called for extraordinary statesmanship from Mao, but as China entered the new decade, the 'statesmen' of the People's Republics were now in hostile confrontation with each other.

The Great Leap policies were effectively given up following a politburo meeting in January 1961. Mao took more of a back seat role while more moderate leaders such as Liu Shaoqi, who had become State President in 1959, and Deng Xiaoping rescued the economy by disbanding the people's communes and introducing elements of private control to peasant small-holdings. They also began importing grain from Canada and Australia to mitigate the worst effects of famine.

Other members of the Communist Party, realizing the disasters of the last decade, including Liu Shaoqi and Deng Xiaoping, decided that Mao should be removed from actual power and only remain in a largely ceremonial and symbolic role. They attempted to marginalize Mao, and by 1959 Liu Shaoqi became State President, but Mao remained chairman of the party. Liu and others began to look at the situation much more realistically, somewhat abandoning the idealism Mao wished for. Mao also genuinely feared that China was slipping in a non-egalitarian direction and he would not stand by while a new elite took over the party and subverted the revolution. To Mao the revolution had to be a permanent process, constantly kept alive through unending class struggle. Hidden enemies in the party and intellectual circles had to be identified and removed.

Facing the prospect of losing his place on the political stage, Mao responded to Liu and Deng's movements by launching the Great Proletarian Cultural Revolution in 1966. Conceived of as a 'revolution to touch people's souls', the aim of the Cultural Revolution was to attack the 'Four Olds' old ideas, old culture, old customs, and old habits in order to bring the areas of educa-tion, art and literature in line with communist ideology. Anything that was suspected of being feudal or bourgeois was to be destroyed: 'Although the bourgeoisie has been overthrown, it is still trying to use the old ideas, culture, customs, and habits of the exploiting classes to corrupt the masses, capture their minds, and endeavour to stage a comeback. The proletariat must do just the opposite: it must meet head-on every challenge of the bourgeoisie in the ideolog-ical field and use the new ideas, culture, customs, and habits of the proletariat to change the mental outlook of the whole of society. At present, our objective is to struggle against and crush those persons in authority who are taking the capitalist road. To criticize and repudiate the reactionary bourgeois academic "authorities" and the ideology of the bourgeoisie and all other exploiting classes. And to transform education, litera-ture and art, and all other parts of the superstructure that do not correspond to the socialist economic base, so as to facilitate the consolidation and development of the socialist system.'

The decision thus took the already existing student movement and elevated it to the level of a nationwide mass campaign. It called on not only students but also 'the masses of the workers, peasants, soldiers, revolutionary intellectuals, and revolutionary cadres' to carry out the task of 'transforming the superstructure' by writing big-character posters and holding 'great debates'. The decision granted the most extensive freedom of speech the People's Republic had ever seen, but this was a freedom severely determined by the Maoist ideological climate and, ultimately, by the People's Liberation Army (PLA, the successor of the Red Army) and Mao's authority over the army. These students, workers and other revolutionaries came to be known as the Red Guards. Millions of Red Guards were encouraged by the Cultural Revolution group to become a 'shock force' and to 'bombard' with criticism both the regular party headquarters in Beijing and those at the regional and provincial levels.

Red Guard activities were promoted as a reflection of Mao's policy of rekindling revolutionary enthusiasm and destroying 'outdated', 'counter-revolutionary' symbols and values. Mao's ideas, popularised in the *Quotations from Chairman Mao*, became the standard by which all revolutionary efforts were to be judged. The 'four big rights', speaking out freely, airing views fully, holding great debates, and writing big-character posters, became an important factor in encouraging Mao's youthful followers to criticize his party rivals. The 'four big rights' became such a major feature during the period that they were later institutionalized in the state constitution of 1975. The result of the unfettered criticism of established organs of control by China's exuberant youth was massive civil disorder, punctuated also by clashes among rival Red Guard gangs and between the gangs and local security authorities. The party organization was shattered from top to bottom. (The Central Committee's Secretariat ceased functioning in late 1966.) The resources of the public security organs were severely strained. Faced with imminent anarchy, the PLA, the only organization whose ranks for the most part had not been radicalized by Red Guard-style activities, emerged as the principal guarantor of law and order and the de facto political authority.

Although the PLA was under Mao's rallying call to 'support the left', PLA regional military commanders ordered their forces to restrain the leftist radicals, thus restoring order throughout much of China. The PLA was also responsible for the appearance in early 1967 of the revolutionary committees, a new form of local control that replaced local party committees and administrative bodies. The revolutionary committees were staffed with Cultural Revolution activists, trusted cadres, and military commanders, the latter frequently holding the greatest power.

The radical tide receded somewhat, beginning in late 1967, but it was not until after mid-1968 that Mao came to realize the uselessness of further revolutionary violence. Liu Shaoqi, Deng Xiaoping, and their fellow 'revisionists' and 'capitalist roaders' had been purged from public life by early 1967, and the Maoist group had since been in full command of the political scene.

Essentially, the Cultural Revolution was an internal coup staged by a political clique surrounding Mao. They wrested power from the government by establishing a rival power base. This they achieved by encouraging and manipulating the young Chinese intelligentsia to overthrow established authorities. All aspects of Chinese life were affected in the process: government, the economy and the family. The upheavals took a great personal toll on countless individuals.

According to *Mao: the Unknown Story*, Mao was bitter that Liu and other party leaders had stopped his Great Leap Forward programme, and he was determined to exact revenge. The Cultural Revolution allowed Mao to circumvent the communist hierarchy by giving power directly to the Red Guards, groups of young people, often teenagers, who set up their own tribunals.

The Cultural Revolution led to the destruction of much of China's cultural heritage and the imprisonment of a huge number of Chinese intellectuals, as well as creating general economic and social chaos in the country. Millions of lives were ruined during this period, which is depicted by such Chinese films as *To Live* and *Farewell My Concubine*. Any vestiges of wealth, current or historical, were confiscated and destroyed and available books became reduced to ones the CPC approved of. During the Cultural Revolution, millions of educated youths were sent to rural areas to work in the country-side and learn from the peasantry. Mao believed that this would ultimately create a new society where there was no gap between urban and rural, labourers and intellectuals.

Mao chose Lin Biao to become his successor. Mao and Lin Biao formed an alliance leading up to the Cultural Revolution in order for the purges of any opposition to succeed. Mao needed Lin's clout for his plan to work. In return, Lin was made Mao's successor. Somewhat later, it is unclear whether Lin was planning a military coup or an assassination attempt but he died trying to flee China, possibly anticipating his arrest, in a suspicious plane crash over Mongolia. It was declared that Lin was planning to depose Mao, and he was posthumously expelled from the CPC. At this time, Mao lost trust in many of the top CPC figures and became more paranoid. He enlisted loyal party supporters to reinforce a personality cult around him.

In the spring of 1968, a massive campaign began, aimed at promoting the already-adored Mao Zedong to a god-like status. On 27 July, the Red Guards' power over the army was officially ended and the central government sent in units to protect many areas still being targeted by Red Guards. Mao had supported and promoted this idea by allowing one of his 'Highest Directions' to be heard by all of the people. A year later, the Red Guard factions were dismantled entirely. Mao feared that the chaos they caused, and could still cause, might harm the very foundation of the Communist Party of China. In any case, their purpose had been largely fulfilled, and Mao had largely consolidated his political power, following the example of the Soviet leader Stalin. He no longer needed them and became suspicious of the influence they possibly could hold.

A poster was created for the Cultural Revolution. The caption on the poster reads (literal translation from the Chinese): 'The People's Liberation Army is a School of Mao Zedong Thought'. One of the reasons Mao is most remembered is the 'Cult of Mao', the personality cult that was created around him. Mao had presented himself as an enemy of landowners, businessmen, and Western and American imperialism, as well as an ally of impoverished peasants, farmers and workers. Some argue that personality cults go against the basic ideas of Marxism. Stalin, however, circumvented this and began cultivating a cult of personality around himself and Lenin, even though Lenin expressly wished that no monuments be created after his death.

Mao said the following about cults at the 1958 party congress in Chengdu, where he expressed support for the idea of personality cults – even those like the one around Stalin: 'There are two kinds of personality cults. One is a healthy personality cult, that is, to worship men like Marx, Engels, Lenin, and Stalin. They hold the truth in their hands. The other is a false personality cult, blind worship without analysis.'

In 1962, Mao proposed the Socialist Education Movement (SEM) in an attempt to 'protect' the peasants against the temptations of feudalism and the sprouts of capitalism that he saw re-emerging in the countryside (due to Liu's economic reforms, which he disliked). Large quantities of politicized art were produced and circulated – with Mao at the centre. Numerous posters and musical compositions referred to Mao as 'A red sun in the centre of our hearts', a 'Saviour of the people'.

The Cult of Mao proved vital in starting the Cultural Revolution. China's youth had mostly been brought up during the communist era, and they had been taught to love Mao. Thus they were his greatest supporters. Their feelings for him were so strong that many followed his urge to challenge all established authority.

In October 1966, Mao's *Quotations from Chairman Mao Tse-Tung*, which was known as the *Little Red Book* was published. Party members were encouraged to carry a copy with them and possession was almost mandatory as a criterion for membership. Over the years, Mao's image came to be displayed almost everywhere, in homes, offices and shops. His quotations were typographically emphasized by putting them in boldface or red type in even the most obscure writings.

Mao believed that 'socialism was the only way out for China' because the United States and other Western countries would not allow China to develop using theories such as imperialism, as described by Lenin. The United States placed a trade embargo on China as a result of its involvement in the Korean War, lasting until Richard Nixon decided that developing relations with China would be useful in dealing with the Soviet Union. Some people claim that while the Tigers (South Korea, Taiwan, Hong Kong and Singapore) obtained favourable trade terms from the United States, most third world capitalist countries did not, and they saw nothing like the economic growth of the Tigers. The other side of this debate argues that the disparity in per capita income between Taiwan and the mainland today demonstrates that Mao's statement may have been a self-fulfilling prophecy.

There is more agreement on Mao's role as a military strategist and tactician during the Chinese Civil War and the Korean War. Even among those who find Mao's ideology to be either unworkable or abhorrent, many acknowledge that Mao was a brilliant political and military strategist. Mao's military writings continue to have a large amount of influence both among those who seek to create an insurgency and those who seek to crush one.

In the remains of Mao's personality cult one of the last publicly displayed portraits of Mao Zedong was at the Tiananmen gate. The ideology of Maoism has influenced many communists around the world, including third world revolutionary movements such as Cambodia's Khmer Rouge, Peru's Shining Path, the Revolutionary Movement in Nepal, and also claims influence of the Revolutionary Communist Party, USA. China has moved sharply away from Maoism since Mao's death, and most people outside of China who describe themselves as Maoist regard the Deng Xiaoping reforms to be a betrayal of Mao's legacy.

According to Deng Xiaoping, who attempted to reform

China along with Liu Shaoqi in 1959, Mao was 'seventy per cent right and thirty per cent wrong', and his 'contributions are primary and his mistakes secondary'. Some members of the Communist Party of China see Mao as responsible for pulling China away from its biggest ally, the USSR, in the Sino-Soviet split. Others admire this break with a country that Mao considered to be 'capitalist-roaders', increasingly heading towards capitalism. The Great Leap Forward and the Cultural Revolution were also considered to be major disasters in his policy by his critics and even many of his supporters. Mao has also been blamed for not encouraging birth control and for creating a demographic bump, which later Chinese leaders responded to with the one-child policy. This eventually caused the deliberate murder or abandonment of baby girls, since Chinese culture demanded that the family of a girl must pay a dowry to any future husband's family and boys had a better chance of earning higher wages to support the family.

Mao Zedong died at the age of 82, on 9 September 1976, in Beijing. Mao had been in poor health for several years and had declined visibly for some months prior to his death. His body lay in state at the Great Hall of the People. A memorial service was held in Tiananmen Square on 18 September 1976. There was a three-minute silence observed during this service. His body was later placed into the mausoleum of Mao Zedong, although he wished to be cremated and had been one of the first high-ranking officials to sign the 'Proposal that all Central Leaders be Cremated after Death' in November 1956.

Until his death, Mao maintained control of the Politburo of the Communist Party of China and the Central Committee of the Communist Party of China through both political acumen and a cult of personality, the latter resulting in such sobriquets as Grand Helmsman and Saviour of China.

As anticipated after Mao's death, there was a power struggle for control of China. On one side were the leftists led by the Gang of Four. The Gang of Four was a group in the Communist Party of China who were arrested and removed from their positions in 1976, following the death of Mao Zedong. They were blamed for the events of the Cultural Revolution. The group consisted of Mao's widow Jiang Qing and three of her close associates, Zhang Chunqiao, Yao Wenyuan, and Wang Hongwen, who wanted to continue the policy of revolutionary mass mobilization. On the other side were the rightists, which consisted of two groups. One was the led by Hua Guofeng who advocated a return to central planning along the Soviet model. The other was the reformers, led by Deng Xiaoping, who wanted to overhaul the Chinese economy based on market-oriented policies and to de-emphasize the role of Maoist ideology in determining economic and political policy.

Eventually, the Restorationist moderates won control of the government. Deng Xiaoping defeated Hua Guofeng in a bloodless power struggle shortly afterwards.

The failure of the Great Leap was partly blamed on Mao's idea of 'the more people, the stronger we are' and the rampant overpopulation thereof. Uneducated families were told to have as many children as possible. China's population growth increased exponentially.

When Deng Xiaoping took power in 1978, his new policies focused on strengthening China's economy. China was the world's most populous nation by far, and he saw overpopulation as a roadblock to economic development. In 1979, Deng began the national initiative of 'birth planning', encouraging families to have only one child to control the population. The policy is not legally enforced nationally, only 'encouraged'. The policy is supervised and enforced usually at the township level. Every township and town has a 'Birth Planning Commission', headed by a commissioner.

Mao's legacy totals more than 50 million dead. Most starved to death, others were executed for any criticism, real or imagined, of the CPC, or for acts considered 'unrevolutionary'. Still, supporters of Mao credit him with advancing the social and economic development of Chinese society. They point out that before 1949, for instance, the illiteracy rate in mainland China was 80 per cent, and life expectancy was a meagre thirty-five years. At his death, illiteracy had declined to less than

7 per cent, and average life expectancy had increased to more than seventy years (alternative statistics also quote improvements, though not nearly as dramatic). In addition to these increases, the total population of China increased by 57 per cent to 700 million, from the constant 400 million, during the span between the Opium War and the Chinese Civil War. Supporters also state that, under Mao's regime, China ended its 'Century of Humiliation' at the hands of Western imperialism and regained its status as a major world power. They believe, too, that Mao also industrialized China to a considerable extent and ensured China's sovereignty during his rule.

As the Chinese government instituted free market economic reform in the early twenty-first century, it put less emphasis on studying Mao. For example, there was little state recognition of the twenty-fifth anniversary of Mao's death. This was a clear contrast with 1993, when the state organized numerous events and seminars commemorating Mao's hundredth birthday. Nevertheless, unlike the denunciations of Stalin and 'Stalinism' by Khrushchev during the Soviet era in Russia, the Chinese government has never officially repudiated the tactics of Mao. The Chinese government also suppresses critics of the government who uphold Mao's critique of the current rulers of China as betraying the core principles of socialism.

Mao left behind him several political treatises written before and after he assumed power. These include:

On Practice (1937)
On Contradiction (1937)
On Protracted War (1938)
On New Democracy (1940)
Talks at the Yan'an Forum on Literature and Art (1942)
On the Correct Handling of the Contradictions Among the People (1957)
In Memory of Norman Bethune
The Foolish Old Man Who Removed the Mountains
Serve the People

Mao also wrote poetry. His poems are all in the traditional Chinese verse style, mainly in the classical *ci* and *shi* forms. His poems are generally considered well written and of high literary quality.

Mao received a rigorous education in Chinese classical literature while a student at university. This probably helped greatly in his ability as a poet. His style was deeply influenced by the great Tang Dynasty poets Li Bai and Li He. He is generally considered to be a romantic poet, in contrast to the realist poets represented by Du Fu.

Many of Mao's poems are still very popular in China. They are frequently quoted in popular culture, literature and daily conversations. Some of his most well-known poems are: *Changsha* (1925), *The Double Ninth* (1929), *Loushan Pass* (1935), *The Long March* (1935), *Snow* (1936), *The PLA Captures Nanjing* (1949), *Reply to Li Shuyi* (1957), and *Ode to the Plum Blossom* (1961).

The general consensus is that his pre-1949 poetic works are better, as it seems that the pre-1949 Mao himself was considered 'better'. He was an idealist, who never really seemed to, or perhaps refused to, grasp that some of his ideas caused only misery and death when he put them into practice.

Emperor Bokassa I

Jean Bedel Bokassa, President of the Central African Republic, made himself president for life in 1972. This, however, was not enough for him. By 1975, Bokassa was an established alcoholic, wallowing in the excesses that the huge wealth he had acquired could buy. In September 1976, Bokassa dissolved the government and replaced it with the 'Central African Revolutionary Council'. At the MESAN congress, he declared the republic a monarchy and announced his intention to become its first emperor. He had an obsession with French history that proved to be very expensive. He decided to spend a third of the country's annual budget on his coronation as Emperor Bokassa I. The former French colony he ruled is still one of the poorest countries in the world and at that time it had an annual gross domestic product of around $70 million, equivalent to the average turnover of major supermarket.

He issued an imperial constitution and converted back to Catholicism from Islam which he had taken as his faith a few years earlier. He had himself crowned Emperor Bokassa I on 4 December 1977. It was a lavish ceremony, clearly trying to copy Napoleon I who converted the French revolutionary republic of which he was First Consul into the First French Empire (but Napoleon had at least conquered a large empire, befitting some kind of ceremony). Bokassa's title was to be 'Emperor of Central Africa by the will of the Central African people, united within the national political party, the MESAN'. Bokassa attempted to justify his actions by claiming that creating a monarchy would help Central Africa 'stand out' from the rest of the continent, and earn the world's respect. He spent nearly $20 million on the coronation celebrations.

Bokassa's coronation ceremony was to faithfully replicate that of his favourite historical figure, Napoleon Bonaparte, with staggering attention to detail. He wore an ankle-length tunic of velvet and shoes of pearls. The imperial mantle was embroidered with gold bees, precisely like Napoleon's. Everywhere, two golden laurel fronds bracketed the gold initial 'B' for Bokassa, replacing the 'N' for Napoleon. Behind him trailed thirty feet of crimson velvet embroidered with gold, with an ermine-trimmed mantle, which weighed, apparently, over seventy pounds. A jewel-encrusted, gold-hilted sword also weighed him down along with an ebony staff of office. The crown, too, was an exact replica of Napoleon's, fronted with the golden French imperial eagle, expensive and heavy. The throne was covered with more crimson velvet, trimmed with gold and backed by another vast golden eagle, the outstretched wings of which threw an ominous shadow over the Emperor and his Empress Catherine, formerly simply Mrs Bokassa, a peasant girl from the same village of mud huts as the Emperor.

The Emperor was carried through the dusty, rutted streets of the capital, Bangui, to his coronation in a gilded coach drawn by eight white imported horses from Normandy. Fourteen horses had actually been sent from France but the rest had died because of the severe African heat. Bokassa's shifty-looking army lined the route cheering obediently. Bokassa, who had trained for the event by watching films of Queen Elizabeth's coronation, gave a much-practised royal wave with his white-gloved hand. Even the church had been renamed Notre Dame de Bangui for the occasion.

Over 2,500 guests attended from all over the world. More had been invited, including every exisiting European leader and monarch. Most had politely returned their invitations. The British dismissed the event out of hand and the US cut off aid to the country. Six hundred of the international dignitaries who came were lodged for several days in the best hotels or in

specially constructed housing and fed and watered at considerable expense to the country. However, despite generous
invitations, no actual foreign leaders attended the event. Many
thought Bokassa was insane, and compared his egotistical
extravagance with that of Africa's other well-known eccentric
dictator, Idi Amin. Tenacious rumours that he occasionally
consumed human flesh were brought up during his later trial.

The French had provided Bokassa with $2.5 million worth of
credit. He used this money to purchase a fleet of Mercedes
limousines in which to ferry his guests about, and also to
provide a ceremonial escort of two hundred BMW motor-
cycles.

During the ceremony, Bokassa promised to continue 'the
democratic evolution of the Empire'. Afterwards, 4,000 guests
sat down to a full, French-style banquet at the Renaissance
Palace in Bangui. The Emperor and Empress waltzed the night
away to music provided by a French naval band.

A few years later when Bokassa's rule had gone from
tyranny to open horror it was said that the 4,000 guests had, in
fact, been dining on human flesh. A few months earlier, as part
of his coronation celebrations, Bokassa had ordered that conditions for a number of political prisoners be made more
lenient. They were taken out of chains and given decent food
and exercise. They were told that after the ceremony they
would be given an imperial pardon. In fact, having been
suitably fed and exercised, it is claimed that they were then
expertly diced and fed to the coronation guests in rich Parisian
coronation sauce.

There was no Central African Republic before the French
came into equatorial Africa at the turn of the century. The area,
remote and unexplored, had been the location of a number of
mythical kingdoms, including that of Prester John, the
legendary Christian Emperor of Ethiopia. In the sixteenth
century, the Portuguese had invaded, lured by these fabulous
stories and looking for gold. In the next century, the Arabs
came to capture the inhabitants of the region in order to sell
them into slavery. The slave trade along with the smallpox,

measles and syphilis that came with it, decimated the people living in the area which had previously had a substantial population.

When the French moved into the area it was known as Ubangi-Shari, and from 1920 was a full-scale colony. The French leased 50 per cent of the country to a mere seventeen French companies, who were given a free hand to exploit the labour and natural products. These companies used forced labour, torture and the taking of hostages to compel most of the population to collect the increasingly rare, but valuable natural rubber vine. In 1927, a local leader, Chief Mindogon, was whipped to death by the territorial guards of one French company, because he had failed to supply enough rubber-collectors. Chief Mindogon was the father of Jean Bedel Bokassa, then aged just six.

After the Second World War, in which many Africans served their French masters obediently and bravely, President de Gaulle sought to retain a looser hold over the African colonies. They were offered two choices: remain willingly as extensions of France, subject to French rule but also able to call on French assistance or accept complete independence, along with the complete withdrawal of the French. The fear of Barthelmy Boganda, then French-appointed ruler of Ubangi-Shari, was that since the colonial powers had carved equatorial Africa into small states, independence for Ubangi-Shari would leave it as a small insignificant province, very likely to be trampled on by its neighbours. Also, while the French could withdraw their troops and administrators, their businessmen still held a large portion of the country's limited wealth. It would be a state, but not yet a nation as it had never had an independent central government. Prior to colonization, the area had comprised a number of tribes, each one following its own leaders. Boganda asked the French for help with the transition. The French refused, there was no compromise available, and, in 1960, the Central African Republic was born. It was a reluctant independence. Barthelmy, the only man with sufficient experience to attempt to solve the nation's dilemmas, died in an aircraft accident the same year.

His successor was David Dacko. After independence was achieved on 13 August 1960, Dacko became Provisional President of the Republic (from 14 August 1960 to 12 December 1960), and then, with the active support of France against his rival Abel Goumba, the first President of the Central African Republic (12 December 1960 to 31 December 1965). In 1960 he also served as President of the Conference of Prime Ministers of Equatorial Africa. During his first term as President, Dacko significantly increased diamond production in the Central African Republic by eliminating the monopoly on mining held by (French) concessionary companies and decreeing that any Central African could dig for diamonds. He also succeeded in having a diamond-cutting factory built in the capital, Bangui. Diamonds eventually became the Central African Republic's most important export and remain so today, even though half or more of the mined diamonds are smuggled out of the country. Dacko encouraged the rapid 'Central Africanization' of the Central African Republic's administration, which was accompanied by growing corruption and inefficiency, and he expanded the number of civil servants, which greatly increased the portion of the national budget needed to pay salaries. The difficulty of securing sufficient revenue to pay such a large number of often inefficient and corrupt bureaucrats has been a major problem for the Central African Republic ever since. After five years of increasing corruption and chaos, on 31 December 1965 Bokassa seized power in a military coup. Troops loyal to Bokassa, many of whom had served with him in the French army, overran Bangui. Dacko handed over the combination of the safe to Bokasssa. Bokassa abolished the constitution of 1959 on 4 January 1965 and began to rule by decree.

Bokassa was born in Bobangi, a village in Moyen-Congo, in the present Central African Republic (then a French colony called French Equatorial Africa) in 1921. His father was the village chief. Bokassa was raised in a French Catholic Mission and joined the French army at the earliest opportunity. A career soldier, Bokassa joined the Free French Forces and ended the

113

Second World War as a sergeant-major, having been awarded the Legion d'Honneur (an award created by Napoleon) and the Croix de Guerre. By 1961 he had risen to the rank of lieutenant. He left the French army in 1964 to join the army of the Central African Republic. In 1965, then forty-four years old, he had served in French Indochina, and risen to the rank of colonel after impressing his French commanders with his loyalty and his fascination with French military history. As a cousin of the current president, David Dacko, and nephew of Dacko's predecessor Barthélémy Boganda, Bokassa rose to the rank of Chief of Staff of the Armed Forces of the Central African Republic. Through his French contacts, he eventually rose to the position of Chief of Staff at the Ministry of Defence. He thought his claims of being related to Barthelmy Boganda gave him a tribal right to position of leader.

His coup was a surprise for the French. Technically, the country was officially independent, but the French still reserved the right to interfere when and where necessary. However, the civil unrest during Dacko's regime had made them fear for their business and strategic interests in the country. Because of what was happening in other parts of Africa at the time, the French were worried about the possibility of a Marxist-led popular uprising. They had actually been planning their own coup until Bokassa, who learned about their intentions, arrested the chosen replacement to Dacko, Colonel Jean Izamo, head of the national gendarme police force, on New Year's Eve. Dacko, who belonged to the same Ngbaka ethnic group as Bokassa, was imprisoned, placed under house arrest in Lobaye, but then was released on 16 July 1969. He was eventually named Personal Counsellor of President Bokassa on 17 September 1976. When Bokassa's rule came under increasing criticism, through his increasingly violent and erratic behaviour during the late 1970s, Dacko managed to escape to Paris. Eventually, the French would convince him to co-operate in a coup to remove Bokassa from power and restore him to the presidency.

Until the lavish coronation twelve years later there was little to distinguish Bokassa's government from any other chaotic, violent and corrupt post-colonial regime common throughout Africa at the time. It was run on the simple maxim of 'to the victors, the spoils'. Bokassa abolished any vestiges of democracy, making himself president and head of the armed forces, the Minister of Information and the Minister for Justice. In a move similar to that of Idi Amin, he appointed people from his own tribal background to ministerial positions. He also regularly shot them, often for minor misdemeanours. The army officers who had supported him were rewarded with vast salaries and promotions. Towards the public, he behaved initially like a benign chieftain, making extravagant public gestures to compensate for his lack of ability to govern. He donated his first month's salary towards the building of a hospital, and even paid in cash one or two of the country's outstanding bills. Work was started on a public transport system; a central market was built. To a population thoroughly accustomed to mere exploitation these seemed like definite signs of improvement. Predictably, however, they were not sustained.

France didn't much care for military leaders who took charge without first obtaining permission from them. However, Bokassa's regime was preferable to the communism they dreaded. Also, Bokassa was so clearly a Francophile that they thought he would be harmless. He never renounced his French citizenship and idolized de Gaulle. Even the death of his father at the hands of the French colonialists only seemed to have filled him with admiration for their power. He remained grateful to the French church and army for taking the position of surrogate parent. He regarded de Gaulle's successor, Giscard d'Estaing, as his 'cousin'. Bokassa was still financially dependent on France, which was the outlet for half its exports and from which it received huge amounts of aid, sometimes up to $20 million a year. However, nearly 90 per cent of that was 'bi-lateral', in that it involved some concession in return from the Central African Republic. France had a big financial interest in the country, and therefore, in Bokassa.

Realizing that the country had almost been better off as an

outright colony, Bokassa persuaded the French to send a small contingent of paratroopers to guarantee the stability of his regime. The original group of eighty quickly swelled until, by 1969, 20 per cent of the armed forces were French. Bokassa was not particular where his money came from and at various times the US, the Soviet Union, Yugoslavia, Romania and South Africa were all involved in 'projects'. After a meeting with Colonel Gaddafi of Libya, Bokassa decided to convert to Islam and changed his name to Salah Eddine Ahmed Bokassa. It is presumed that this was a ploy calculated to ensure ongoing Libyan financial aid.

In April 1969, an attempted coup was the impetus for Bokassa to further consolidate his power. Bokassa's private bank account and that of the government's had never been entirely separate entities. The line that did exist between them was removed when his Minister of Finance, Colonel Alexander Banza, was arrested, tortured and executed. He had foolishly attempted to restrict the tide of Bokassa's personal enrichment. From then on, Bokassa began a process of what he termed 'privatization' of state assets and revenue. This meant that the diamond and uranium mining interests, obviously the most important of the country's assets, became the property of a handful of closely related people, with French companies owning the mining concessions. Diamonds and uranium accounted for around 50 per cent of the country's exports. Bokassa had a complete monopoly on internal trade and shares in every national business, and, through bribery and fear, he completely subjugated the whole civil service to his will. Out of 4,000 government officials, few bothered to do any work, and even fewer had any power at all. They lived in the old colonial villas and clubs, a seeming life of luxury, with little to do. Because its currency was still the French franc, and France protected its value, the country was saved from bankruptcy by the skin of its teeth. The situation, however, was still desperate.

In March 1972, Bokassa declared himself president for life. He survived another coup attempt in December 1974 and an assassination attempt in February 1976. There was always a plot in the offing somewhere, but they became a regular, bi-annual event in the following years, generally launched by those who were jealous of the success of Bokassa's 'privatization' and wanted a piece of the action. Bokassa was desperately attached to even the tiniest portion of the fortune he had amassed. In 1973, after an attempted robbery at his palace, he became insane with anger at the idea of being robbed. He went to a nearby prison and personally beat to death three convicted thieves being held there. They had had nothing to do with the failed burglary but he had had to make someone pay. The following day he passed a decree sanctifying property, with ears, limbs or anything else to be cut off for the most minor theft.

When Bokassa announced his intention to become Emperor in 1976 he started building himself an imperial palace at Berengo. This was still not yet finished by his coronation. It was to have had landscaped lawns, swimming pools, fountains, bulletproof glass and fortress-like defences. The cost of this folly, in addition to his absurdly lavish coronation, devastated the nation's finances. No one could stop him, though, as, a year later he announced yet more publicly financed celebrations to commemorate the anniversary of his coronation. The government ran out of money, and was unable to pay any of its civil service salaries or any student grants. In January 1979, Bokassa decided that all school children had to purchase and wear ludicrous French-style school uniforms, the sole manufacturer of which was an establishment owned by his wife. Given the Central African heat, this was not only financially but also physically ridiculous as well. Most school children in Bangui had no books, and many went barefoot. It was not a popular decision. Bokassa, however, was quite resolute, and students found themselves turned away from school for being incorrectly dressed. General unrest began to spread, and a certain amount of looting began in the town centre. Bokassa sent in the army who gunned down and killed two hundred 'disruptive' students and children. Bokassa then blamed it on the Russians and denounced the 'stupid' government decree about school uniforms; he was Emperor, he could overrule it and make sure that whoever was responsible was punished. The French eventually bailed out the country, and civil service salaries were raised by 50 per cent to keep them quiet.

Though it was claimed that the new empire would be a constitutional monarchy, no significant democratic reforms were made, and the suppression of dissent remained widespread. Torture was said to be especially rampant, with allegations that even Bokassa himself occasionally participated in beatings. Despite the country's decline into dictatorship, France remained a supporter of Bokassa. French president Valéry Giscard d'Estaing was a friend and loyal supporter of the Emperor, and supplied the regime with much financial and military backing. In exchange, Bokassa frequently took d'Estaing on hunting trips in Africa to his personal game reserve, which took up most of the eastern half of the country. He often greeted d'Estaing with a handful of diamonds and supplied France with uranium, a mineral that was vital for France's nuclear weapons programme. Bokassa, by now, had annexed the major portion of his country's wealth, and showered it on visiting diplomats.

By January 1979, French support for Bokassa had all but eroded after the riots in Bangui led to the massacre of civilians, and the regime became international news. In April 1979, Bokassa arrested a number of students and teachers for circulating leaflets denouncing his wealth. Strikes and 'sit ins' began. Between 18 and 20 April, the 'Imperial Guard' rounded up one hundred students and children and took them to Ngaragbo prison. They were then systematically beaten to death, with the active participation of Bokassa. Their bodies secretly disappeared. The cannibalism stories that emerged during and after his overthrow received a boost from the discoveries made at his imperial palace, where it seems he had been butchering children and allegedly feeding the bits he couldn't manage to his four pet crocodiles. In some lurid accounts, the bodies of up to forty children were found at the bottom of his swimming pool, with another dozen in the cold-storage room, left over from the feasting of the previous night. Ironically, 1979 was the 'International Year of the Child'.

The French were becoming horribly embarrassed by the stories coming out of Bangui. However, they still had a number of businesses in the country. To give them more time to access their assets and possibly remove Bokassa from power in the country, they set up an African Mission of Inquiry with representatives from five other African states to investigate the allegations. In the meantime, they tried desperately to get rid of Bokassa before the inquiry could find him guilty. This would put them in the position of being the principal sponsors of a mass-murdering dictator. Their efforts were in vain, Bokassa refused all their invitations to take trips outside his own country, and stayed in his fortified palace.

The inquiry found Bokassa guilty in August 1979. Protesting that he was a fervent Christian – although he once briefly converted to Islam – and the father of a large family himself, Bokassa protested that he could never have harmed children. In September, amid mass civil unrest caused by the sanctions his barbarous behaviour had brought on his country, Bokassa was forced to flee to Libya. While he was out of the country, the French launched 'Operation Barracuda', and in a bloodless coup brought David Dacko back from Paris and put him back in the presidential palace in Bangui. Dacko remained president until André Kolingba overthrew him on 20 September 1981.

Bokassa found himself stranded in Libya. The French initially refused him an entry visa to their country. He eventually fled to the Ivory Coast, where he sold swimwear. In 1983, France finally gave him asylum because of his French Foreign Legion history and he later lived in exile in France in a villa outside Paris. Miraculously, he ended up flat broke and had his water, gas and electricity supplies cut off. His children were arrested for shoplifting and he was unable to bail them out.

In 1986, he returned to Bangui, where, in his absence, he had been sentenced to death. After he returned from exile in France on 24 October 1986, he was arrested and tried for treason, murder, cannibalism and embezzlement. Following an emotional trial over some months he was sentenced to death on 12 June 1987. His sentence was commuted to solitary life imprisonment in February 1988 and then reduced further to twenty years. He was released in 1993, as part of a general amnesty for all prisoners, called for by out-going President Andre Kolingba. Bokassa returned to his family village and his seventeen wives and fifty children. At the end of his life he proclaimed himself the thirteenth apostle and claimed to have secret meetings with the Pope. The only state leader ever to be tried for cannibalism died of a heart attack on 3 November 1996.

After his death, the Central African state radio described him as 'illustrious' and said he would be buried in his home village of Berengo. Ten years earlier, during his disgrace, the same radio called him 'the Ogre of Berengo'.

Nicolae Ceauşescu

When one thinks about Romania, its fairytales and mythological history are what first come to mind. The Transylvanian
forests are inhabited, in legend at least, by vampires and
ghouls. Vlad Dracul, thought to be the basis for Bram Stoker's
vampire tale of Dracula, hails from this part of the world. There
are many monsters and tyrants in Romanian folktales; in
Nicolae Ceauşescu, Romanians found themselves a real
monster and tyrant.

Nicolae Ceauşescu was born on 26 January 1918 in a two-
room peasant dwelling in the tiny village of Scorniceşti, Olt
County (in the informal region of Oltenia), around a hundred
miles from Bucharest. He was one of ten children. His mother
was a devout Christian and was illiterate, his father a well-
known drunk and bully. The only distinguishing feature of the
young Nicolae was a severe stammer, which caused him to be
bullied at school, perhaps adding to his future paranoia.

Ceauşescu moved to Bucharest at the age of eleven to
become a shoemaker's apprentice. He enthusiastically joined
the then illegal Communist Party of Romania in Bucharest in
early 1932 and was first arrested in 1933, charged with
agitating during a strike. He was again arrested in 1934,
initially for collecting signatures on a petition protesting the
trial of railway workers sympathetic to the communists and
twice more for other similar activities. These arrests earned
him the description of a 'dangerous communist agitator' and an
'active distributor of communist and anti-fascist propaganda'

121

on his police record. He consequently went underground, but was captured and imprisoned in 1936 for two years at Doftana for anti-fascist activities. It is rumoured that when Ceauşescu converted to communism he learned to repeat a huge amount of party dogma without stammering to prove his devotion to the cause. Unfortunately he never quite overcame his speech problem which was always secretly mocked to the end of his life.

As is common with communist leaders, his history was more or less rewritten for propaganda purposes and the early life of Ceauşescu was no different. Accordingly his young life was full of idealized rosy-cheeked and barefoot peasants, oppressed but cheerfully and determinedly socialist. His birthplace was opened to the public as a sort of shrine after his ascension to power. The peasant cottage was rebuilt, retimbered, whitewashed and the floor spread with suitably working-class straw (in reality it would have been a mixture of dirt and sawdust which would have been less picturesque). There is scarcely a document relating to his life that has not been altered or simply faked and inserted into the files years afterwards. This fanatical remodelling of his life extended to the smallest incidents. Photographs of Ceauşescu had to be retouched to remove any unsightly wrinkles before they were used in publications (often making him look like he had been sanded down like a rough piece of wood). There is one photograph that appeared in the official newspaper *Scienteia* in 1989 where Ceauşescu is posing with Zhikov, the Bulgarian leader, which shows Ceauşescu with three hands. Zhikov had been holding a hat and Ceauşescu thought it necessary that he should have a hat too so one was painted in along with a hand to hold it. The problem was that the artist forgot to erase one of Ceauşescu's hands.

While out of jail in 1939, he met Elena Petrescu (they married in 1946). She would play an increasingly strategically important role in his political life over the decades. The Ceauşescus had one adopted son, Valentin Ceauşescu (he was adopted in order to give a personal example of how people should take care of orphans, a big problem in Romania), a daughter Zoia Ceauşescu (born 1950) and a younger son, Nicu Ceauşescu (born 1951).

Ceauşescu was arrested and imprisoned once more in 1940, again for political agitating. In 1943, he was transferred to Târgu Jiu internment camp where he shared a cell with Gheorghe Gheorghiu-Dej, the famous communist leader, becoming his protégé.

During the Second World War, under the rule of fascist General Ion Antonescu, Romania actively supported Germany, particularly after the German invasion of Russia. Ceauşescu, who had met the future leader of the Romanian Communist Party in jail, worked his way up through the ranks of the outlawed party. In 1944, during a coup that was afterwards portrayed as a great communist uprising, King Michael ousted Ion Antonescu, restored democracy and pulled Romania out of the war. A coalition government, of which the communists were part, gave them a back door to power. After the Second World War, when Romania was beginning to fall under Soviet influence, Ceauşescu was made Secretary General of the Communist Youth Movement (a post he held from 1944 to 1945).

At the end of the Second World War the fate of the Romanians, though they did not know it, was being decided at Yalta where Churchill and Stalin sat down to carve up the wreckage of post-war Europe. The Russians were given a large chunk of the Eastern Bloc, including a 90 per cent influence in Romania. In the years that followed, the fascists were replaced by the Securitate and Russian troops. Virtual occupation by the communists followed. The communists were now the dominant party. Any opposition to their rule was savagely suppressed with the unrestrained use of violence. Democrats were branded as Nazis, their confessions extracted under torture.

In the general election of 1946, the Romanians over-whelmingly rejected their communist rulers. The results were suppressed by Gheorghiu-Dej who branded the opposition 'fascist traitors' and put the leaders of opposing parties on trial, fraudulently keeping the communist government in power. He proceeded to abolish the popular National Peasants Party and King Michael was forced to abdicate at gunpoint, under threat of the communists starting a civil war. It was now virtually an open war between the opposing parties. Between 1945 and 1955, 200,000 members of the National Peasants Party were arrested and jailed for a total of 900,000 years between them. Seventy-two per cent of them died in prison, principally of torture or murder that was often publicly labelled as suicide – almost all deaths in prison during those years were the result of unnatural causes.

Throughout this period Ceauşescu generally did very well for himself. There was a brief period in 1945 when he was fired for falling out with Moscow's communist representative, who thought him backward and dim, mainly because of his speech impediment. However, he bounced back in the dubious 1946 elections to become deputy to the Romanian Parliament. By 1948 he had become Deputy Minister for Agriculture. He took to wearing a badly fitting general's uniform to signify his new-found importance. His passionate nationalism made him popular with the other Romanian communists who were growing increasingly distant from Moscow. He was particularly interested in Joseph Stalin whose method of rule impressed him; he followed him closely. In a typically Stalinist way, he used his promotion to 'Secretary to the Central Committee in charge of Party Organization', to ensure that everybody appointed to the endless bureaucratic committees owed their positions to him and knew it. Every application passed across his desk and had to be verified by him. He now controlled the access to power and privilege in a society where luxuries were few and far between. Like Stalin, he learned how to control through bureaucracy and hard work.

There was a strong nationalist streak and a hatred of Russia among the Romanian people. Consequently the gap between Russia and Romania continued to widen. However, Stalin and his methods were approved of objectively within the Romanian leaders and he continued to be revered even after his death. Russia wanted Romania to become a supplier of grain for the Eastern Bloc's common market. The Romanians, however, wanted to copy Stalin's industrialization policy. They resented being cast in the role of a peasant-like agricultural society; they wanted the big factories and the power they assumed this would give them. When Gheorghiu-Dej died of cancer in 1965, the Romanian Communist Party looked to elect a leader who would continue, if not advance, Romania's relative independence from Russia. This was how, at the age of forty-seven, Nicolae Ceauşescu, with his strong Stalinist and patriotic views, became Secretary General of the Romanian Communist Party and with this the ruler of his country. There were other candidates but no one stood against him knowing that if they opposed him and failed, they were unlikely to survive for much longer. Ceauşescu became leader with Stalin's methodology as his only idea of how to run a country.

Ceauşescu then proceeded with a manic period of diplomatic visits and long, elaborately staged public speeches and appearances. This ostentatious, if professionally styled, time became known as 'the Frenzy' which marked the beginning of his PR-driven personality cult. There were motorcades, flower-draped cars, balcony appearances and long speeches in front of stage-managed crowds. He wanted to be seen on a large international world stage as a major world leader.

He got lucky when, in Czechoslovakia, communism was undergoing a thaw in what became known as 'the Prague Spring'. In 1968, the Russians, who had just crushed similar resistance in Hungary, sent the tanks in. This was Ceauşescu's big break. He made a speech in which he voiced Romania's terror of Russian interference: 'There is no justification whatsoever for military intervention in the affairs of a fraternal socialist state . . . the entire Romanian people will never allow anybody to violate our homeland.'

Overnight the poor boy from Scorniceşti became a national hero and international sensation. Initially, the Western powers were so delighted to discover an Eastern Bloc country seemingly opposed to the Soviet Union that they thought of him as an ally, misinterpreting his patriotic rhetoric as progressive thinking. From then on many Western leaders flocked to meet with this anti-Soviet communist leader. Those he met included de Gaulle, Richard Nixon and Margaret Thatcher. Ceauşescu was very popular and could do no wrong. Nixon called him 'one of the great leaders of the world'.

Without a doubt, all this went to his head. He deliberately recultivated his personality cult to keep up to date with his burgeoning ego. Public appearances now became completely artificial with the use of 'canned laughter' and pre-recorded applause for use whenever necessary. When he visited North Korea, the clearly demented Kim Il Sung forced his entire population to wear badges with Ceauşescu's face on them. Every road had a separate lane just for Kim Il Sung's use. Ceauşescu was impressed – both he and his wife Elena thought that the totalitarian state of North Korea showed the way forward for communism. Elena, in particular, thought assuming greater power would bring her husband the respect she thought he deserved. After the visit to Korea she egged on her already egotistical husband to claim even greater power. Apparently her favourite phrase was, 'They don't deserve you; you are too great for them.'

An entourage of sycophants was quickly acquired, all willing to protect Ceauşescu from the realities of life in Romania in return for power and privilege. Ceauşescu began to believe his own hype: in his mind he was a national hero and the people loved him for it.

Suddenly things began to shift and disappear mysteriously. Ceauşescu's father, drunk in a bar in Bucharest, was overheard telling people not to take his son so seriously, adding that he told 'nothing but lies'. The next day the pub had vanished and been replaced by a 'long-established' dairy outlet. It was not advisable to make any remark on this sort of thing. The favourite treatment for those who questioned what they were seeing was a long stay in a psychiatric hospital. At institutions like the Doctor Petra Groza hospital in Bucharest patients were often referred for treatments such as 'political paranoia'. Those treated included priests if they complained about corruption; journalists and writers diagnosed with 'senile dementia' if they wrote about human rights abuses. These 'politically insane' cases were locked up with the genuinely disturbed; there was no distinction drawn between them. When prisoners were finally genuinely crazed and sick they were made to build their own coffins and killed with drug overdoses.

Ceauşescu's whims began to border on the ridiculous. On one occasion he decided that he wanted to make a welcome speech to the new students at the Polytechnic Institute in Bucharest. The problem was that the proposed rallying point was at that time taken up by a vast, 12,000-cubic-metre access hole for the new Bucharest metro. The morning after Ceauşescu had made his request, the engineers arriving for work on the metro found, instead of the hole they expected, mature trees, grass, flowers and a very pleasant park, perfect for a rally. No one dared to tell Ceauşescu that his plans were in any way inconvenient, so he got what he wanted.

In 1974, Ceauşescu declared himself to be President of Romania and awarded himself a regal sceptre. By now the rampant nepotism and the extent of Ceauşescu's family's control during his rule was almost beyond belief. His wife Elena acquired a string of fake degrees and became a member of the Central Committee, effectively becoming deputy leader of the country. Ceauşescu's brother, Floria, was the chief journalist on the official newspaper *Scienteia*. His brother Ioan was also made a member of the central committee and became Vice President of State Planning. His sisters did equally well in politics, business and the health service. Ceauşescu's son, Nicu, was placed in charge of the Communist Youth Organization, even though he had had a reputation as a rapist from the age of fourteen. Nicu inherited the family penchant for alcohol, developing cirrhosis of the liver years later in prison. Ceauşescu's daughter, Zoia, became a melancholy nymphomaniac. Corruption and prostitution reigned at the highest levels of government.

Next, Ceauşescu decided that Romania should repay its national debt. There was no reason for this other than as a rampant nationalist he wanted Romania to be completely self-sufficient and not owe anybody any money. He thought if this was the case no one on the international scene could interfere with what went on inside Romania. It was another idea that he had picked up from North Korea's Kim Il Sung. This now meant that the Romanian people had even less to eat, as everything had to be exported. Internationally, Ceauşescu began to be seen as unsophisticated, mean and untrustworthy. Elena was desperate to be invited to stay at Buckingham Palace. Accordingly, Ceauşescu offered a £300-million aircraft deal to the British for this coveted photo opportunity. When that was refused he offered ice cream, yoghurt and strawberries along with the aircraft. It is rumoured that the Queen found all of this extremely distasteful.

Ceauşescu became obsessed with food and hygiene. He arrived everywhere with a personal taster and several bottles of alcohol with which he constantly sterilized his hands after shaking hands with anybody. It had been rumoured that Gheorghiu-Dej's cancer had been caused by radiation beamed at him by the Russians to get rid of him. Consequently Ceauşescu had every room swept by a Geiger counter before he entered. Fidel Castro told Ceauşescu that he had uncovered a CIA plot to smear the inside of his clothes with poison that would make his hair fall out. Ceauşescu then decided it would be unsafe to wear any of his clothes more than once. It became a matter of state priority. The Securitate designed and made all his clothes, keeping a year's supply hermetically sealed in a climate-controlled warehouse at a secret location outside Bucharest. He did eventually visit the Queen of England but palace staff were amazed to find him holding a conference with his staff in the grounds at 6 a.m. He had naturally assumed that his rooms would be bugged. His paranoia was now rampant.

He developed a passion for eavesdropping; claiming that it was the only way to create an 'honest population'. Behind his office was a personal monitoring room where he could select households like TV channels. A new telephone was created which doubled up as a microphone direct to central government. It became the only one available in Romania. Even televisions came with built-in transmitters. By 1980, every restaurant was equipped with ceramic ashtrays and vases stuffed with listening devices. Dissident Carol Kiraly said in 1984: 'The atmosphere of terror is beyond description. It permeates every aspect of everyday life. Distrust is so prevalent that no one dares to communicate with anyone else . . .'

In 2006, it was discovered that Ceauşescu had recruited thousands of children to spy on school friends, parents and teachers. The Securitate recruited children across Romania and blackmailed them into becoming informants in the late 1980s as the winds of change began to blow across the former Eastern European communist countries. 'In every county there were complex networks of children allegedly working for Ceauşescu.' The children were expected to tell their Securitate handlers of their friends' and families' opinions on the Communist Party and whether they listened to Western radio stations or had contact with foreigners or made jokes about Ceauşescu. It seems that Ceauşescu's paranoia was such that he would stop at nothing in attempting to discover any threat to his leadership, however small and insignificant.

In spite of all this, the West still regarded him as an ally and turned a blind eye to his absurd behaviour. As late as 1988, President Bush paid him a friendly visit. Many leaders went hunting with him, although he was such a bad shot he hired snipers to stand behind him and be responsible for his own 'hits'.

His wife Elena had as many delusions of grandeur as her husband. On official visits she devoted herself to receiving luxury free gifts, honorary titles and diamonds. She even opened a 'National Museum of Gifts to the Ceauşescus'. Neither she nor Ceauşescu ever set foot inside a shop and were officially paid an annual salary of 18,000 lei (equivalent to US$3,000 at the official exchange rate at the time). Nevertheless, there was a slush fund with over $400 million in cash from Securitate operations, something that would later be used against them during their trial. The money came from 'selling' the Jewish population of Romania to Israel at up to $50,000 a head and from arms deals and, notoriously, drug smuggling.

Ceauşescu's dogs were another passion of his and he treated these with extreme kindness, giving them their own luxury doggy villa complex, complete with telephone and television. His motorcades that drove through Bucharest often contained no one other than Corbu, his favourite black Labrador on a trip to the countryside.

Despite the wealth of the Ceauşescus and the luxury lifestyles that their other family members and even their dogs lived, the country was in a terrible state. Eventually, animal feed had to be used, instead of flour, for making bread. Petrol queues were up to three miles long and, without fuel, people were freezing to death in winter temperatures of down to −30 degrees Centigrade. Erratic gas supplies meant that fires would go on and off at irregular intervals. Many people who fell asleep by their working gas fires died by them as the gas supply ran out then came on again while they slept. The suicide rate soared and many people have described the entire population at the time as suffering from acute depression. Because of all the deaths, Ceauşescu banned contraception and abortion to increase the population of the country. The birth rate rose by 92 per cent but the infant mortality rate rose by 146 per cent. There were not enough hospitals, doctors, nurses, milk or clothes to deal with so many children. Undeterred, Ceauşescu continued with his repopulation policy. It was a horribly botched attempt at social engineering. Women had to have regular tests to make sure they were not using contraceptive devices. AIDS began to spread unrecognized, spread by contaminated blood and re-used needles. Mentally handicapped and unwanted children were dumped in remote orphanages where many died of hepatitis and cholera.

The industries Ceauşescu had established were appallingly

inefficient. He spent more time and money organizing his grand rallies and speeches than he did on Romania's industries. In one particularly absurd act, Ceauşescu had 20,000 Bibles sent to Romania by a Christian organization made into toilet paper – odd words such as 'Esau', 'Jeremiah' and 'God' were still legible on it. A parrot, formerly a pet at one of the Ceauşescus' households, was arrested and then throttled by the Securitate after it was heard saying 'Stupid Nicu', in reference to Ceauşescu's son Nicu. It was throttled when, under interrogation, it refused to give the name of the person who had taught it the insult.

Ceauşescu's megalomania continued. His next project, again following Stalin's lead, was the 'systemization' of the ancient, rural communities. He also wantonly destroyed a huge part of the old Bucharest to make his monolithic 'House of the People', a huge, grey concrete slab designed as a tribute to his own achievements. One of the world's largest buildings and often referred to one of the world's most boring buildings, it now stands empty and decaying because it has no practical use. Its staterooms are so vast as to be impossible to heat and in winter icicles hang from the ceiling. To light and heat the House of the People would take more power than all of Bucharest's domestic users have at their disposal.

The rural 'systemization' programme involved obliterating thousands of villages and moving the populations into 'urban collectives' or 'agro-industrial complexes' where workers would have to rent tiny flats on vast concrete estates. This sheer vandalism of pretty rural villages was all part of Ceauşescu's distrust of the peasants and his desire to put people where they could be more easily spied on by him and encouraged to inform on each other. Elena agreed; she thought the new concrete buildings would look much more 'tidy and modern' than the higgledy-piggledy village cottages and huts.

In a different way to other Warsaw Pact leaders at the time, Ceauşescu had not been pro-Soviet but had pursued an 'independent' foreign policy for Romania. While Soviet leader Mikhail Gorbachev spoke of reform, Ceauşescu was more in favour of the political hard-line, megalomania, and personality cults of East Asian communist leaders like North Korea's Kim Il Sung, whom he greatly admired. Even after the Berlin Wall fell and Ceauşescu's southern comrade, Bulgarian leader Todor Zhivkov, was replaced in November 1989, Ceauşescu ignored the threat to his position and held out as the last old-style communist leader in Eastern Europe.

It was a priest who eventually started the uprising in Romania. On 16 December 1989, a protest broke out in Timişoara in response to an attempt by the government to evict a dissident Hungarian reformed pastor, László Tökés. Tökés had recently made critical comments against Ceauşescu's regime in his sermons, which reached the international media. The government alleged that he was inciting ethnic hatred. Afraid of the government, the bishop had removed him from his post at Ceauşescu's request. He was also deprived of the right to use the apartment he was entitled to as a pastor. For some time, his parishioners gathered around his home to protect him from harassment and eviction by the Securitate. Passers-by, including religious Romanian students, having been told by the pastor's supporters that this was yet another attempt by the communist regime to restrict religious freedom, spontaneously joined in. The whole town resisted and the unrest spread. Ceauşescu furiously called an emergency meeting, shouting, 'You do not quieten your enemy by talking to him, but by burying him. Some hooligans want to destroy socialism and you make it child's play for them.'

Securitate were dispatched to Timişoara with orders to kill. While the Securitate sprayed tear gas and water jets, the police beat up rioters and arrested many of them. Around 9 p.m. the rioters withdrew. They regrouped eventually around the Romanian Orthodox Cathedral and started a protest march around the city, but again the security forces confronted them. Riots and protests resumed the following day, 17 December. The rioters broke into the District Committee building and threw party documents, propaganda brochures, Ceauşescu's writings, and other symbols of communist power out of the windows. Again, the protesters attempted to set the building on fire, but this time they were stopped by military units. In the ensuing violence and confusion it was reported that there were 60,000 dead, although after the revolution the number was reduced to one hundred with several hundred injured.

By the morning of 18 December, soldiers accompanied by Securitate agents in plain clothes, guarded the centre. The town's mayor, Moţ, ordered a Communist Party gathering to take place at the university, with the purpose of condemning the 'vandalism' of the previous days. He also declared martial law, prohibiting people from congregating in groups of more than two. Defying the curfew, a group of thirty young men headed for the Orthodox Cathedral, where they stopped and waved a Romanian flag from which they had removed the Romanian Communist coat of arms.

On 19 December, Securitate members, Radu Bălan and Ştefan Guşă visited the workers in the city's factories, but failed to make them resume work. By 20 December, massive columns of workers were entering the city. Some 100,000 protesters occupied Piaţa Operei (Opera Square, today Piaţa Victoriei, or Victory Square), and started to chant anti-government protests. The events in Timişoara were widely reported by Radio Free Europe, Voice of America and by students returning home for Christmas holidays.

Previously, in November 1989, Ceauşescu had visited Mikhail Gorbachev, in Moscow, who had suggested that he should resign. Ceauşescu flatly refused. The question of a possible resignation arose again on 17 December 1989, when Ceauşescu assembled the CPEx (Political Executive Council) to decide upon the necessary measures to crush the Timişoara uprising. Again Ceauşescu refused to release his grip on power. Members of CPEx, including Gheorghe Oprea and Constantin Dăscscălescu, called for Ceauşescu not to resign, but to sack those who opposed his decisions instead. Later that day, Ceauşescu left Romania to visit Iran, leaving the task of resolving the uprising of Timişoara to his wife and other acolytes. On 20 December 1989 Ceauşescu returned to

Romania only to find out that the situation had worsened. At 7 p.m. on 20 December, he gave a televised speech from a TV studio located inside the Central Committee building, in which he labelled the people protesting in Timişoara as enemies of the socialist revolution.

Ceauşescu, still believing in his own god-like status as his nation's saviour and genius, called for a huge rally to woo the people as he had done in 1968. He could not and would not believe he was hated, and began to show signs of confusion and strain. As usual, his court sycophants humoured him and arranged a 200,000-strong rally on 21 December. It was a disaster. The people remained apathetic with only the front rows showing support for Ceauşescu with cheers and applause (completely staged and performed under orders). In front of the world's press his own people had turned on him and began to boo. Ceauşescu offered, as an act of desperation, to raise the salaries for workers by the ridiculous amount of 100 lei (about US$4 at the time) per month. The rally turned into a protest demonstration and in the end a revolution emerged. Ceauşescu retreated in disbelief, demanding to his army that the protesters be dealt with.

It is likely that in the small hours of 22 December, Ceauşescu must have thought that his desperate attempts to crush the protests had succeeded, because he apparently called another meeting for the next morning. However, before 7 a.m., his wife Elena received the bad news that large columns of workers from many industrial platforms (large communist-era factories or groups of factories concentrated into industrial zones) were heading towards downtown Bucharest. The police barricades that were meant to block access to Piaţa Universitaţii (University Square) and Piaţa Palatului (Palace Square), proved useless. By 9.30 a.m., University Square was jammed with people. Security forces (army, police and others) re-entered the scene, but only to defect to the revolutionaries. These included several of the central army commanders, who, sensing the way things were going, also switched sides. The regime was attempting to use them in the repression of the mass protests, but they finally ended up joining the protestors. Of these generals the most important were Ilescu and Stanculescu, who had actually initiated the killing in Timişoara, but suddenly became revolutionaries when the trouble started in Bucharest. General Milea was shot before he could defect for failing to disperse the crowds. Ceauşescu and his wife went into hiding.

That night on 22 December 1989, demonstrations finally broke out in the capital, Bucharest. The Securitate were under orders to shoot anything which moved. Using their mass of tunnels underneath Bucharest to move about, they fought a bloody battle with the army and the general public as other countries were preparing for Christmas. The fighting stopped only after the capture and execution of the Ceauşescus.

There are several conflicting views on the events in Bucharest that led to the fall of Ceauşescu in 1989. One view is that a portion of the Romanian Communist Party CPEx (Political Executive Council) tried and failed to bring about a scenario similar to that in the rest of the Eastern Bloc communist countries at the time. The idea was that the communist leadership would resign *en masse*, allowing a new government to emerge peacefully. Another view is that a group of military officers successfully staged a conspiracy against Ceauşescu. As we have seen above it is true that certain officers did join the opposition. Several officers have claimed that they had been part of a conspiracy directed against Ceauşescu, but evidence beyond their own claims is scant, at best. The latter view is supported by a series of interviews given in 2003 and 2004 by former Securitate Lieutenant Colonel Dumitru Burlan, Ceauşescu's long-time bodyguard. The two theories are not necessarily mutually exclusive. It remains a matter of dispute whether army and other leaders turned against Ceauşescu out of sincere revulsion at his policies (as many later claimed) or simply out of sheer opportunism.

Ceauşescu, babbling incoherently with rage and disbelief at what he was seeing, had fled with his wife Elena and their bodyguard by helicopter. Two of their loyal collaborators, Emil Bobu and Tudor Postelnicu accompanied them. They headed for Ceauşescu's Snagov residence, and, from there, further to Târgoviflte. Hearing news of what was happening in Bucharest, their pilot casually abandoned them on a lonely road in the middle of nowhere. By that time, the army had closed the entire Romanian airspace. Reduced to hitchhiking, the Ceauşescus flagged down a doctor's car as he drove past and arrived in Târgovişte. Elena actually held a loaded gun to his head as he drove them aimlessly around not knowing where to leave them. After some wandering through the industrial outskirts of the town, the couple decided to enter a building near a local steel plant. An engineer there called the police, who showed up in the form of a nearby traffic police unit who took the Ceauşescus to the local police headquarters, from where they were sent to an army barracks across the street. Their bodyguard disappeared into the night and, still in denial that anything bad was happening, the Ceauşescus gave themselves up. However, it was here that the Ceauşescus were informed that they had actually been arrested. On 25 December, Christmas Day, the two were sentenced to death by an *ad hoc* military court on a range of charges including genocide. Footage of the trial and execution was promptly released in France and other Western countries; an edited version (lacking footage of the actual execution) was released on television the same day for the Romanian public.

They were most likely executed because it was felt that while they were alive, the Securitate would not surrender, particularly if it meant losing their comfortable lifestyle. There were also many army officers who were keen that Ceauşescu should not have the public opportunity to implicate them in his atrocities, especially now that the revolution had fallen into their hands. That Nicolae Ceauşescu was fêted by so many Western world leaders was regarded as shameful on the part of the Romanian people. The rest of the world had no idea how much they had suffered until it was too late. Nicoloae and Elena Ceauşescu were executed by firing squad on

25 December 1989 as the world toasted the arrival of Christmas. For the Romanians it was perhaps the first celebration they had had for many years.

Historically, the Romanian revolution of 1989 was seen as a week-long series of riots and protests in late December of 1989 that overthrew the communist regime of Nicolae Ceauşescu. While the Romanian revolution was unfolding, other central and Eastern European nations were peacefully making the transition to non-communist, multi-party democracy; Romania was the only Eastern Bloc country which violently overthrew its communist regime and executed its leaders.

Former member of the Communist Party leadership and Ceauşescu ally (prior to falling into the dictator's disgrace in the early 1980s) Ion Iliescu became the leader of the short-lived post-revolution National Salvation Front Party. The National Salvation Front, comprised mainly of former members of the second echelon of the Communist Party, immediately assumed control over the state institutions, including the main media outlets, such as the national radio and television. They used their control of the media in order to launch virulent propaganda-style attacks against their political opponents, especially against the traditional democratic parties, which were about to re-emerge after more than fifty years of underground activity. In May 1990, partly due to the National Salvation Front's use of the media and of the partly preserved Communist Party infrastructure to silence the democratic opposition, Ion Iliescu became Romania's first democratically elected president with a majority of 85 percent.

The revolution brought Romania vast attention from the outside world. Initially, much of the world's sympathy inevitably went to the National Salvation Front government. However, much of that sympathy was squandered during the Mineriad of June 1990, when miners and police, responding to Iliescu's appeals, invaded Bucharest. They brutalized students and intellectuals who were on the streets protesting against what they described as the hijacking of the Romanian revolution by former members of the communist leadership, under the auspices of the National Salvation Front. They saw it as an attempt by the communists to suppress any genuine political opposition.

Ion Iliescu remained the central figure in Romanian politics for more than a decade, being re-elected for the third time in 2000, after a term out of power between 1996 and 2000. The survival of Ceauşescu's former ally demonstrated the ambiguity of the Romanian revolution, at once the most violent in 1989 and yet one that, according to some, did not cause enough change. Iliescu's protégé and successor at the head of the ruling ex-communist Social Democratic Party, Adrian Năstase, was defeated by the Justice and Truth coalition candidate Traian Băsescu in the 2004 presidential elections. In 2005, the Memorial of Rebirth was inaugurated to com-memorate the victims of the revolution. Exactly how many victims there were over the nearly forty-year period of Ceauşescu's communist rule will never be known due to the secrecy under which all bureaucratic states operate. Even a conservative rough estimate would run into hundreds of thousands.

During their trial, the couple recited the 'Internationale'. They began to sing it just before their execution. After only the fourth word they were shot dead.

Idi Amin

Idi Amin was quite literally a madman. He was clinically insane and after his death in 2003 his doctor released information that corroborated this theory. He was being treated with anti-psychotic drugs and was also receiving drugs to treat syphilis. The problem was either no one noticed or dared reveal this until it was too late. For over eight years there was no one to stop him in his constant quest for grandeur, power and most of all bloodshed.

Amin was born in the north of Uganda near the Sudanese border on 1 May 1928. He was part of one of Uganda's smallest tribes, the Kakwa, who lived in tiny villages of mud and wattle huts. Shortly after giving birth to her son, his mother left her husband, Amin's father, and moved to the south of the country where she raised Amin alone on money earned from selling love potions and lucky charms. He became a natural leader among the village children, he was unusually large and even at a young age there are tales of his violent behaviour towards other children, particularly those with whom he 'fell out'.

Having had an obsession with the military from an early age, he joined the King's African Rifles in 1946 at the age of eighteen. He loved the rituals and traditions of the British army.

He had never learned to read or write and it took him several years to make any progress in his career even in a regiment where illiteracy was accepted as commonplace. Obedience and enthusiasm were what he excelled at. He was proud of his regiment, his boots were always shiny, his uniform tidy and he was excellent at sports. He was six feet, four inches tall and at his heaviest weighed twenty stone. During those early years in the army he became the heavyweight boxing champion of Uganda, perhaps a testament to his predilection for violence. According to British officers at this time he was a likeable character to have about, always making people laugh – 'Not much grey matter, but a splendid chap to have about.' When the British made Africans officers they opted for those who, like Amin, were strong and loyal even if illiterate. In spite of failing military courses in England and Israel he was nevertheless made a lieutenant in 1960. A contemporary of his at the time said, 'He was just the type that the British rulers liked, the type of African they used to refer to as from the "warrior tribes": big, uncouth, illiterate and willing to obey orders.'

One story originating from Amin's time in the British army draws attention to just how mentally unstable he was even then. His commanding officer persuaded him to open a bank account. He deposited £10 but then spent £2,000 in the next few hours, buying new suits, a car and a huge amount of food and drink. He then posed around town in his uniform acting like a king. There were other stories, too, regarding atrocities committed in distant frontier villages by soldiers of the King's African Rifles. Tales of rapes and captives being tied up and bayoneted were consistently linked with reference to the presence of an unusually large, happy, laughing officer. Instead of tackling the issue, the British turned a blind eye. They were too busy preparing for the independence of the country and also, in general, Lieutenant Amin was loyal and seemed to get the job done.

Winston Churchill described Uganda as a 'fairy tale' commenting on its beautiful landscape. It was seen as the pearl of Africa and contains the famous Mountains of the Moon which rise 17,000 feet to produce snowfields on the equator. Uganda is green, rich and fertile with forests, rolling green plains and hills. The British arrived there at the end of the nineteenth century and found it inhabited by ancient and varied tribal groups practising cruelties such as burying alive and roasting as popular punishment. The many tribal groups fought constantly, sometimes regarding ancient feuds, some of which continue to this day. There are over forty tribes in Uganda, and each one has local and family loyalties making them more sympathetic to their own local leaders than to any central government.

In 1888, control of the emerging British 'sphere of interest' in East Africa was assigned by royal charter to the Imperial British East Africa Company, an arrangement strengthened in 1890 by an Anglo-German agreement confirming British dominance over Kenya and Uganda. In 1894, the Kingdom of Buganda within Uganda was placed under a formal British protectorate. When the British arrived, the ruling monarch was Kabuka Butesa I, king of the large and dominant Buganda tribe who was renowned for being cruel and despotic. The 1900 Uganda Agreement formed the basis of the relationship between the Buganda on the one hand, and the British colonial administrators of what became known as the Uganda Protectorate on the other hand. A key element of the agreement was the allocation of land to the Buganda as a form of freehold tenure that came to be known as 'mailo land'. This more or less excluded European settlers from acquiring land and consequently there were virtually no white settlers in Uganda during the period of British rule. The agreement was ostensibly made between willing equal partners – the British having first given 'protection' to the Buganda at the Buganda's own invitation – and in general the British time there was uneventful.

After the Second World War, Africa began to change. Britain granted internal self-government to Uganda in 1961, with the first elections held on 1 March 1961. Benedicto Kiwanuka of the Democratic Party became the first Chief Minister. Democratic elections were hastily arranged in April 1962 to elect members to a new National Assembly. Milton Obote, leader of the majority coalition in the National Assembly, became prime minister of a socialist government and led Uganda to formal independence on 9 October 1962. Uganda maintained its Commonwealth membership. Still, however, when the British withdrew, they left behind them a country unprepared for independence and democracy. The tribal disputes were as bad as ever and, politically, the country was dogged by uncertainty. Those who had acquired authority as loyal servants to their British rulers benefited from their head start in the leadership positions and tightened their grip on power. Idi Amin, by now deputy commander of the army, was one of these. Obote had tried to resolve the issue of the warring tribes by appointing the traditional king, from the large Buganda tribe, as president to reassure the Buganda that they still held some authority in a government dominated by members of other, smaller tribes. Obote himself was from the small Langi tribe, a minority in Uganda. Edward William Walugembe Luwangula Mutesa III, otherwise known as 'King Freddie' assumed what was mainly a ceremonious position. Trouble started in February 1966 when Obote tried to reduce his powers and the Buganda tribe (the largest in Uganda) rebelled. Obote turned to Idi Amin for help.

Amin's response was typically violent, and disproportionate. He attacked the presidential palace with a 122-mm gun mounted on his own jeep. Chunks were knocked out of the walls and 1,500 Buganda died in the ensuing fighting. Obote suspended the constitution, assumed all government powers, and removed the ceremonial president and vice-president. King Freddie escaped to England where he remained for the rest of his life. Obote began to rely on Amin and his direct approach to problems; Amin's career had now really taken off. There were still many allegations of his cruelty and of his smuggling gold, ivory and coffee. Crucially however, no one ever lived long enough to testify against him in public.

Throughout the early 1960s, the country was still undergoing political struggle. Supporters of a centralized state vied with those in favour of a loose federation and a return to a strong role for tribally based local kingdoms. In September 1967, a new constitution proclaimed Uganda a republic, gave the president even greater powers, and abolished the traditional kingdoms altogether. There was by now growing discontent in the country with the government's increasing bureaucracy and corruption. In 1969 there was a failed assassination attempt on Obote. Gradually the relationship between Obote and Amin cooled. Obote had, quite rightly, begun to feel afraid of Amin and Amin suspected he was to be distanced from the government. There were also rumours of his impending arrest. In January 1971, Obote flew to Singapore to attend the Commonwealth conference. He was to be unable to return for nine years. Amin launched a military coup on 25 January. Beginning at 3 a.m. the army stormed the parliament, the airport (where two priests were killed) and the radio station. All telephone lines were cut and Amin himself watched it all from his heavily fortified luxury home.

In the days following the coup there was an almost carnival atmosphere. The anti-Obote protesters took to the streets hailing Major-General Amin as their saviour and hero. These protesters were mainly from the Buganda tribe who had resented Obote's expulsion of their king.

Amin declared Obote to be a corrupt communist and promised that he would ensure free elections for the people to elect a new leader and that he himself would then return to his barracks and his troops. He took to the streets, stopping looting and handing out personal cheques to passers-by. He also freed some political prisoners and allowed the Buganda to bring back the body of King Freddie for ceremonial burial. One person noted at the time, 'I have never encountered a more benevolent and popular leader as Idi Amin.' The reality could have been further from that assessment. No one could have had any idea of what was to follow.

Amin declared himself president, dissolved the parliament, and amended the constitution to give himself absolute power. Within three weeks of Amin's coup, 2,000 army officers and men had been killed on his orders. Some 10,000 civilians were murdered within three months. The murders were secret and systematic. At first the main targets were people belonging to the Acholi and Langi tribes. Obote had been a Langi and his closest allies were from the Acholi tribes. Amin wanted to be rid of them all, every single tribe member. Obote's family were all slaughtered, including his brother-in-law. Amin had created killer squads in his army and they were now put to work. When in doubt about a person's heritage they simply looked at the names. Names beginning with 'O' were common in the Acholi and Langi tribes so all people with names beginning with 'O' were killed. The killer squad soldiers had absolute powers of arrest and were given ridiculously inappropriate names, 'the Public Safety Unit' and 'the State Research Bureau'.

Amin discovered that there were thirty-six officers in his army from the targeted tribes. These officers were summoned to Mackindye for 'training in internal security'. They were all locked in cells and subsequently murdered with bayonets. Amin also ordered the death of the former army chief of staff, Brigadier Hussein Suleiman, whom he had resented since Obote appointed him. He had him slowly beaten to death with wrenches and then had his head cut off and frozen, the beginning of what was to become a large collection which would eventually need its own room and refrigerator. A year later Amin apparently brought out Suleiman's frozen head to show it off proudly to his guests at a dinner party.

Next, without reason, he began to destroy his own army. At Jinja and Mbarara barracks the officer corps was crushed by tanks as they stood on the parade ground to salute Major-General Amin. At other barracks officers were pushed into rooms then grenades were thrown through the windows. In the prisons at Mackindye, Naguru and Nakasero limbs were smashed with sledgehammers and prisoners forced to kill each other in the hope of saving their own lives but other prisoners were then turned on them in the same way in an endless chain of murder. The human remains were put into trucks and dumped in rivers and lakes outside Kampala. According to legend, when the lights went out in Kampala, the locals knew that forty miles away at the Owen Falls Dam on Lake Victoria, the hydro-electric generators were yet again clogged with bodies.

At first the outside world didn't know what was going on in

Uganda. Idi Amin's government was officially recognized by many international governments including Britain, and he launched himself as an international statesman with great relish. On his visits to both England and Israel, he presented himself as ruler of an empire and always dressed in full military regalia with a ridiculous number of medals (the vast majority awarded by himself) pinned to his chest. On his first official visit to England he had dinner with Conservative Prime Minister Edward Heath and also Prince Philip and the Queen. His official reception in Scotland impressed him so much that he acquired a fetish for all things Scottish believing that the Scots wanted him as king, a position he said he would be delighted to accept.

Israel initially took him seriously. They regarded Amin as a friendly Muslim leader of an African country and hoped that he would help in their relations with Sudan. Eventually it became clear that all was not well inside the head of Idi Amin. In one conversation he is rumoured to have asked the Israelis for twenty-four Phantom jets. When Israel asked why he needed them, he informed them that it was because he needed to bomb Tanzania. Israel declined, for obvious reasons, and Amin changed in his attitude towards them. When Palestinian terrorists murdered Israeli athletes at the 1972 Munich Olympics he sent the following telegram to both Kurt Waldheim, the United Nations Secretary General, and the Israeli Prime Minister Golda Meir: 'Germany is the right place, where, when Hitler was Prime Minister and Supreme Commander, he burnt over six million Jews. This is because Hitler and all the German people know that the Israelis are not people who are working in the interest of the people of the world and that is why they burned the Israelis alive with gas in the soil of Germany . . .' (sic).

Other incoherent messages were sent to many world leaders whenever Amin thought it necessary, often giving them 'advice' on various problems and sometimes just taunting them. The British Prime Minister and the Queen of England were among his favourite targets. When he was inaugurated as

President of Uganda he had white men carry him aloft through the streets of Kampala and declared himself to be 'the Conqueror of the British Empire'. Amin also made a request to England for Harrier jets so that he could bomb South Africa, Tanzania and Sudan. Leaders across the globe began to realize that all was not well with Idi Amin, but they had no idea of the atrocities being committed inside Uganda.

Back in Uganda the shortage of living cabinet ministers meant that the incompetence of Amin was beginning to take its toll. His only economic policy was that of extortion and he began to believe he had been appointed by God to rule the country. He insisted he was in touch with God who guided him in his rule of Uganda through visions. According to one minister at the time, 'The problem takes on fantastic dimensions. He cannot concentrate . . . he does not read . . . he cannot write. He has to have recourse to people of his own intelligence and calibre – the illiterate army officers who rule the country for him . . .' The army officers in question were men who used to be cooks, drivers and cleaners who were now majors and colonels. Military spending went up 500 per cent. Inflation soared to 700 per cent to the point where a bar of soap cost two weeks' wages. Amin's solution was simply to print more money. He often took private flights to Paris or London to go on luxury spending sprees with his closest friends.

Meanwhile, his killer squads had complete control of the country. Deaths of politicians and civilians continued at breathtaking speed. The Church became a new target. The Archbishop of Uganda died in a 'motor accident' with two government ministers. Archbishop Luwum was shot dead by Amin himself whose explanation was that he had lost his temper. Many people were killed simply for their possessions. Some civilians were taken off the street, killed, and had relatives charged for the return of the often badly mutilated bodies.

As news of the horrors in Uganda slowly reached the rest of the world, the carnage was on such a staggering scale that it took a while for it to be believed. It was also very difficult to confirm. Nicholas Stroh and Robert Siedle, two American journalists, began to ask questions. They were shot at Mbarara barracks. Following their deaths, their murderer Major Juma Aigu proudly drove around Kampala in their Volkswagen. Slowly, however, refuges and exiles began to emerge from the country with tales of terrible evils being committed. Education Minister Edward Rugomayo fled from Uganda and put together a detailed list of atrocities including slow deaths by bleeding and amputation, genital mutilation, people being fed on their own flesh until they died, reproductive organs being set on fire, electric shocks and the gouging out of eyes. Idi Amin had sympathy for no one and was implacable after any disagreement. Bob Mckenzie, a former Kenyan minister, had a quarrel with Amin and on his leaving the country was given a gift of a lion's head trophy. It exploded on his aircraft shortly after take-off killing everyone on board.

At home, Amin kept a harem of wives and an estimated twenty-five to thirty-five children. He had in his home a collection of 'trophies' from those he had killed. When one of his wives, Kay, died in a bungled abortion attempt he insisted that her legs and arms be removed and reattached with the legs at the shoulders and the arms at the pelvis as a warning to the other wives. He kept the head of Jesse Gitta, the former husband of his wife Sarah, in his freezer (referred to as his 'botanical room'). Among many others was the head of Ruth Kobusinje, a one-time girlfriend whom he had suspected of infidelity. One nurse testified to decapitating six bodies and sending their shaved and preserved heads to Amin's home. He also confessed proudly to Henry Kyemba, the Ugandan Health Minister, during a dinner party that he had eaten the flesh of his human victims on many occasions

Back on the international scene he turned his loyalty towards Libya and Colonel Gaddafi, supporting his anti-Western and anti-Jewish policies. Gaddafi was under the mistaken impression that Uganda was a Muslim country. Amin had assured Gaddafi that Uganda was an 80 per cent Muslim country when the truth was that it was nearer 15 per cent. To please and impress Gaddafi, Amin expelled the Israeli engineers who had built Entebbe airport and who were also working on crucially important dam projects. He sent offers to England to sort out the Northern Ireland problem and offers to the USA to sort out Vietnam. He confiscated all British property in Uganda and set up a 'Save Britain Fund' to help with Britain's economic recession, even going so far as to send a telegram to Edward Heath describing the state of Britain as a 'disgrace to the Commonwealth'.

Eventually it was two internationally important events that served the purpose of showing to the world the true extent of Idi Amin's madness. The first of these was his decision to expel all Asians from the country, and the second was the Entebbe hijack.

The expulsion of the Asian population was the final blow to Uganda's economy. Amin's excuse was that the Asians had only come to the country to build the railways and now that they were finished, they should all go home. In reality Asians ran about 80 per cent of Uganda's small businesses. As they left the country Asian families were usually stripped of all their possessions including all jewellery and watches. Most of the Asian families from Uganda sought asylum in Britain. However, when Amin decided that the British High Commission was not processing them fast enough he kidnapped one hundred British citizens and held them until the High Commission agreed to work twelve-hour days and hire more premises and staff. All previously Asian businesses were handed over to Amin's army henchmen and shops were emptied and then closed within a few weeks. By now the Ugandan people were near starvation but Amin, still in his fantasy world, did not or would not notice; he was still offering help to over thirty third world countries affected by drought. He continued to write cheques with absolutely no idea of the desperately bad shape the country's economy was in.

The Entebbe hijack began with the hijacking by Palestinians of an Air France airliner, carrying around three hundred passengers, travelling from Tel Aviv to Paris. Since Amin had aligned himself with the Palestinian Liberation Organization as part of his anti-Jewish, anti-Western outlook, the aeroplane was allowed to land at Entebbe airport. From Entebbe, the hijackers publicized their demands. All passengers would be killed within forty-eight hours unless fifty-three Palestinian prisoners charged with terrorism were released from jails in Israel and Europe. The world's press was now watching Uganda. Amin was delighted, revelling in the attention and thinking he could now hold the West to ransom. The deadline was extended under negotiation and the non-Jewish passengers released. The rest of the hostages were taken to the airport terminal where Amin wandered, smiling, through them. A British-Israeli passenger choked on her food and had to be taken to hospital in Kampala. While she was receiving treatment the Israeli army staged a spectacular rescue. Flying into Entebbe airport, they destroyed a flight of Mig fighter planes and routed Amin's army. In just under an hour and a half they flew out of Entebbe leaving twenty Ugandan army troops and all seven hijackers dead. They took with them, alive, all the hostages, except the woman who had been taken to hospital.

When he heard about this, Amin went wild with fury. Never one to allow anyone to humiliate him, he had the hospitalized passenger, an old lady called Dora Bloch, taken out of the hospital and killed. Her body was found dumped on the outskirts of Kampala. Within Uganda it was made a capital offence to talk about the affair. Amin sent a telegram to the Israeli government threatening to attack them unless they paid compensation for his destroyed aircraft and 'expenses' he had incurred while 'entertaining' the hostages. The telegram was typically meandering and insane. The Israelis ignored it.

It seems unbelievable that the West did nothing about Amin's eight-year reign of terror. Politically, many countries were reluctant to get involved in a country that had only just gained independence. Libya still supported him and even though most African countries were appalled at his actions they were also unwilling to get involved due to internal problems of their own as they built independent nations themselves. Amin surrounded himself with military hardware, carried a loaded and ready gun at all times, and people have said that it was unwise to make any sudden movements in his presence. He ruled by exploiting the fear of others. He was incoherent, illiterate and clinically insane, but he knew how to control people through fear. One way or another his reign had to end.

In 1978 some units of his Ugandan army mutinied and fled across the border to Tanzania. Amin accused Nyerere of having started a war with Uganda and, in October, he invaded Tanzania. Amin's invading force of three thousand troops raped and murdered their way through Tanzania. A bit prematurely, though with great pride, Amin announced that he had conquered Tanzania. Nyerere mobilized the Tanzania People's Defence Force and counterattacked.

Within a few weeks, the Tanzanian army expanded from fewer than 40,000 troops to over 100,000, including members of the police, prison services, national service and the militia. Several anti-Amin groups of Ugandan exiles, which had united as the Uganda National Liberation Army (UNLA), joined the Tanzanians. Amin's troops were driven back. Insane as ever, Amin asked Nyerere if he would like to settle the dispute with a boxing match between the two of them. Nyerere simply sanctioned the continued advance of his troops into Uganda.

The Ugandan army retreated steadily. Since he was still Amin's supporter, Colonel Gaddafi sent 3,000 troops to aid him, but the Libyans soon found themselves on the front line. The Ugandan army units were using supply trucks to carry their newly plundered wealth in the opposite direction out of Uganda. Tanzanian and UNLA forces met little resistance, and invaded Uganda, taking Kampala in April 1979. Idi Amin fled to Libya to seek refuge with Gaddafi. He lived there for the next few years until Gaddafi threw him out. The reason for this is unclear. Perhaps Gaddafi realized the extent of Amin's madness but there is also a rumour of a rape or attempted rape of Gaddafi's fourteen-year-old daughter by Amin. Whatever the reason, he ended up in Saudi Arabia where he lived a life of luxury on stolen Ugandan money until his death in August 2003. The Tanzanian army remained in Uganda to maintain peace while the UNLF (the political wing of the UNLA) organized elections to return the country to civilian rule.

Idi Amin's doctor John Kibukamusakie revealed that before his sudden death in Saudi Arabia, he had been having treatment for a cocktail of psychiatric illnesses, hypermania bringing on rapid and wildly conflicting ideas, syphilis causing grand paranoia and schizophrenia with a 'general paralysis of the insane'. He had recently made plans to have statues of his favourite figures, Adolf Hitler and Queen Victoria, created and erected in his house and had tried to put in motion plans to have a bodyguard of bagpipe-playing Scottish bodyguards to look after him.

At the hands of this huge and dangerously mentally ill man, untold millions of government officials, military officers, religious professionals and civilians were murdered. Often, Amin was present, smiling benevolently or laughing happily, so insane that he was unable to know the value of life and so deluded he believed he was following God's orders. By removing all educated people from the government in Uganda and appointing illiterate thugs to run the country for him, he created a world where he could not, and also need not, read, hear or see any opposition to his system of dictatorial rule by fear.

François 'Papa Doc' Duvalier

Papa Doc's tyrannical reign over Haiti dated from 1956 to 1971. He declared himself President for Life in 1964. He then founded his own appreciation movement that he called the 'Praise Papa Doc' movement. He had abolished the Catholic Church in Haiti and so, in accordance with this, he published a tome of self-flattery called *Catechisms of the Revolution*, a parody of the Catholic prayer book with himself as the Holy Trinity. There was now a new Lord's Prayer that began:

Our Doc, who art in the National Palace for life,
hallowed be thy name by present and future generation.
Thy will be done in Port-Au-Prince and in the Provinces . . .

Haiti, which shares the Caribbean island of Hispaniola with the Dominican Republic, has never been governed well by its rulers, whether white or black. Almost all of them have acquired power by violence and have, therefore, been obliged to maintain it through fear. Hispaniola was conquered by the Spanish who established settlements there. Within eighteen years of Columbus's discovery of America, the Spanish settlers had worked the native population of Arawak Indians to death in their frantic search for gold. The Spanish also brought with them myriad diseases that killed those indigenous inhabitants who had not already been worked to death. For a while, Haiti became a haven for pirates, but eventually it came under French control. The French created an affluent plantation economy, worked by slaves imported from West Africa. The Africans brought with them their tribal customs and gods. Despite the efforts of French missionaries to convert the population of the island to Christianity, they made little headway. The teachings of the Catholic missionaries were simply absorbed into the African belief systems to create what came to be known as voodoo.

In voodoo, the Catholic Creed, the Apostles' Creed and the Hail Mary are all used in ceremonies. The Virgin Mary becomes Grande Erzulie, Goddess of Fertility, Saint Peter is Papa Legba and the cross of Christ is a symbol of Baron Samedi, Lord of the Dead. God exists but is aloof, remote and indifferent. Those who practise voodoo appeal to the lesser spirits or 'loas' to help them meet their daily needs with regard to food, sex, shelter, cures from diseases and protection against enemies. There are two types of these spirits: 'Rada', which are African, and 'Petro', which are peculiarly Haitian, much more violent and unpredictable. Voodoo priests are known as 'houngans'. Papa Doc became a houngan quite early in his life and voodoo remained heavily influential during his years in power. In addition to the houngans, there are the 'bocors', the sorcerers who cast spells and curses that are called 'ouanga'. The most important religious part of a peasant's life in the voodoo faith is their death. They frequently pay huge sums of money, even mortgaging their homes to a houngan to give a service at the burial to make sure the corpse does not become a zombie slave of an enemy and ensure that their own personal god will be returned to the mystical Guinea.

The first slave rebellions of 1791 began in an atmosphere of nightly voodoo sacrifices. The first slave leader was a famous houngan called Brookman. It was Brookman who mobilized the slaves to gain their freedom during the reign of the French leader Toussaint Louverture. They were to lose it again when Napoleon sent 43,000 troops to Haiti to restore slavery. The French also imported dogs from Cuba, trained to pursue and kill the black fighters but the fight for freedom continued. Dessalines, the great Haitian ex-slave hero, thrashed the French so severely that they surrendered to the British rather than face the anger of his ragged ex-slave army. Papa Doc was fond of comparing himself to Dessalines and often used a similar 'fight against the white man's oppression' rhetoric in his speeches and writings. One of Dessalines's officers, when he came to write the Act of Independence in 1804, said: 'To write this Act of Independence we must have a white man's skin for parchment, his skull for an inkwell, his blood for ink and a bayonet for a pen.'

In a violent and racist world that was still dependent on slavery, Haiti became an isolated country, an unwanted example of a free black nation. It was deeply in debt, which crippled the economy, and between 1843 and 1915 alone was ruled by twenty-two different dictators, most of whom were assassinated by those who were to take their jobs. In the twentieth century Haiti was still characterized by violence and racism. The better-educated mulattos (those of mixed race, usually with white fathers and black mothers) tended to be born into more comfortable circumstances and they became a kind of aristocratic elite. The black majority became an embittered underclass. It was because of this that the expression *Negritude* – the idea of raising the pride and consciousness of the Negro majority, who, for so long, had felt cursed by their colour – began to be used in the twentieth century. Papa Doc would eventually use this notion as an excuse to tell people that only he knew what was good for them. He was never slow to play the race card to justify his atrocities or explain why the country was in a mess (usually, to his mind, this was the outcome of the racism of other countries).

François Duvalier was born in 1907 in a tin-roofed shack, just a few streets away from the National Palace. His mother was a baker and his father was a teacher. Haiti, during his childhood, had an atmosphere of continuous tyranny, as the British, French, Germans and Americans fought constantly over the country, each underwriting their favourite dictators. Eventually the USA sent in the marines and they were to remain in Haiti until 1934. During their occupation they built hospitals, bridges and schools and installed telephones. Their presence, however, was deeply resented and there were frequent suicide bombings.

After the marines left, the population set about destroying the network of bridges and telephone systems that had been left by their American overlords. The Haitians subsequently had an instinctive hatred for Americans. It was something that François 'Papa Doc' Duvalier was later to harness for his own ends. He was a quiet and forgettable pupil during his early education and later went on to medical school where he became involved on the fringes of student politics and protests. Most significantly for his future life, he fell under the influence of Lorimer Denis, a twenty-four-year-old voodoo mystic and the mainspring of the *Negritude* movement. Duvalier began to write for *Action National*, the nationalist newspaper. In his articles he criticized the US occupation, and praised the flowering of traditional Haitian culture hoping that, 'A man will come to correct injustice and set things right.'

The years that followed the marines departure were so strife-torn that one colleague of Duvalier's joked that he was the only one of his generation who never knew the inside of a prison. Duvalier kept his head down and worked on his strategy of doing nothing, which was later to serve him so well in his rise to the top. As a committed nationalist, he continued to dabble in 'Haiti's traditional culture' and became a houngan by virtue of his knowledge, learned through the teachings of Denis. He also continued to write, but under an assumed name and always needing the support of his voodoo mystic Lorimer Denis. His articles were always focused on restoring the national pride of Haiti; throughout his life he would repeat the following sentiment: 'We swear to make our motherland the Negro miracle.'

Duvalier, by now a doctor, worked in a series of government hospitals as a consultant, and in 1943 was chosen to work alongside some US doctors on a project intended to wipe out the terrible, contagious disease called 'yaws' that afflicted over 70 per cent of the population. Because of this association the

Americans later thought he might be a suitable candidate for their support.

From only ever having done what he was told, he eventually gained the position of Director of Public Health, where he did nothing, unless he was told to. He regarded himself as an 'intellectual' and this secured him a prominent position in the new Nationalist Party. He gained a position in government by default when the existing dictator failed in his attempt to rig the elections sufficiently and had to 'buy' the nationalists' support in a coalition with a few 'ministerial prizes'. Again, Duvalier did nothing. While everyone around him indulged in frenzied corruption and disastrous blunders, he kept his head down which ensured he kept his job and was eventually promoted to Cabinet Minister for Public Health and Labour. He never expressed a view, made no enemies and because he did nothing there was nothing to criticize him for. And, although he was known for his support of *Negritude*, he married a mulatto on the advice of a colleague in the government at the time.

A new black elite began to emerge under the rule of Dumarsais Estime, who had won power with the support of the army, and Duvalier was a part of this. The new elite began to break in to the world of business and government, challenging the traditional hold on power that the mulattos had enjoyed up until then. Unfortunately those now attaining this power were no better to their fellow humans than their predecessors, and displayed the same talent for indiscipline and greed. The mulattos persuaded the army to turn on their former ally and, in 1950, Colonel Paul Magloire became the umpteenth dictator in Haiti's brief history.

His governmental career thwarted, Duvalier left his post before Magloire could devise a nasty end for him. He returned to medicine and treating yaws. He had nevertheless acquired a lasting distrust of the army that would continue throughout his rule; as a result he never allowed the army to carry guns. His behaviour became paranoid and he took to switching plates with dinner companions because he thought someone might try to poison him.

Magloire had an infamous reputation as a playboy and under his rule Haiti became a decadent and sexy international attraction. In particular, the international literati – Noël Coward, Truman Capote and Graham Greene – flocked to the capital Port-au-Prince. The Americans were providing considerable financial support, but in return demanded that Haiti be maintained as a communist-free zone. Magloire took this literally and shot anyone suspected of promoting unrest. In 1954, he set his sights on Duvalier, who spent the next couple of years in hiding, dressed as a woman. There was considerable unrest in the country and though Duvalier had done very little, if anything, to agitate, the government needed someone to blame. Hence, Duvalier found himself named leader of the opposition. His enemies, however, did him a favour. They created in him a plausible leader. In 1956, he came out of hiding and threw off his women's clothes. He immediately disassociated himself from the continued killings and bombings. It was, predictably, nothing to do with him. However, he had changed tack. He began using voodoo to frighten the peasants into economically ruining the government. He still did nothing himself, but now he was telling other people to bomb and shoot. He remained untarnished by action.

Magloire escaped to Jamaica and in Haiti elections were called. Newspaper reporters found Duvalier quite odd. He was unable to tell them what he stood for, merely offering a bit of unintelligible philosophy here and there. The election campaign was a virtual civil war, featuring six changes of leadership. In one incident over 1,000 of Duvalier's supporters were massacred in Port-au-Prince. However, many people believed in the softly spoken, bespectacled Doctor François Duvalier. What they were to get, however, was an outright gangster. The election results were astounding. In some areas Duvalier's share of the vote was double that of the entire population of that area. This kind of 'popularity' had been a traditional element of the 'support' enjoyed by Haitian dictators, the justification for their rule often having been 'in the hands of the gods'. Over 90 per cent of the population was illiterate, and most people earned the equivalent of £1 per week or less. The elections also saw the death of his long time friend and guru, Lorimer Denis. There were rumours that Duvalier had given his friend to the voodoo spirits in order to ensure his election as president. Once he had secured his position as president, he christened himself 'Papa Doc', and in a clear sign of what was to come he announced in his inauguration ceremony: 'As President I have no enemies and can have none. There are only enemies of the nation.'

Duvalier had two priorities as the new President of Haiti. Firstly, he had to guarantee that he was well paid for the job and secondly, ensure he could keep it. Because of Haiti's turbulent history, many people thought the President's chair had an evil spell over it. Duvalier's solution was to turn to the USA.

His approach was to exploit the American fear of communism. Cuba was shortly to fall to Castro and Duvalier raised the US fear of communism spreading throughout the Caribbean. He reportedly sent a message to the US government stating: 'Communism has established centres of infection – nowhere in the world is as vital to US security as the Caribbean.' He flirted with communism for the next fifteen years to keep the dollars coming. By 1960, apart from the vast loans he gained through extortion, the USA had given Duvalier $22 million. In addition, on his election, he had promised Cuba's dictator, Batista, that he would, for a price, not help Castro's communist rebels. Batista's henchmen got a million-dollar kickback for arranging the deal. Duvalier personally got $3 million, and Haiti got the few cents left over. After Cuba fell to Castro and the communists, he could hold the USA to ransom. His strategy had paid off handsomely.

Huge loans were received from the USA for education and health projects, hotels and airports that were never completed. Over 50 per cent of Haiti's entire budget came from the USA. It has been estimated that the personal income and fortune amassed in this way by Duvalier could have funded an aid programme for the entire nation. Within a few years of his election, the annual bill for his personal security amounted to a staggering $28 million, half of the country's yearly expenditure. His secret police, the Ton Ton Macoute, cost another $15 million. Duvalier resented any idea that the US should supervise the funds it gave to Haiti, and encouraged left-wing student disturbances to scare America. He even dressed his troops in the same colourful style of Castro's revolutionaries. Likewise, he exploited the Cuban missile crisis, when it was discovered that the Soviet Union was building nuclear missile launching sites in Cuba capable of reaching American soil. After procrastinating, he came out in support of the USA, who were then forced to keep paying him. When President Kennedy cut off aid to Haiti, Duvalier threatened to 'bring him to his knees', and reputedly put an 'ouanga' on him. Whether this had anything to do with it or not, shortly afterwards, Kennedy was shot.

All this influx of aid money made it seem that, as president, Duvalier was actually doing something. In reality, he was doing absolutely nothing. It seemed that all he needed to do was to keep implying that in the future he might switch to communism and everybody paid him to keep him sweet, and absolutely immobile. The magazine *Newsweek* described him as 'Big Brother masquerading as the Mad Hatter', a reference to the top hats he took to wearing. He continued practising voodoo, consulting the entrails of sacrificed goats and communicating with God from his bathtub in which he would wear one of his top hats. He never managed to offer an intelligible soundbite to any journalist. As *Newsweek* put it: 'He moves hyper-slowly, speaks in a whisper; his eyelids droop. Wearing a slightly bemused unshakeable half-smile, he does nothing for disconcertingly long periods of time and Haitian people, susceptible to this sort of thing, are awed.'

Although the USA provided the major part of his income, the rest had to be extracted from other people by any means necessary. He put this project in the hands of Clement Barbot, who organized an armed gang that eventually evolved into the Ton Ton Macoute, Duvalier's own secret 'police' force. The name came from an ancient Haitian folktale about a giant bogeyman who strides through the country from mountain to mountain, stuffing little boys and girls into his knapsack or 'macoute'. He was referred to in Haitian as Ton Ton Macoute (Uncle Knapsack). Duvalier's Ton Ton Macoute uniformly wore dark glasses to avoid being recognized and they used machine guns at will. At times there were up to 10,000 of these Ton Ton Macoute, unrestrained by any law. Any government employee could join; extortion was seen as a kind of perk for the civil service.

Another of the government's sources of revenue was the sale and resale of gambling and hotel concessions associated with the tourist trade in Port-au-Prince. There were also monopolies on everything else from sugar to cement, and even matches. Each time these businesses changed hands, huge sums of money fell into the hands of Duvalier and Barbot. Barbot even managed to sell the same gambling concession three times in a couple of months, even though it was still technically owned by an Italian. Barbot's mistake was to try to sell the gambling concession yet again, but this time to try to cut Duvalier out of the deal. As a result, he was arrested and imprisoned. He had told the purchasers that Duvalier needed the money to build a hospital.

Barbot, who was a thoroughly evil man himself, was to become Duvalier's most hated enemy. Barbot escaped from prison to the USA where he told the *Washington Post* that Duvalier had told him that he wished, personally, to kill at least three hundred people a year. The peasants muttered that Barbot had magical powers himself and could assume the shape of a black dog at will, presumably a throwback to the days of Haiti's slave wars with the French who used dogs to kill rebelling slaves. Duvalier duly ordered all black dogs to be shot on sight.

Barbot's successor was Luckner Cambronne, a great admirer of Duvalier, who once declared that 'a good Duvalierist stands ready to kill his children, or children to kill their parents'. This is probably the best explanation of Duvalierism ever offered; Duvalier was to be worshipped and obeyed above everything and everybody else.

Cambronne was set to work to raise funds for Duvalier's next project, Duvalierville, a new town named after him to commemorate his greatness. Cambronne set about this enthusiastically, using every means imaginable, including tolls, threats, beatings and torture. Even schoolchildren were mugged on their way to school for donations to 'the National Renovation Fund', a bottomless pit of money which poured into the private bank accounts of officials. One of Cambronne's 'inspired' ideas for fundraising involved sending people extortionate bills for telephones that had never worked (the destroyed phone lines were never rebuilt) or, in some cases, had never been installed. Cambronne explained that once all the bills were paid the telephones would be restored to working order. He continued to publicly support Duvalier, announcing his greatness in often quite ridiculous and clearly insane speeches: 'Duvalier has performed an economic miracle. He has taught us to live without money and eat without food. Duvalier has taught us how to live without life.'

Duvalierville was supposed to be finished in six months. In the end there was only a pile of building rubble and a fading sign swinging in the wind. The project never came to fruition. The money had once again disappeared into the bottomless pit of private bank accounts.

As rumours of the internal state of Haiti reached the international community, tourism, a vital source of income, fell by 70 per cent. Duvalier launched a $40,000 drive to bring the tourists back. Typically, he ruined his chances by simultaneously hanging up the decomposing body of one of his opponents opposite the 'Welcome to Haiti' sign at the airport.

Eventually, with aid and hard currency now hard to find, he compelled peasants to donate blood in exchange for a few days' wages. This was then sold to America at $20 a litre. The peasants continued to live in dire poverty. Disease and premature deaths were common and none of the 'building' programmes for schools, hospitals, houses, roads and bridges were ever completed. The general daily lives of the Haitians were disorganized misery, even when they weren't terrified that the Ton Ton Macoute were about to arrive on their doorstep to take what little they had left.

The country was still in some disorder, with growing discontent, when Duvalier had the bright idea of persuading the USA to send a small unit of marines over to 'help train his own forces'. Since the previous occupation by the US marines, the Haitian people had regarded USA with superstitious terror. Once the marines had arrived, Duvalier clung to them. Their presence, even if neutral, seemed to give his regime international approval.

By the late 1950s, all opposition was outlawed and a state of emergency was declared with a permanent curfew. Homes of potential opponents were bombed. Since he had declared that he 'could have no enemies', he told the world's press that Haiti had only two political prisoners and one of them was a friend of his.

Eventually, under US pressure, Duvalier held an election in 1961, after which he declared himself president for the next six years. Regardless of what name people chose to write on the ballot paper, most of the population was illiterate and, anyway, Duvalier's name appeared on every one. All ballot papers given to his voters had his name printed on the bottom with the title 'President' beside it. Following this election he told the people: 'I am and I symbolize an historic moment in your history as a free and independent people. God and the people are the source of all power. I have taken it, and damn it, I will keep it for ever.' He explained his success as a divine sign: 'I am already an immaterial being . . . this giant capable of eclipsing the sun because the people have already consecrated me for life.'

At the next election, he was the only candidate and he thereafter regarded elections as an unnecessary activity. He therefore declared himself to be president for life in 1964. Finally he changed the constitution to ensure the dynastic succession of his son 'Baby Doc' to the role of president following his death.

Instead of taking charge and putting to rights Haiti's terrible economic problems and dire poverty, Duvalier divided his time between practising voodoo and writing tributes to himself for the press to print: 'Duvalier is the professor of energy, electrifier of souls . . . powerful multiplier of energy . . . renovator of Haitian Fatherland . . . synthesises all there is of courage, bravery, genius, diplomacy, patriotism and tact.' None of it made any sense nor was it in any way true, but, with only a small percentage of the population literate, who was to know, and how many were brave enough to challenge Duvalier's utterances?

It was Duvalier's reputed use of voodoo that was his strongest means of maintaining a powerful hold over Haiti. Catholic priests were persecuted and expelled. The Vatican excommunicated the Haitian authorities. In response, Duvalier's militia chief held a voodoo ceremony on the steps of the cathedral in Port-au-Prince, where he smeared the steps with pig's blood. The funeral procession of Clement Joumelle, a prominent opponent, was hijacked by the Ton Ton Macoute. They drove off with the body, refusing to let a Catholic priest bless the burial. There were more voodoo stories of Duvalier burying people alive at the foot of a giant cross in the Bel Air region, and also sacrificing babies, which had become cheap and plentiful in a nation so poverty stricken that mothers openly sold their children for just forty cents.

In Haiti it had become traditional that the violence of the few oppresses the many; the people had such a bloody history that they were profoundly fatalistic and cynical about all governments and tended simply to endure the latest horrors.

There were many bizarre attempts to dethrone Papa Doc. Not long after he first took power, eight men rode into town, took the main barracks and narrowly failed to capture the palace and the president. This became known as the famous 'Dade County Sheriff's Invasion', so called because the 'army' included a couple of deputy sheriffs from Florida. They did have reinforcements but these never made it from Miami. The Haitians were terrified of white invaders and the small 'invasion' force found itself confronted by thousands of Haitians armed with large sticks and broom handles. Duvalier didn't trust his own army enough to give them guns, so they always remained unarmed. They nevertheless saw off the invading force and afterwards Duvalier posed in his full army uniform, with helmet and gun, as a triumphant warrior who had seen off an army of thousands. Duvalier sent out word that an 'international invasion' had been defeated. It eventually transpired that the eight invaders were mercenaries who were only going to receive $2,000 each if they had been successful.

The USA, which by now had begun desperately to hope that Duvalier would be overthrown, ended up in the ironic position of supporting his regime with aid money, while the CIA attempted to undermine him through supporting the sad, ineffectual efforts of the rebels. It just wasn't working.

Eventually, Duvalier died from diabetes and heart failure in 1971, but that was not the end of the misery for Haiti. Jean Claude 'Baby Doc' Duvalier succeeded him. As a youth, 'Baby Doc', the only son among five children, enjoyed the nicknames at school of 'Fat Potato' and 'Baskethead'. He was so unintelligent that he compelled the teachers at his school to stop publicizing his grades. He was, reportedly, terrified of taking over his father's job and missed the funeral after taking an overdose of Valium. He was only interested in acting the playboy, spending his time with expensive fast cars and women. He left Mama Doc to get on with the serious business of running the country. Still, he kept busy in the traditional presidential mode of acquiring personal wealth. By the time he was overthrown in 1986, he had diverted at least $120 million dollars into his own pockets. His wife had flowers flown in from Miami weekly at a cost of $50,000 a time. Her jewellery collection required its own mobile vault and she was reportedly, and understandably, utterly loathed by the people.

In 1986, in the middle of major civil unrest, the Duvalier clan finally left Haiti aboard a US air force plane that took them to France. Baby Doc lives in Cannes, the wealthy sunspot on the riviera. He sits alone in expensive restaurants and drives his expensive cars up and down the seafront. It is reported that about every six weeks, his courier disappears and returns with around $100,000 in cash in his car.

In 1991, Haiti held its first ever truly democratic elections which resulted in a Roman Catholic priest, Father Jean-Bertrand Aristide, becoming president. Several months later he was forced out of office and into exile by yet another military coup. Over the next few years, Aristide put pressure on the international community to oust the illegal government and, in 1994, his efforts paid off. A UN task force of 20,000 troops (mostly from the US) forced the dictatorship out and reinstated Aristide. He ruled until 1995 when the new constitution forced him to stand down (he was not allowed to stand in consecutive elections). A close colleague of his, Rene Preval, became president until 2000 when Aristide stood again and became President of Haiti.

There have been many debates over the years as to whether Aristide was just as corrupt, or became as corrupt, as Papa Doc ever was. What is not disputed is that Haiti remains one of the most hopeless places on earth. Its population still live in extreme poverty and major floods and mudslides have killed thousands over the years. These have mostly been a result of deforestation caused by Papa Doc's indiscriminate awards of lucrative logging contracts. The trees sold abroad left the Haitian landscape, as well as its population, diminished, and all simply as a result of the greed of only a handful of people. Perhaps Haiti has yet to be governed by a regime that works to develop the wealth of the nation, rather than simply lining its own pockets.

General Augusto José Ramón Pinochet Ugarte

Of the bloody coup d'état in Chile, in 1973, in which he played a major commanding role, General Pinochet has said, 'We only set about the task of transforming Chile into a democratic society of free men and women.' What followed were the deaths of over 3,197 people, mainly on his orders. In contrast to most other nations in Latin America, prior to the coup, Chile had a long tradition of democratic civilian rule; military intervention in politics had been rare. Some political scientists have ascribed the relative violence of the coup to the stability of the existing democratic system, which required extreme action to overturn.

Chile was invaded and colonized by the Spanish in the first half of the sixteenth century. The country achieved full independence in 1818 and slowly emerged as one of the most stable and representative democracies in the world. However, after the Second World War, the country's economy eventually began to suffer a downturn.

In September 1970, Salvador Allende Gossens, of the Marxist Popular Unity leftist coalition party, became president. He promised to extend social reforms and to introduce a socialist system. Allende had a long-standing association with the KGB (Komitet Gosudarstvenoi Bezopasnosti), the Soviet secret police force, and his election campaign was heavily financed by the Soviets. Blaming the capitalist system for Chile's economic woes, Allende's Popular Unity (UP) govern-

ment moved quickly to socialize the economy. They nationalized the country's US-controlled copper mines, other foreign-
controlled businesses and industries, banks and large rural
estates. The management of many factories was turned over to
the workers and the state. Salaries and wages were lifted and
prices held down. The subsequent growth in demand saw
employment levels rise.

The socialization programme was initially popular and
successful but by 1972 the economy went into a dramatic
decline and opposition to Allende and the UP began to escalate.

Already strained, relations with the US became further
stretched by the Chilean government's recognition of Cuba,
China, North Korea and North Vietnam and by its cultivation
of ties with the Soviet Union. The US responded by
withdrawing financial assistance and blocking loans, although
aid to the Chilean military was doubled. The US had sources
within the Chilean military that knew they were planning a
coup. With the economy contracting, the government
attempted to spend its way out. The result was hyperinflation,
reaching an annual rate of more than 500 per cent, and
complete economic paralysis. Racked by internal divisions and
external opposition the government became unable to act.
Meanwhile Soviet agents began to move into Chile in large
numbers following Allende's victory. Soviet paramilitary
instructors used Chile as a base for the training of insurgents
from across Latin America.

In September 1970, following Salvador Allende's victory in
the Chilean presidential vote, United States President Richard
M. Nixon had ordered the Central Intelligence Agency (CIA)
to do all it could to prevent the Marxist Allende from being
inaugurated. Under the supervision of national security adviser
Henry Kissinger, the CIA developed the so-called 'Track II'
plan to oust Allende, allocating US$10 million to the project,
while formally insulating the US embassy in Chile from any
involvement.

The CIA attempted to bribe key Chilean legislators and
funded a group of military officers plotting a coup, providing a

further payment of US$35,000 after the assassination on 22 October of General Rene Schneider, the commander-in-chief of the army, who had refused to approve the coup plan. One CIA document from October states, 'It is firm and continuing policy that Allende be overthrown by a coup . . . It is imperative that these actions be implemented clandestinely and securely so that the USG [US Government] and American hand be well hidden.' In January 1971, Pinochet rose to Army Division General, and was named General Commander of the Santiago Army Garrison. Covertly the CIA continued to work to destabilize the UP government, providing up to US$7 million in funding to opposition groups in order to 'create pressures, exploit weaknesses, magnify obstacles' and hasten Allende's downfall. At the beginning of 1972, Pinochet was appointed General Chief of Staff of the Army.

In the face of growing civil unrest in the country, Allende appointed Pinochet – whom, as his Masonic brother of the same lodge, he thought he could trust – as Army Commander in Chief on 23 August 1973. Just one day later Parliament voted a resolution calling for Allende's removal, by force if necessary.

Pinochet was born in Valparaíso on 25 November 1915, the son of Augusto Pinochet Vera, who worked as a customs official, and Avelina Ugarte Martínez. He went to primary and secondary school at the San Rafael Seminary of Valparaíso, the Rafael Ariztía Institute (Marist Brothers) in Quillota, the French Fathers' School of Valparaíso. He entered military school in 1933. After four years of study, in 1937 he graduated with the rank of *alférez* (second lieutenant) in the infantry.

Pinochet rose quickly through the military ranks. In September 1937, he was assigned to the 'Chacabuco' Regiment, in Concepción. Two years later, in 1939, then with the rank of sub-lieutenant, he moved to the 'Maipo' regiment, garrisoned in Valparaíso, before returning to infantry school in 1940. On 30 January 1943, he married Lucía Hiriart Rodríguez, with whom he had five children: three daughters (Inés Lucía, María Verónica, Jacqueline Marie) and two sons (Augusto Osvaldo and Marco Antonio).

At the end of 1945, he was assigned to the 'Carampangue' regiment in the northern city of Iquique. Then in 1948, he entered the War Academy, but he had to postpone his studies, because, being the youngest officer, he had to carry out a service mission in the coal zone of Lota. The following year, he returned to his studies in the Academy.

After obtaining the title of Officer Chief of Staff, in 1951, he returned to teach at the military school. At the same time, he worked as a teacher's aide at the War Academy, giving military geography and geopolitics classes. In addition to this, he was active as editor of the War Academy's institutional magazine *Cien Águilas* ('One Hundred Eagles').

Eventually reaching the rank of major, in 1953, Pinochet was sent for two years to the 'Rancagua' regiment in Arica. While there, he was appointed Professor of the War Academy and he returned to Santiago to take up his new position. He also obtained a baccalaureate, and with this degree he entered the University of Chile's Law School.

In 1956, Pinochet was chosen, together with a group of other young officers, to form a military mission that would collaborate in the organization of the War Academy of Ecuador in Quito, which forced him to suspend his law studies. He remained with the Quito mission for three and a half years, during which time he dedicated himself to the study of geopolitics, military-geography, and intelligence. Pinochet returned to Chile at the end of 1959 and was sent to General Headquarters of the First Army Division, based in Antofagasta. The following year, he was appointed commander of the 'Esmeralda' regiment. Due to his success in this position, he was appointed Sub-Director of the War Academy in 1963.

His military career continued to progress successfully. In 1968, he was named Chief of Staff of the Second Army Division, based in Santiago, and at the end of that year, was promoted to Brigadier General and Commander in Chief of the VI Division, garrisoned in Iquique. In his new function, he was also appointed Intendant of the Tarapacá Province.

Pinochet was then, to everyone's surprise, appointed Army

Commander by the president shortly before parliament voted a resolution calling for President Allende's removal, by force if necessary.

The Chilean coup of 1973 began on 22 August when the Chamber of Deputies of Chile passed, by a vote of eighty-one to forty-seven, a resolution calling for Allende's removal. The measure failed to obtain the two-thirds vote in the Senate constitutionally required to convict the president of abuse of power, but represented a dramatic challenge to the Marxist head of state. Street demonstrations against the government become an almost daily event, with protests coming from both the left and the right. Workplace shutdowns and lockouts were also commonplace. It has been said by some historians that the CIA financed strikes by transport workers and shopkeepers, and was implicated in the sabotage of public infrastructure, and had also infiltrated all of the parties in the UP. In 1975, a US Senate investigation in Washington found that the Nixon administration had indeed backed the 1973 coup.

The military intervened in the mounting social crisis, staging a violent coup d'état under the direction of Pinochet. The military surrounded and attacked the presidential palace while the air force bombed it. President Allende died before being captured. The exact circumstances of his death are still disputed, although an autopsy in 1990 found that Allende's wounds were consistent with the most commonly accepted explanation that he had committed suicide.

In his memoirs, Pinochet affirmed that he was the leading plotter of the coup, and used his position as commander-in-chief of the army to co-ordinate a far-reaching scheme with the other two branches of the military and the national police. In recent years, however, high military officials from the time have said that Pinochet reluctantly got involved only a few days before it was scheduled to occur (he had, after all, just been given the top military job by Allende). Pinochet apparently eventually followed the lead of other branches of the military (especially the navy) as they triggered the coup.

Many of Allende's aides were arrested then transported to a

military base, where they were executed and buried. After the military's seizure of power, Pinochet engaged in brutal political repression, aiming to destroy all remaining support for the defeated Popular Unity (UP) government. In October 1973, General Pinochet despatched General Aurellano Starck on the operation that notoriously became known as the Caravan of Death. General Starck flew out of Santiago by helicopter on 30 September, heading first south, then turning towards the copper-rich north of the country. Everywhere Starck's helicopter landed, prisoners were taken out and murdered. Four in Cauquenes, twelve in Valdivia, fifteen in La Serena – until the final stop in Calama on 19 October, where twenty-six political prisoners were killed. The Caravan had lasted nineteen days. In total, seventy-two prisoners were dead. This was by no means the most deaths in one operation but it is one of the few with evidence of direct instruction to murder by Pinochet.

Almost immediately after taking power, the junta banned all the leftist parties that had constituted Allende's UP coalition. Much of the Pinochet regime's violence was directed towards those it viewed as socialist or Marxist sympathizers, though dissidents who spoke out against the government were also persecuted. In the first few months after the coup, thousands were murdered or became what were eventually called 'the disappeared'. Thousands more were jailed. Torture was commonplace. Up to one million fled into self-imposed exile. A state of siege was declared and martial law introduced. Parliament was temporarily closed. The media was censored, universities purged, books burned, Marxist political parties outlawed and union activities banned. At least five new prison camps had to be established for the increasing number of political prisoners.

Some accounts state that up to 250,000 people were detained in those first months. Stadiums, military bases, and naval vessels were initially used as short-term prisons. The newly formed secret police (National Intelligence Directorate – DINA) created a reign of terror at home and organized the assassinations of opponents in exile overseas. Civilian courts were supplanted by military tribunals.

It is not known exactly how many people were killed by the government and military forces during the seventeen years that Pinochet was in power; the exact numbers of 'the disappeared' will probably never be known. The Rettig Commission listed 2,095 deaths and 1,102 'disappearances', with the vast majority of victims coming from the opposition to Pinochet at the hands of the state security apparatus. In 2004, the National Commission on Political Prisoners and Torture produced the Valech Report after interviewing an estimated 35,000 people who claimed to have been abused by the regime. About 28,000 of those testimonies were regarded as legitimate. According to the Commission, more than half of the arrests occurred in the months immediately following the coup (approximately 18,000 of those testifying claimed they were detained between September and December of 1973).

A military junta was established immediately following the coup, made up of General Pinochet representing the army, Admiral José Toribio Merino representing the navy, General Gustavo Leigh representing the air force, and General César Mendoza representing the carabineros (uniformed police). The new junta embarked on a campaign to remove the influence of the UP from all social institutions.

Once the junta was firmly in power, Pinochet consolidated his control. First, he retained sole chairmanship of the junta. Pinochet, an admirer of Spanish dictator Francisco Franco, was appointed president on 27 June 1974. He immediately began ruling as an iron-fisted autocrat. The US, pleased to be rid of the Marxists, were quick to recognize the junta and reinstated financial aid to help rebuild the country. The new junta quickly broke off the diplomatic relations with Cuba that had been established under the Allende government.

According to General Manuel Contreras, the head of DINA, Pinochet received daily briefing about the activities of the secret police. The US Defense Intelligence Agency also reported that in 1975 Pinochet 'in fact heads the DINA'. The US embassy corroborated the report, stating that 'DINA reported directly to Pinochet and was ultimately controlled by him alone'.

During 1976, the body of the communist activist Marta Ugarte was found washed up on a beach in Chile. It was later revealed that Ugarte's body, along with those of up to 500 other Chileans executed following the coup, were weighted with a piece of railroad track then dumped from a helicopter into the Pacific Ocean. This was part of an organized programme to hide evidence of any abuse of human rights. The military later extended its programme to hide the evidence of human rights violations committed during the coup, going so far as exhuming the remains of the 'disappeared' and disposing of them elsewhere. As with the bodies of the executed many of these remains were dumped from helicopters into the Pacific Ocean. Many others were burned. The order for the clean-up came directly from Pinochet, who threatened to 'retire' any commander if bodies continued to be found in his jurisdiction. The situation in Chile came to international attention in September 1976, when Orlando Letelier, a former Chilean ambassador to the USA and a minister in Allende's cabinet, was assassinated in Washington DC by a bomb in his car. General Carlos Prats, Pinochet's predecessor and army commander under Allende, who had resigned rather than support the moves against the democratic system, was assassinated under similar circumstances in Buenos Aires, Argentina, two years earlier.

In mid-1975, Pinochet had set about making economic reforms variously called 'neo-liberal' or sometimes 'free market' by its supporters. He declared that he wanted 'to make Chile not a nation of proletarians, but a nation of proprietors'. To formulate his economic policy, Pinochet relied on the so-called Chicago Boys, who were economists trained at the University of Chicago and heavily influenced by the monetarist policies of Milton Friedman.

Pinochet launched an era of deregulation of business and privatization. To accomplish his objectives, he abolished the minimum wage, rescinded trade union rights, privatized the pension system, state industries, and banks, and lowered taxes on income and profits. Supporters of these policies (most notably Milton Friedman himself) have dubbed them 'the Miracle of Chile', due to the country's sustained economic growth since the late 1980s.

General Leigh, head of the air force, became increasingly opposed to Pinochet's policies and was forced into retirement on 24 July 1978. General Fernando Matthei replaced him. Pinochet was, in general, during these years paranoid about consolidating his power over the country, and maintaining his flourishing economy. During 1977 and 1978, Chile was on the brink of war with Argentina (also ruled by a military government) over a disagreement regarding the ownership of the strategic Picton, Lennox and Nueva islands at the southern tip of South America. Antonio Samoré, a representative of Pope John Paul II, successfully prevented full-scale war. The conflict was finally resolved in 1984, with the Treaty of Peace and Friendship. Chile now holds undisputed sovereignty over the islands and Argentina over the surrounding sea.

In 1977, making it clear that he had started as he meant to go on, Pinochet announced that there would be no early return to democracy. The junta alone would determine when civilian government could be reinstated. As head of state and commander-in-chief of the military he exerted absolute control over the country and ensured that his cronies controlled all key posts. The state of siege was lifted and replaced with a state of emergency. The National Intelligence Directorate was abolished and replaced by the National Information Centre. The state of emergency gave Pinochet the right to assume complete dictatorial control. In the same year, the United Nations (UN) Human Rights Commission condemned the Pinochet regime for its practice of torturing detainees.

Pinochet allowed a referendum on the legitimacy of his regime in 1978. He then claimed that more than 75 per cent of the population endorsed his role. Pinochet's position had by now become unassailable. He passed an amnesty law to protect military officers accused of human rights abuses committed since the 1973 coup. Decree law 2191, personally drafted by the then justice minister, Monica Madariaga, a relative of

Pinochet, was published on 19 April 1978. Anyone who committed crimes, was an accomplice in committing crimes or covered up crimes between the day of the coup and 10 March 1978 is exculpated from criminal responsibility. The law is technically still in force today.

In 1981, Pinochet promoted himself to the supreme army rank of Captain General, a title previously borne only by colonial governors and by Bernardo O'Higgins, a hero of Chile's war of independence. The rank was reserved only for someone who was simultaneously head of the government and of the army. He introduced a new constitution allowing him to remain as president until 1989. The new constitution also entrenched the military's domination of the government and allowed Pinochet to restrict freedom of association and speech and to arrest or exile any citizen, with no rights of appeal except to Pinochet himself.

The political activities of unions and community organizations were restricted and politicians were barred from advocacy roles for such groups. Local governments were abolished and Pinochet gave himself the power to dissolve the House of Representatives. This meant that now the constitution could not be amended without approval from Pinochet. A plebiscite was scheduled for 1988–89 to determine if he would have an additional eight years in office. With the abolition of the minimum wage, people in rural or poor urban areas were becoming poorer and more desperate and there began to be murmurs of unrest again.

Pinochet's rule was frequently made unstable by protests and isolated violent attacks. These attacks by armed groups opposed to the regime allowed the dictatorship to justify what they termed the 'cycle' of oppression. The attacks made the 'state of emergency' continue, allowing Pinochet to rein in control even tighter. Having come to power with the self-proclaimed mission of fighting communism, Pinochet found common cause with the military dictatorships of Bolivia, Brazil, Paraguay, Uruguay, and, later, Argentina. The six countries eventually formulated a plan that became known as

Operation Condor, in which one country's security forces would target suspected 'Marxist subversives', guerrillas, and their sympathizers in allied countries. Meanwhile, the CIA established contact with Manuel Contreras, the head of the Chilean secret police. Contreras was a key player in Operation Condor. In August, Pinochet travelled to Washington to meet with the CIA deputy director, General Vernon Walters. During this visit, he also received a one-off payment from the CIA for his work in Operation Condor.

Back in Chile the junta turned its attention to the economy and decided that the best policy was slashing welfare. Inflation was curbed and property returned to its original owners. All companies nationalized by the Allende government were returned to private ownership. However, unemployment stayed high and was worsening, and with no appropriate welfare state the people were suffering. There were numerous violent uprisings and demonstrations. As the country's economy floundered and began to go into recession in the 1980s, the Communist Party of Chile called for armed insurrection. In May 1983, the opposition and labour movements began to organize demonstrations and strikes against the regime, provoking violent responses from government officials.

In 1986, security forces discovered eighty tons of weapons smuggled into the country by the Manuel Rodríguez Patriotic Front (FPMR), the armed branch of the outlawed Communist Party. The shipment of Carrizal Bajo included C-4 plastic explosives, RPG-7 and M72 LAW rocket launchers as well as more than three thousand M-16 rifles. The operation was overseen by Cuban intelligence. It also involved East Germany and the Soviet Union. In September, weapons from the same source were used in an unsuccessful assassination attempt against Pinochet by the FPMR. Pinochet suffered only minor injuries, but five of his military bodyguards were killed. The violent retribution for this – the beheading of leftist professor José Manuel Parada, journalist Manuel Guerrero and Santiago Nattino by the uniformed police (*carabineros*) – led to the resignation of junta member General César Mendoza in 1985.

According to the transitional provisions of the 1980 constitution (supposedly approved by 75 per cent of voters in what has been said to be 'a highly irregular and undemocratic plebiscite') a plebiscite was scheduled for 5 October 1988 to vote on a new eight-year presidential term for Pinochet. The Constitutional Tribunal ruled that the plebiscite should be carried out as stipulated by the Law of Elections. That included an 'Electoral Space' during which all positions, in this case two, *Yes* and *No*, would have two free slots of equal and uninterrupted TV time, broadcast simultaneously by all TV channels, with no political advertising outside those spots. The allotment was scheduled in two off-prime-time slots: one before the afternoon news and the other before the late-night news, from 22:45 to 23:15 each night (the evening news was from 20:30 to 21:30, and prime time from 21:30 to 22:30). The opposition *No* campaign headed by Ricardo Lagos produced colourful, upbeat programmes, telling the Chilean people to vote against the extension of the presidential term. Lagos, in an interview, called on Pinochet to account for all the 'disappeared' persons. The *Yes* campaign did not argue for the advantages of extension, but was instead negative, claiming that voting 'no' was equivalent to voting for a return to the chaos of the UP government.

Pinochet lost the 1988 referendum. Fifty-five per cent of the voters rejected the extension of the presidential term, while 42 per cent voted 'yes', and, although a plebiscite is technically non-binding, this one triggered multi-candidate presidential elections in 1989 to choose his replacement. Open presidential elections were held the following year, during the same period that congressional elections would have taken place anyway. Pinochet left the presidency on 11 March 1990 and transferred power to Patricio Aylwin, the new democratically elected president.

Due to the transitional provisions of the constitution, Pinochet remained as commander-in-chief of the army, until March 1998. He was then sworn in as a Senator-for-Life, a privilege first granted to former presidents with at least six years in office by the 1980 constitution. His senatorship and consequent immunity from prosecution protected him, and legal challenges began only after Pinochet had been arrested in the United Kingdom. In the 1990s, the Spanish government indicted Pinochet. In 1998 Pinochet, who still had much influence in Chile, travelled to the United Kingdom for medical treatment. While there, he was arrested under an international warrant issued by judge Baltasar Garzón of Spain, and was placed under house arrest, at first in the clinic where he had just undergone back surgery, and later in a rented house. The charges included ninety-four counts of torture of Spanish citizens, and one count of conspiracy to commit torture. The government of Chile opposed his arrest, extradition to Spain, and trial.

He was arrested and released by the British government and, finally, arrested and prosecuted by the Chilean government itself. In April 1999, along with Margaret Thatcher, Pope John Paul II, and George Bush Senior, the Dalai Lama called upon the British government to release Augusto Pinochet. They all urged that Pinochet be allowed to return to his homeland rather than be forced to go to Spain.

There were questions at the time about Pinochet's allegedly fragile health. After medical tests, the Home Secretary Jack Straw ruled, despite the protests of legal and medical experts from several countries, that he should not be extradited, and on 2 March 2000, he returned to Chile. His poor health has led the British and Chilean governments to dismiss the idea of prosecution.

Shortly after the verdict, Pinochet resigned from the Senate and lived quietly. He rarely made public appearances and was notably absent from the events marking the thirtieth anniversary of the coup on 11 September 2003. Almost two years after his resignation, on 28 May 2004, the Court of Appeals voted fourteen to nine to revoke Pinochet's dementia status and, consequently, his immunity from prosecution. In arguing their case, the prosecution presented a recent television interview Pinochet had given for a Miami-based television network. The judges found that the interview raised doubts about the mental incapacity of Pinochet.

In a rare interview broadcast by the Miami-based Spanish language television station WDLP-22 on 24 November 2002, Pinochet said he had no regrets about his time in power and refused to apologize for the abuses of his regime: 'I never aspired to be a dictator because . . . I considered that to be a dictator would end badly . . . I always acted in a democratic way . . . Who shall I ask to be pardoned by? They say I should ask for forgiveness, what shall I ask to be forgiven for? . . . I feel like an angel. I have no resentment . . . I am a man who does not carry any hate in his heart . . . I don't want future generations to think badly of me. I want them to know what really happened.'

As well as trials for human rights abuses, Pinochet stands accused of tax evasion and fraud. On 14 July 2004 the US Senate Permanent Sub-Committee on Investigations released a report into the Washington-based Riggs Bank, which found that from 1994 to 2002 the bank helped Pinochet hide US$4–8 million in multiple accounts and two offshore shell companies. According to the report, Riggs 'served as a long-standing personal banker for Mr Pinochet and deliberately assisted him in the concealment and movement of his funds while he was under investigation (in Britain) and the subject of a world-wide court order freezing his assets'. The report also cited a Riggs client profile estimating Pinochet's entire fortune at between US$50 million and US$100 million. A judicial investigation was also opened into whether Pinochet had been involved in multiple tax fraud and the misappropriation of funds, while in government.

Chileans remain deeply divided on his legacy. Many see him as a brutal dictator who ended democracy and led a regime characterized by torture and favouritism towards the rich. Others believe that he saved the country from communism, safeguarded Chilean democracy, and led the transformation of the Chilean economy into Latin America's most stable and fastest growing. He has many international supporters, including, famously, ex-UK Prime Minister, Margaret Thatcher, who thanked the General for 'bringing democracy to Chile'. Apparently they often enjoyed tea together and indeed Pinochet's free-market policies were not so different from the ones introduced by Thatcher that decimated Britain in the late 1980s and 1990s.

However, when in power, Pinochet gave a series of speeches that rather clearly indicated that the 1973 coup targeted not only Allende's Popular Unity government, but Chilean democracy itself, which the General saw as hopelessly flawed. A recurrent claim in his speeches was that Chile had been 'slave and victim of the Congress since 1925, and slave and victim of the political parties'. Arguing for an 'organic' type of democracy, Pinochet argued, 'Merely formal democracy dissolves itself, [it is a] victim of a demagogy that substitutes simple, unattainable promises for social justice and economic prosperity.' According to Pinochet, democracy inevitably leads to a Marxist dictatorship.

Supporters of Pinochet credit him with staving off the beginning of communism, fighting terrorism from radical groups such as MIR, and implementing free market policies that laid the groundwork for rapid economic growth that continued into the 1990s. His opponents charge him with destroying Chile's democracy. Their main charges were the repression of radical groups such as MIR who were pushing for change, pursuing a policy of state terrorism, catering exclusively for private interests, and adopting economic policies that favoured the wealthy and hurt the country's middle- and low-income sectors. While his supporters originally denied it, it is now generally accepted that Pinochet's government was responsible for torturing and killing thousands of people perceived to be opponents of his regime.

In 1998, the new government of Chile established the National Commission on Truth and Reconciliation to inquire into human rights abuses committed during Pinochet's rule. Its report found the security forces responsible for 2,115 deaths, including those of 957 detainees who disappeared. The secret police, accused of responsibility for 392 of the disappearances, was disbanded.

As is so often the case in Latin America, the US government and the local military, headed by a despotic strongman, became the culprits in the massacre and exile of hundreds of thousands of people. As now, in the Middle East and elsewhere, the US government supports those militia which oppose the governments which the USA dislikes, regardless of the policies those militia are likely to implement once in charge. It is debatable whether the USA will grudgingly recognize its responsibility in Chile; Pinochet will no doubt go to his grave believing he is blameless.

Pol Pot

The man who was to become known to the world as the ruthless and paranoid dictator Pol Pot, the leader of the Khmer Rouge, was born Saloth Sar in Prek Sbauv in Kampong Thum province, Cambodia, to a fairly wealthy family. Once he was absolutely in control of the Khmer Rouge and the area it controlled, he boasted on the state-controlled radio that only one or two million people were needed to create the new agrarian communist utopia that he envisioned. As for others, as the Khmer Rouge's proverb put it, 'To keep you is no benefit, to destroy you is no loss.'

In order to explain how Pol Pot and his Khmer Party took control of Cambodia, it is necessary to give a brief account of the very complicated history of this area of south-east Asia. Long before Pol Pot, the area had had many struggles for power, both within its own territory and with its neighbouring states: Laos, Thailand and Vietnam, and, historically, with the ancient Kingdom of Champa.

The golden age of Khmer civilization was the period from the ninth to the thirteenth centuries, when the kingdom of Kambuja, which gave Kampuchea, or Cambodia, its name, ruled large territories from its capital in the region of Angkor in western Cambodia.

Under Jayavarman VII (1181–*circa*. 1218), Kambuja reached its zenith of political power and cultural creativity. Jayavarman VII gained power and territory in a series of successful wars against its close enemies the Chams and the Vietnamese.

Following Jayavarman VII's death, Kambuja experienced gradual decline. Important factors were the aggressiveness of neighbouring peoples (especially the Thai), chronic strife between dynasties and the gradual deterioration of the complex irrigation system that had ensured rice surpluses. The Angkorian monarchy survived until 1431, when the Thai captured Angkor Thom and the Cambodian king fled to the southern part of his country.

The fifteenth to the nineteenth century was a period of continued decline and territorial loss. Cambodia enjoyed a brief period of prosperity during the sixteenth century, because its kings, who had built their capitals in the region south-east of the Tonle Sap along the Mekong River, promoted trade with other parts of Asia. This was the period when Spanish and Portuguese adventurers and missionaries first visited the country. But the Thai conquest of the new capital at Lovek in 1594 marked a downturn in the country's fortunes and Cambodia became a pawn in power struggles between its two increasingly powerful neighbours, Siam (Thailand) and Vietnam. Vietnam's settlement of the Mekong Delta led to its annexation of that area at the end of the seventeenth century. Cambodia thereby lost some of its richest territory and was cut off from the sea. Such foreign encroachments continued through the first half of the nineteenth century because Vietnam was determined to absorb Khmer land and to force the inhabitants to accept Vietnamese culture.

In 1863, King Norodom signed an agreement with the French to establish a protectorate over his kingdom. The country gradually came under French colonial domination. During the Second World War, the Japanese allowed the Vichy French government (governing that part of France not under the direct control of Nazi Germany) to continue administering Cambodia and the other Indo-Chinese territories, but they also fostered Khmer nationalism. Cambodia enjoyed a brief period of independence in 1945 before allied troops restored French control. King Norodom Sihanouk, who had been chosen by France to succeed King Monivong in 1941, rapidly assumed a central political role as he sought to neutralize leftist and republican opponents and attempted to negotiate acceptable terms for independence from the French. Sihanouk's 'royal crusade for independence' resulted in grudging French acquiescence to his demands for a transfer of sovereignty. A partial agreement was struck in October 1953. Sihanouk then declared that independence had been achieved and returned in triumph to Phnom Penh.

In the middle of this Pol Pot was undertaking his education. He attended the Preah Sihanouk College at Kompong Cham, after failing the admission exams for the Lycée Sisowath (a prestigious school). He qualified for a scholarship that allowed for technical study in France. Thus, he studied at the EFR in Paris from 1949 to 1953. He briefly participated in an international labour brigade, building roads in Yugoslavia in 1950. However, he failed his exams two years running, and was forced to leave France in 1953, whereupon he returned to Cambodia. After the Soviet Union recognized the Viet Minh as the government of Vietnam in 1950, French communists (PCF) took up the cause of Vietnam's independence from France. The PCF's anti-colonialism would eventually attract many young Cambodians including the young Pol Pot. In 1951, he joined a communist cell in a secret organization known as the Cercle Marxiste that had taken control of the Khmer Student's Association (AER) that same year. Within a few months, Pol Pot had also joined the PCF. Historian Philip Short has said that Pol Pot's poor academic record was a considerable advantage within the anti-intellectual PCF and helped him to quickly establish a leadership role for himself among the Cercle Marxiste.

He was the first member of the Cercle to return to Cambodia, from France, and was given the task of evaluating the various groups rebelling against the government. He recommended the Viet Minh, and in August 1953, Pol Pot, along with Rath Samoeun, travelled to the Viet Minh eastern zone headquarters in the village of Krabao at the Kompong Cham/Prey Veng border area of Cambodia.

After his return to Phom Penh in 1953, Pol Pot had become the liaison between the above-ground parties of the left (Democrats and Pracheachon) and the underground communist movement. Pol Pot took a job teaching French literature and history at a private school.

Pol Pot and the others found, disappointingly, that the People's Revolutionary Party of Cambodia (PRPK) was little more than a Vietnamese front organization. In 1954, the Cambodians at the eastern zone headquarters split into two groups. One group followed the Vietnamese back to Vietnam as a basis for cadres to be used by Vietnam in a future war to liberate Cambodia. The other group, including Pol Pot, returned to Cambodia. It was at this time that Pol Pot married Khieu Ponnary, the sister of Ieng Thirith, in 1956.

After Cambodian independence following the 1954 Geneva Conference, right- and left-wing parties struggled against each other for power in the new government. King Norodom Sihanouk played the parties off against each other while using the police and army to suppress any extreme political groups. In 1955, King Norodom Sihanouk abdicated and became the country's new political leader of the Popular Socialist Party. What many saw as corrupt elections, in 1955, led many leftists in Cambodia to abandon any hope of taking power by legal means. The communist movement, while ideologically committed to armed struggle in these circumstances, did not launch a rebellion because of the weakness of their party. Sihanouk had survived on the political stage through a mixture of political acumen and ruthlessness.

Neutrality was the central element of Cambodian foreign policy during the 1950s and 1960s. However, by the mid-1960s, parts of Cambodia's eastern provinces were serving as bases for North Vietnamese Army and Viet Cong (NVA/VC) forces operating against South Vietnam, and the port of Sihanoukville was being used to supply them. Throughout the 1960s, domestic Cambodian politics polarized. Opposition grew within the middle class and among leftists including Paris-educated leaders such as Son Sen, Ieng Sary and Pol Pot, who led an insurgency under the clandestine Communist Party of Kampuchea (CPK). Sihanouk called these insurgents the Khmer Rouge, literally the 'Red Khmer'.

Throughout the 1960s, Sihanouk struggled to keep Cambodia neutral as neighbouring countries of Laos and South Vietnam came under increasing communist attack during the Vietnam War.

In January 1962, the government of Cambodia rounded up most of the leadership of the far-left Pracheachon Party ahead of parliamentary elections due in June. The newspapers and other publications of the party were also closed. This event effectively ended any above ground political role for the communist movement in Cambodia. In July 1962, the underground communist party secretary Ton Samouth was arrested and afterwards was killed while in custody. When Ton Samouth was murdered, Pol Pot became the acting leader of the communist party. At a party meeting attended by at most eighteen people in 1963, he was elected to be secretary of the central committee of the party. In March 1963, Pol Pot went into hiding after his name was published in a list of leftist suspects put together by the police for Sihanouk. He fled to the Vietnamese border region and made contact with Vietnamese units fighting against South Vietnam.

In early 1964, Pol Pot convinced the Vietnamese to help the Cambodian communists set up their own base camp. The central committee of the party met later that year and issued a declaration calling for armed struggle. The declaration also emphasized the idea of 'self-reliance' in the sense of extreme Cambodian nationalism. In these border camps, the ideology of the Khmer Rouge was gradually developed. The party, breaking with Marxism, declared rural peasant farmers to be the true working-class proletariat and the life blood of the revolution. This is in some sense explained by the fact that none of the central committee was in any sense 'working class'. All of them had grown up in a feudal peasant society.

After another wave of repression by Sihanouk in 1965, the Khmer Rouge movement under Pol Pot grew rapidly. Many teachers and students left the cities for the countryside to join the movement. In April 1965, Pol Pot went to North Vietnam in order to gain approval for an uprising in Cambodia against the government. North Vietnam refused to support any uprising because of agreements being negotiated with the Cambodian government. Sihanouk had continued to promise to allow the Vietnamese to use Cambodian territory and Cambodian ports in their war against South Vietnam.

After returning to Cambodia in 1966, Pol Pot organized a party meeting where a number of important decisions were made. The party was officially, but secretly, renamed the Communist Party of Kampuchea (CPK). Lower ranks of the party were not informed of the decision. It was also decided to establish command zones and prepare each region for an uprising against the government.

In the spring of 1967, Pol Pot decided to launch a national uprising in Cambodia. The Khmer Rouge and Pol Pot decided to launch the uprising even after North Vietnam refused to assist it in any real way. The uprising began on 18 January 1968 with a raid on an army base south of Battambang. The Battambang area had been an area of great peasant unrest for the past two years. The army drove off the attack, but the Khmer Rouge had captured a number of weapons and was therefore able to drive the police out of surrounding villages.

By the summer of 1968, Pol Pot began the transition from a party leader working with a collective leadership into the absolutist leader of the Khmer Rouge movement. Where before he had shared communal quarters with other leaders, he now had his own compound with a personal staff and a troop of guards. Outsiders were no longer allowed to approach him. Rather, people were summoned into his presence by his staff.

At the beginning of 1969, the movement was estimated to consist of no more than 1,500 regulars. But the core of the movement was supported by a number of villagers many times that size. While weapons were in short supply, the insurgency was still able to operate in twelve of nineteen districts of Cambodia. In the middle of the year Pol Pot called a party conference and decided on a change in propaganda strategy. It was decided at the conference to shift the party's propaganda to attack the right-wing parties of Cambodia and their supposed pro-American attitudes. Much of this had to do with the US bombings along the Ho Chi Minh trail.

The Ho Chi Minh trail was a network of routes from North Vietnam to South Vietnam in the neighbouring countries of Laos and Cambodia to provide logistical support to the Viet Cong and the North Vietnamese army during the Vietnam War. It was a combination of truck routes and paths for foot and bicycle traffic. Parts of the trail had actually existed for centuries as primitive footpaths that facilitated trade in the area. The trail did not simply run north to south. From 1965 to 1970 military supplies were offloaded from China and Russia into Cambodian ports (with Cambodian knowledge and approval) and then moved into South Vietnam. The trail also involved base areas inside Laos and Cambodia. Instead of being called a trail, it is better described as a zone of military occupation in Laotian and Cambodian territory along the entire border north to south.

In October 40,000 North Vietnamese soldiers entered central Cambodia with Sihanouk's approval. As NVA/VC activity grew in Vietnam, the United States and South Vietnam became concerned, and, in 1969, the United States began a fourteen-month-long series of bombing raids on NVA/VC elements, contributing to destabilization. Sihanouk tacitly supported the bombing, but suspected the communists would win. The United States claimed that the bombing campaign took place no further than ten then later, twenty miles inside the Cambodian border, areas where the Cambodian population had been evicted by the NVA. This was not true.

Though the Khmer Rouge were only a minor threat, the war in Vietnam was rapidly becoming a major one. The presence of the sanctuaries was a source of constant frustration for the Americans. At first, with rare and relatively minor exceptions, American forces did not pursue guerrillas beyond the border. Later, however, American commanders began to believe that the Cambodian sanctuaries were crucial for Vietnamese logistics, and that they also served as the headquarters for the communist war efforts throughout Vietnam. In February 1969, General Creighton Abrams, the commander of US forces in Vietnam, requested permission to attack Vietnamese troops inside Cambodia. President Richard Nixon quickly agreed, and on 18 March 1969, American B-52s launched the first of many secret bombing raids over Cambodia. Sihanouk had, in fact, confidentially told an American ambassador that he would not object if American forces engaged in 'hot pursuit' of Vietnamese forces in unpopulated areas of Cambodia. But the extent of the attacks would later become a source of bitter recriminations. Former American Secretary of State Henry Kissinger would claim that Sihanouk was 'inviting this sort of pressure as a means of evicting these invading forces' from Khmer territory. Sihanouk himself would dispute that contention: 'I did not know about the B-52 bombing in 1969 . . . the question of a big B-52 campaign was never raised.' In the end, the arguments between the politicians were immaterial. Either way, the war had come to Cambodia.

The leader of Cambodia, however seemingly complicit, fully understood what the American presence in Vietnam meant. Sihanouk had led Cambodia since its independence from France in 1953. As American involvement in Vietnam deepened, Sihanouk realized that maintaining his rule would require a delicate balancing act. He could not afford to make enemies of either the USA or the Vietnamese communists.

When the Vietcong began to use areas inside Cambodia, particularly around the Ho Chi Minh trail, as a sanctuary from which to launch guerrilla attacks into South Vietnam, Sihanouk's position became increasingly precarious. Keeping the Vietnamese out by force was scarcely an option; his own army consisted of fewer than 30,000 poorly equipped troops. In comparison, by the end of 1964 the Vietnamese communists were fielding an army of roughly 180,000. Sihanouk's reluctance to move against the Vietnamese was strengthened by his conviction that the communists would eventually be victorious. But the 1966 national assembly elections showed a significant swing to the right, and General Lon Nol formed a new government, which lasted until 1967.

The leftists in Cambodia had originally concentrated on a political struggle against Sihanouk. By 1967, however, as it became clear that political opposition was both futile and increasingly dangerous, the Cambodian communists began to focus on armed struggle. They did not, however, constitute a serious threat to Sihanouk's regime. Even as late as 1969, the communists or the Khmer Rouge were estimated to have only about 2,500 troops.

The Khmer Rouge Party ceased to be anti-Sihanouk in public statements and became more anti-right or opposed to pro-American groups. This helped to raise support among the peasants in rural areas that had been bombed by the US military during their fight with Vietnam. However, in private, the party had not changed its view of him. In November, Pol Pot went again to Hanoi to ask for direct support of the Khmer Rouge. He was turned down and the Vietnamese even attempted to convince him to end his insurgency. He asked the Vietnamese about visiting North Korea and Laos. The Vietnamese turned down both requests, something that created a very bad impression with Pol Pot. The Vietnamese strongly suggested that he visit Moscow and cease his independent contact with the Chinese government.

During 1968 and 1969 political insurgency in Cambodia had worsened. In August 1969, General Lon Nol formed a new government – eventually he would overthrow Sihanouk. Sihanouk went abroad, to France, for medical reasons in January 1970. This was the point at which the road to power opened for Pol Pot and the Khmer Rouge. Sihanouk, safely out of the line of fire in Paris, ordered the government to stage anti-Vietnamese protests in the capital. The protesters quickly went out of control and wrecked the embassies of both North Vietnam and the Viet Cong. Sihanouk, who had actually ordered the protests, denounced them from Paris and blamed unnamed individuals in Cambodia for them. These actions, along with other intrigues by Sihanouk's followers in Cambodia, convinced the government that he should be removed as head of state. The National Assembly voted to remove Sihanouk from office.

The government, led by General Lon Nol, closed Cambodia's ports to Vietnamese weapons traffic and demanded that the Vietnamese leave Cambodia. For North Vietnam this could have been disastrous. The North Vietnamese reacted to the political changes in Cambodia by sending Premier Pham Van Dong to meet Sihanouk in China and recruit him into an alliance with the Khmer Rouge. Pol Pot was also contacted by the Vietnamese who now offered him whatever resources he wanted for his insurgency against the Cambodian government. Pol Pot and Sihanouk were actually in Beijing at the same time but the Vietnamese and Chinese leaders never informed Sihanouk of the presence of Pol Pot or allowed the two men to meet. Shortly afterwards, Sihanouk issued an appeal by radio to the people of Cambodia to rise up against the government and support the Khmer Rouge.

In May 1970, Pol Pot finally returned to Cambodia and the pace of the insurgency picked up. Earlier, on 29 March 1970, the Vietnamese had taken matters into their own hands and launched an offensive against the Cambodian army. In March 1970, while Sihanouk was absent, Prime Minister Lon Nol deposed Sihanouk and assumed power through a vote of the National Assembly. Son Ngoc Thanh announced his support for the new government. After the Lon Nol coup overthrew Sihanouk in 1970, he became a minister in the new government and put his Khmer Serei troops at its service. In 1972, he again became Prime Minister, but after being dismissed by Lon Nol, he exiled himself to South Vietnam. Thanh was arrested after the communist victory, and died in their custody in 1977.

On 9 October, the Cambodian monarchy was abolished, and the country was renamed the Khmer Republic. A force of 40,000 Vietnamese quickly overran large parts of eastern Cambodia reaching to within fifteen miles of Phnom Penh before being pushed back. In these battles the Khmer Rouge and Pol Pot played a very small role.

Pol Pot issued a resolution in the name of the central committee. The resolution stated the principle of independence mastery, which was a call for Cambodia to decide its own future independent of the influence of any other country. The resolution also included statements describing the betrayal of the Cambodian communist movement in the 1950s by the Viet Minh. This was the first statement of the anti-Vietnamese/self-sufficiency-at-all-costs ideology that would be a part of the Pol Pot regime when it took power years later.

Through 1971, the invading Vietnamese (North Vietnamese and Viet Cong) did most of the fighting against the Cambodian government, while Pol Pot and the Khmer Rouge functioned almost as auxiliaries to their forces. Pol Pot took advantage of the situation, to gather in new recruits and to train them to a higher standard than had previously been possible. Pol Pot also put many of the resources of the Khmer Rouge organization into political education and indoctrination. While accepting anyone regardless of background into the Khmer Rouge army at this time, Pol Pot greatly increased the requirements for membership of the party. The party now rejected students and so-called middle peasants. Those with clear peasant backgrounds were the preferred recruits for party membership. These restrictions were ironic in that most of the senior party leadership, including Pol Pot, came from student and middle peasant backgrounds. They also created an intellectual split between the educated old guard party members and the uneducated peasant new party members, which was very useful for Pol Pot's absolute control.

In early 1972, Pol Pot toured the insurgent/Vietnamese-controlled areas of Cambodia. He saw a regular Khmer Rouge army of 35,000 men taking shape supported by around 100,000 irregulars. China was supplying five million dollars a year in weapons and Pol Pot had organized an independent revenue source for the party in the form of rubber plantations in eastern Cambodia using forced labour.

After a central committee meeting in May 1972, the party under the direction of Pol Pot began to enforce new levels of discipline and conformity in areas under their control. Minorities such as the Chams were forced to conform to Cambodian styles of dress and appearance. (The Cham people are descendants of the ancient kingdom of Champa. Their population of approximately 100,000 is centred on the cities of Phan Rang and Phan Thiet in central Vietnam. Neighbouring Cambodia has the largest concentration of Chams where their numbers range from as low as half a million to perhaps as high as a million. The Cham people form the core of the Muslim communities in both Cambodia and Vietnam.) These policies, such as ones forbidding the Chams from wearing jewellery, were soon extended to the whole population. A haphazard version of land reform was undertaken by Pol Pot. Its basis was that all land holdings should be of uniform size. The party also confiscated all private means of transportation at this time. The 1972 policies were aimed at reducing the peoples of the liberated areas to a form of feudal peasant equality. These policies were generally favourable at the time to poor peasants and extremely unfavourable to refugees from towns who had fled to the countryside.

In 1972, the Vietnamese army forces began to withdraw from the fighting against the Cambodian government. They handed over the fighting to the Khmer Rouge army they had helped to train. Pol Pot issued a new set of decrees in May 1973 which started the process of reorganizing peasant villages into co-operatives where property was jointly owned and individual possessions banned.

The Khmer Rouge advanced during 1973. After they reached the edges of Phnom Phen, Pol Pot issued orders during the peak of the rainy season that the city be taken. The orders led to futile attacks and wasted lives among the Khmer Rouge army. By the middle of 1973, the Khmer Rouge under Pol Pot controlled almost two-thirds of the country and half the population. Vietnam realized that it no longer controlled the situation and began to treat Pol Pot more like an equal leader.

In the autumn of 1973, Pol Pot made strategic decisions about the future of the war. His first decision was to cut the capital, Phnom Phen, off from outside contact and effectively put the city under siege. The second decision was to enforce tight control on people trying to leave the city through the Khmer Rouge lines. The city people were considered almost a disease that needed to be contained so that it not infect the communist areas run by the Khmer Rouge.

He also ordered a series of general purges, in which most opposition were rounded up and killed. Former government officials and anyone with an education was singled out in the purges. A set of new prisons was also constructed in Khmer Rouge-run areas. The Cham minority attempted an uprising around this time against attempts to destroy their culture. While the uprising was quickly crushed, Pol Pot ordered that harsh physical torture be used against most of those involved in the revolt. As usual, Pol Pot tested out harsh new policies against the Cham minority before extending them to the general population of the country.

The Khmer Rouge had also created a policy of evacuating urban areas to the countryside. When the Khmer Rouge took the town Kratie in 1971, Pol Pot and other members of the party were shocked at how fast the liberated urban areas shook off socialism and went back to the old ways. Various ideas were tried to recreate the town in the image of the party, but nothing worked. In 1973, out of total frustration, Pol Pot decided that the only solution was to send the entire population of the town to the fields in the countryside. He wrote at the time, 'If the result of so many sacrifices was that the capitalists remain in control, what was the point of the revolution?' Shortly after, Pol Pot ordered the evacuation of the 15,000 people out of Kompong Cham for the same reasons. The Khmer Rouge then moved on in 1974 to evacuate the larger city of Oudong.

Internationally, Pol Pot and the Khmer Rouge were able to gain recognition as the true government of Cambodia from sixty-three countries. A move was made at the United Nations to give the seat for Cambodia to the Khmer Rouge. The government prevailed by two votes. Mostly, news of his purges and evacuations had not yet reached the rest of the world.

In September 1974, Pol Pot gathered the central committee of the party together. As the military campaign was moving towards a conclusion, Pol Pot decided to move the party towards implementing a socialist transformation of the country in the form of a series of decisions. The first one was that after their victory, the main cities of the country would be evacuated with the population moved to the countryside. The second was that money would cease to be put into circulation and would quickly be phased out. The final decision was the party's acceptance of Pol Pot's first major purge. In 1974, Pol Pot had purged a top party official named Prasith. Prasith was taken out into a forest and shot without any chance to defend himself. His death was followed by a purge of cadres who, like Prasith, were ethnically Thai. Pol Pot offered as explanation that the class struggle had become acute and that a strong stand had to be made against the enemies of the party.

The Khmer Rouge were positioned for a final offensive against the government in January 1975. At the same time, Sihanouk in Beijing proudly announced, at a press event, Pol Pot's 'death list' of enemies to be killed after victory. The list, which originally contained seven names, expanded to twenty-three, including all the senior government leaders along with the military and police leadership. The rivalry between Vietnam and Cambodia also came out into the open. North Vietnam, as the rival socialist country in Indochina, was determined to take Saigon before the Khmer Rouge took Phnom Penh. Shipments of weapons from China were delayed and in one instance the Cambodians were forced to sign a humiliating document thanking Vietnam for shipments of what were, in fact, Chinese weapons.

In April 1975, the government formed a Supreme National Council with a new leadership with the aim of negotiating surrender to the Khmer Rouge. The Supreme National Council was headed by Sak Sutsakhan. He had studied in France with

Pol Pot and was cousin to the Khmer Rouge deputy secretary Nuon Chea. Pol Pot's reaction to this was to add the names of everyone involved to his post-victory death list. Government resistance finally collapsed on 17 April 1975.

The Khmer Rouge captured Phnom Penh on 17 April 1975. A new government was formed and the name of the country was changed to Democratic Kampuchea. Phnom Penh was full of refugees from the war. The new government drove all the refugees into the countryside without regard for the human consequences of their actions. Pol Pot also drew up death lists of former government officials who were to be executed on sight.

Out of a population of approximately eight million people, Pol Pot's regime killed one quarter. The Khmer Rouge targeted Buddhist monks, Western-educated intellectuals, educated people in general, people who had contact with Western countries, people who appeared to be intelligent (for example, individuals with glasses), the crippled and lame, and ethnic minorities like Laotians and Vietnamese. Some were thrown into the infamous S-21 camp for interrogation involving torture in cases where a confession was useful to the government. Many others were subject to summary execution.

Immediately after the fall of Phnom Penh, the Khmer Rouge ordered the complete evacuation of Phnom Penh and all other recently captured major towns and cities. Those leaving were told that the evacuation was due to the threat of severe American bombing and it would last for no more than a few days.

Pol Pot and the Khmer Rouge had been evacuating captured urban areas for many years. The only thing unique about the evacuation of Phnom Penh was the scale of the operation. The first operations to evacuate urban areas occurred in 1968 in the Ratanskri area. Those operations were aimed at moving people deeper into Khmer Rouge territory to better control them. From 1971 to 1973, the motivation changed. Pol Pot and the other senior leaders were frustrated that urban Cambodians were retaining old habits like trade and business. When all other methods had failed, evacuation to the countryside was adopted to solve the problem. The return to the land was intended to purify the people as a whole and create a basis for a new communist society that would eventually return to modern technology.

In 1976 people were reclassified as full-rights (base) people, candidates and depositees – so called because they included most of the new people who had been deposited from the cities into the communes. Depositees were marked for destruction. Their rations were reduced to two bowls of rice soup, or 'juk' per day. This led to widespread starvation.

Hundreds of thousands of the new people, and later the depositees, were taken out in shackles to dig their own mass graves. Then the Khmer Rouge soldiers beat them to death with iron bars and hoes or buried them alive. A Khmer Rouge extermination prison directive had ordered, 'Bullets are not to be wasted.' These mass graves are often referred to as the Killing Fields.

The Khmer Rouge also classified by religion and ethnic group. They abolished all religion and dispersed minority groups, forbidding them to speak their languages or to practise their customs. These policies had been implemented in less severe forms for many years previous to the Khmer Rouge taking power.

According to Father Ponchaud's book *Cambodia: Year Zero*, 'Ever since 1972 the guerrilla fighters had been sending all the inhabitants of the villages and towns they occupied into the forest to live and often burning their homes, so that they would have nothing to come back to.' The Khmer Rouge refused offers of humanitarian aid, a decision that proved to be a humanitarian catastrophe: millions died of starvation and brutal government-inflicted overwork in the countryside. To the Khmer Rouge, outside aid went against their principle of national self-reliance.

Property became collective, and education was dispensed at communal schools. Children were raised on a communal basis. Even meals were prepared and eaten communally. Pol Pot's regime was extremely paranoid. Political dissent and opposition was not permitted. People were treated as opponents based on their appearance or background. Torture was widespread. In some instances, throats were slit as prisoners were tied to metal bed frames.

Thousands of politicians and bureaucrats accused of association with previous governments were killed. Phnom Penh was turned into a ghost city, while people in the countryside were dying of starvation and disease or were being executed.

Pol Pot aligned the country politically with the People's Republic of China and adopted an anti-Soviet line. This alignment was more political and practical than ideological. Vietnam was aligned with the Soviet Union so Cambodia aligned with the rival of the Soviet Union and Vietnam in south-east Asia. China had been supplying the Khmer Rouge with weapons for years before they took power.

In 1976, Sihanouk was placed under house arrest and Pol Pot became Prime Minister and the official Cambodian head of state, with colleague Khieu Samphan as President.

In December 1976, Pol Pot issued directives to the senior leadership to the effect that Vietnam was now an enemy. Defences along the border were strengthened and unreliable deportees were moved deeper into Cambodia. Pol Pot's actions were in response to the Vietnamese Communist Party's fourth congress, which approved a resolution describing Vietnam's special relationship with Laos and Cambodia. It also talked of how Vietnam would forever be associated with the rebuilding and defence of the other two countries.

In May 1977, Vietnam sent its air force into Cambodia in a series of raids. In July, Vietnam forced a Treaty of Friendship on Laos, that gave Vietnam almost total control over the country. In Cambodia, Khmer Rouge commanders in the eastern zone began to tell their men that war with Vietnam was inevitable and that once the war started their goal would be to recover parts of Vietnam (Khmer Krom) which had long ago been part of a Cambodian empire. It is not clear if these statements were the official policy of Pol Pot.

In September 1977, Cambodia launched division-scale raids over the border that once again left a trail of murder and destruction in villages. The Vietnamese claimed that around 1,000 people had been killed or injured. Three days after the raid, Pol Pot officially announced the existence of the formerly secret Communist Party of Kampuchea (CPK) and finally announced to the world that the country was a communist state.

In late 1978, in response to threats to its borders and the Vietnamese people, Vietnam invaded Cambodia to overthrow the Khmer Rouge. While Vietnam could justify the invasion on the basis of self-defence, it quickly became clear that Vietnam intended to stay in Cambodia and turn it into a dependent state similar to Laos. The Cambodian army was defeated, and Pol Pot fled to the Thai border area. In January 1979, Vietnam installed a new government under Heng Samrin, composed of Khmer Rouge who had fled to Vietnam to avoid the purges. Pol Pot eventually regrouped with his core supporters in the Thai border area where he received shelter and assistance. At different times during this period, he was located on both sides of the border. The military government of Thailand used the Khmer Rouge as a buffer force to keep the Vietnamese away from the border. The Thai military also made money from the shipment of weapons from China to the Khmer Rouge. Eventually Pol Pot was able to rebuild a small military force in the west of the country with the help of the People's Republic of China.

Vietnam used the existence of Pol Pot and the Khmer Rouge forces to justify their continued military occupation of the country. After the Vietnamese drove the Khmer Rouge from power in 1979, the Western powers refused to allow Vietnam's puppet regime to take the seat of Cambodia at the United Nations. The seat, by default, remained in the hands of the Khmer Rouge. Various countries considered that however bad allowing the Khmer Rouge to hold on to the seat was, recognizing Vietnam's occupation of Cambodia was worse.

Pol Pot officially resigned from the party in 1985, but

continued as de facto Khmer Rouge leader and dominant force within the anti-Vietnam alliance. He handed day-to-day power off to Son Sen whom he had picked as his successor. Opponents of the Khmer Rouge claimed that they were sometimes acting in an inhumane manner in territory controlled by the alliance, justifying it by pointing out that none of the forces fighting in Cambodia could be said to have clean hands. In 1986, his new wife Meas gave birth to a daughter named Sitha. Shortly afterwards, Pol Pot moved to China for medical treatment for cancer. He remained there until 1988.

Pol Pot ordered the execution of his life-long right-hand man Son Sen and eleven members of his family on 10 June 1997 for attempting to make a settlement with the government (the news did not reach outside of Cambodia for three days). Pol Pot then fled his northern stronghold, but was later arrested by Khmer Rouge military chief Ta Mok, and sentenced to life-long house arrest. In April 1998, following a new government attack, Ta Mok fled into the forest taking Pol Pot with him. A few days later, on 15 April 1998, Pol Pot died, reportedly of a heart attack. His body was burned in the Cambodian countryside, with several dozen Khmer Rouge in attendance.

It is unknown, even today, whether Pol Pot's death was, as reported, from natural causes or whether he was murdered by the very army he had helped to build.

Saddam Hussein

Saddam Hussein gained power over a nation riddled with profound tensions. Long before Saddam, Iraq had been split along social, ethnic, religious, and economic fault lines: Sunni versus Shi'ite, Arab versus Kurd, tribal chief versus urban merchant, nomad versus peasant. Stable rule in a country rife with factionalism required the improvement of living standards. Saddam moved up the ranks in the new government by aiding attempts to strengthen and unify the Ba'ath Party and taking a leading role in addressing the country's major domestic problems and expanding the party's following.

However, even as he rose to power through the Ba'ath Party, the Kurdish and Shia Muslim populations of Iraq hated him. They would eventually discover, disastrously for them, that the feeling was mutual.

Saddam was born in 1937, in Al Ouja, a village outside Takrit. He remains proud of his humble origin in a mud hut, in the middle of a poor, watermelon-growing Sunni Muslim community. Iraq is an overwhelmingly Muslim society, but as mentioned above, within it there are innumerable religious and tribal groups. Sunni Muslims, the majority orthodox doctrine of Islam, comprise only a fifth of Iraq's population. Saddam himself, nominally a Sunni, used religion only as a political tool, posing hypocritically as an Islamic hero in his efforts to present his opposition to the West as a holy war. His weaknesses for cigars, Scotch whisky and adultery (all banned under Islamic law) were too well known for the sight of him kneeling in prayer to be taken seriously.

His father, Hussein 'Abd al-Majid, died or disappeared six months before Saddam was born. The gossip was that he was illegitimate. As Saddam developed his later obsession with history, he would try to glamorize this rumour by claiming that he was the illegitimate child of the Iraqi Hashemite king, through which he traced his direct descent from the Prophet Mohammed himself. Shortly before he was born, Saddam's thirteen-year-old brother died of cancer, leaving his mother severely depressed in the final months of the pregnancy. Saddam's mother also tried to abort the baby by attempting suicide. The infant Saddam was sent to the family of his maternal uncle, Khairallah Talfah, until he was three, where he was generally very happy.

His mother remarried, and Saddam gained three half-brothers through this marriage. His stepfather, Ibrahim al-Hassan, treated Saddam harshly after his return to his maternal home. He was abusive, beat the boy remorselessly and forced the young boy to steal chickens and sheep for resale. With the shadow of his illegitimacy hanging over him, Saddam was something of an outcast in the custom-bound society of his village. It is said that he walked to school in Takrit with an iron bar to protect himself from the other boys.

He had only two allies, one was his cousin, Adnan Khairallah, who would eventually be rewarded for his kindness with a position in government as Defence Minister. Also protecting him was his uncle, Kharaillah Tulfah, who eventually became Governor of Baghdad. Although kind to Saddam, Tulfah was generally seen as a monstrous bigot who wrote a tract that there are 'three who God should not have created: Persians, Jews and flies'. Even Saddam's cousin, Adnan, would eventually die mysteriously in a helicopter crash, after complaining about Saddam's blatant infidelity to his wife, who was Adnan's sister.

At about the age of ten, Saddam fled the family and returned to live in Baghdad with his uncle, Kharaillah Tulfah. Tulfah, the father of Saddam's future wife, was a devout Sunni Muslim. Later in his life, relatives from Saddam's native Tikrit would become some of his closest advisers and supporters. According to Saddam, he learned many things from his uncle, who was a prominent leader in the failed 1941 Nazi-backed coup in Iraq. Especially significant to Saddam was the lesson that he should never back down from his enemies, no matter how superior their numbers or how capable their armies.

They were small-time gangsters, feared as local brigands. In his search for acceptance and prestige, Saddam was eventually drawn into their web of corruption, crime and murder. At the age of ten, Saddam's cousins gave him his first real possession, a revolver. In his teens he commited his first killings on Tulfah's behalf. By the 1950s, in Baghdad, he had a considerable reputation as a thug and an assassin.

He enrolled in law school, but crime kept him too busy to attend. Under the guidance of his uncle, he attended a nationalistic secondary school in Baghdad. In 1957, at the age of twenty, Saddam joined the revolutionary pan-Arab Ba'ath Party, of which his uncle was a supporter.

At the time it was a fledgling movement espousing the creation of a single Arab state. Anti-Western, anti-Persian and anti-Jewsish, it was a synthesis of Arab nationalism and socialism founded by a Syrian secondary school teacher, Michel Alfaq. Saddam became highly useful as a hit man and tough enforcer in the Ba'ath Party's violent opposition to the Hashemite monarchy. In 1958, a year after Saddam had joined the Ba'ath Party, army officers led by General Abdul Karim Qassim overthrew Faisal II of Iraq. The Ba'athists opposed the new government, and in 1959, Saddam was involved in the attempted United States-backed plot to assassinate Prime Minister Qassim.

Saddam Hussein was one of an eight-man hit squad selected for the task. They planned to shoot at Qassim's car as he drove between his house and his office at the Defence Ministry. When the plan finally went into operation on 7 October 1959, it was a total farce. One of the assassins was supposed to block the street and force Qassim's car to a halt. Unfortunately, he lost his keys, and while the would-be killers fell to arguing about whose fault it was, Qassim arrived at the designated spot. They managed to shoot the driver, but in the cross-fire, the successful marksman was then shot dead by his comrades. Several others, including Saddam, also wounded each other. The assassins hobbled off, convinced that some of the mass of flying lead must have hit Qassim. When Saddam came to power the debacle was rewritten as a great battle against overwhelming odds, in which Saddam, although grievously wounded, was the hero, pulling fragments of cannon-shell out of his leg with a pair of scissors. The doctor who actually treated him remembers a tiny superficial wound. Needless to say, the doctor later fled Iraq when he discovered a huge bomb under his car.

While his fellow assassins were rounded up, Saddam escaped to Syria and from there to Egypt. He was sentenced to death in absentia and he studied law at the University of Cairo during his exile. The Egyptians were generally sympathetic towards the Ba'ath Party, but distrusted the naked ambition of Saddam.

In 1950s Iraq, and indeed throughout the Middle East, revolutionary sentiment was characteristic of the era. The stranglehold of the old elites (the conservative monarchists, established families, and merchants) was breaking down in Iraq. Moreover, the populist pan-Arab nationalism of Gamal Abdel Nasser in Egypt would profoundly influence the young Ba'athist, even up to the present day. The rise of Nasser foreshadowed a wave of revolutions throughout the Middle East in the 1950s and 1960s, which saw the collapse of the monarchies of Iraq, Egypt, and Libya. Nasser challenged the British and French, nationalized the Suez Canal, and strove to modernize Egypt and unite the Arab world politically.

Army officers with ties to the Ba'ath Party overthrew Qassim in a bloody coup in 1963. Saddam returned as a gun-toting bodyguard on the right of the party. He won favour by his willingness to dispose of opponents by the most direct methods. He even offered to blow away the leader of the party's left faction. His offer was politely refused by Hassan-al-Bakr, his boss, who didn't want to set a precedent which he guessed he might subsequently fall victim to. However, the new government was torn by factionalism. The Ba'ath government were booted out of power by the army, disgusted at the violence and chaotic in-fighting. Abdul Rahman Arif briefly became ruler of the country and Saddam was imprisoned in 1964. He escaped from prison in 1967 and went underground. Going underground suited Saddam Hussein. This was the kind of electioneering he understood, proceeding via violence and intrigue. Saddam was apparently never without a machine gun and at least one revolver. In this environment, he flourished. Michel Alfaq thought his limited skills particularly appropriate to the Ba'ath's need for violence rather than diplomacy, and supported his claim to the position of secretary and, eventually, leader. The job was to be shared. It was an unprecedented appointment, as Saddam had no credentials and no experience, and was not accepted by the rest of the party. Saddam would have to resort to his customary methods to achieve power. His co-appointee, Abdel al Shaikhili, was later purged and murdered.

In 1966, Saddam seized the post of Deputy Secretary General at gunpoint, and began to build up a network of intimates, dependent upon him for favour. These were usually relatives, or failing that, from his home town of Tikrit. At this time, he was known to the public only as a lowly gunman, entirely uncultured, vulgar and with a complete absence of moral values. Yet, he had a growing fascination for history, particularly the great figures of the mythic Arab past, and began to see himself as a man of destiny, following in the footsteps of Nebuchadnezzar, the enslaver of Israel and Emperor of Babylon.

Ahmad Hassan al-Bakr, Saddam, and others overthrew Abdul Rahman Arif in the bloodless coup of 1968, again with the backing of the CIA. Hassan al-Bakr needed Saddam's sheer ruthlessness to create a Ba'athist state. Saddam became the real strongman, and was soon named deputy to the president, al-Bakr. According to biographers, Saddam never forgot the tensions within the first Ba'athist government, which informed his measures to promote Ba'ath Party unity as well as his ruthless resolve to maintain power and programmes to ensure social stability. Saddam was the power behind the throne, instrumental in implementing the policies of repression and terror that evolved. He established a 'Department of Internal Security', the official state torture service, run by Nadlum Kazar, a notorious psychopath who ran the central interrogation unit at Qasr al Nihayyah in Baghdad. It was there in 1973 that a survivor saw Saddam Hussein, Deputy President of Iraq, bodily pick up a still struggling prisoner and toss him into a vat of acid, watching fascinated as the wriggling man dissolved.

Saddam actively fostered the modernization of the Iraqi economy along with the creation of a strong security apparatus to prevent coups within the power structure and insurrections outside of it. Ever concerned with broadening his base of support among the diverse elements of Iraqi society and mobilizing mass support, he closely followed the administration of state welfare and development programmes.

At the centre of this strategy was Iraq's oil. On 1 June 1972, Saddam Hussein oversaw the seizure of international oil interests, which, at the time, had a monopoly on the country's oil. A year later, world oil prices rose dramatically as a result of the 1973 world oil shock, and skyrocketing revenues enabled Saddam to expand his agenda.

Within just a few years, Iraq was providing social services that were unprecedented among Middle Eastern countries. Saddam established and controlled the 'National Campaign for the Eradication of Illiteracy' and the campaign for 'Compulsory Free Education in Iraq'. Largely under his auspices, the government established universal free schooling up to the highest education levels; hundreds of thousands learned to read in the years following the initiation of the programme. The government also supported families of soldiers, granted free hospitalization to everyone who needed it, and gave subsidies to farmers. Iraq created one of the most modern public health systems in the Middle East, earning Saddam an award from the United Nations Educational, Scientific and Cultural Organization (UNESCO).

To diversify the oil-dependent economy, Saddam implemented a national infrastructure campaign that made great progress in building roads, promoting mining, and developing other industries. The campaign revolutionized Iraq's energy industries. Electricity was brought to nearly every city in Iraq, and many outlying areas.

Before the 1970s, most of Iraq's people lived in the countryside, where Saddam himself was born and raised, and roughly two-thirds were peasants. But this number would decrease quickly during the 1970s as the country ploughed much of its oil profits into industrial expansion.

Nevertheless, Saddam focused intensely on fostering loyalty to the Ba'athist government in the rural areas. After nationalizing foreign oil interests, Saddam supervised the modernization of the countryside, mechanizing agriculture on a large scale, and distributing land to peasant farmers. The Ba'athists established farm co-operatives, in which profits were distributed according to the labours of the individual and the unskilled were trained. The government's commitment to agrarian reform was demonstrated by the doubling of expenditures for agricultural development in 1974–75. Moreover, agrarian reform in Iraq improved the living standard of the peasantry and increased production, though not to the levels Saddam had hoped for.

Saddam became personally associated with Ba'athist welfare and economic development programmes in the eyes of many Iraqis, widening his appeal both within his traditional base and among new sectors of the population. These programmes were part of a combination of 'carrot and stick' tactics to enhance support in the working class, the peasantry, and within the party and the government bureaucracy.

Saddam's organizational prowess was credited with Iraq's rapid pace of development in the 1970s. Development went forward at such a fevered pitch that two million people from other Arab countries and from Yugoslavia worked in Iraq to meet the growing demand for labour.

In 1976, soon after becoming deputy president, Saddam demanded and received the rank of four-star general despite his lack of military training. At the time Saddam was considered an enemy of communism and radical Islam. Saddam was integral to US policy in the region, a policy that sought to weaken the influence of Iran and the Soviet Union. As Iraq's weak and elderly president Ahmed Hassan al-Bakr became increasingly unable to perform his duties, Saddam took on an increasingly prominent role as the face of the government both internally and externally. He soon became the architect of Iraq's foreign policy and represented the nation in all diplomatic situations. He was the de facto ruler of Iraq some years before he formally came to power in 1979. He slowly began to consolidate his power over Iraq's government and the Ba'ath Party. Relationships with fellow party members were carefully cultivated, and Saddam soon gained a powerful circle of support within the party.

The Ba'ath state that Saddam inevitably inherited on 16 July 1979 was well on the way to being run on the only emotional lines he understood, those of terror. He had systematically eradicated everyone who posed a threat, real or imagined, often with his own hands. Yet, unlike his over-enthusiastic sons, who regarded rape and torture as family perks, there seems little evidence that Saddam sadistically enjoyed killing people; for him it was simply a means to maintaining his power – all in a day's work.

In 1979 Iran's Shah, Mohammad Reza Pahlavi, was overthrown by the Islamic revolution, thus giving way to an Islamic republic led by the Ayatollah Khomeini. The influence of revolutionary Shi'ite Islam grew apace in the region, particularly in countries with large Shi'ite populations, especially Iraq. Saddam feared that radical Islamic ideas – hostile to his secular rule – were rapidly spreading inside his country among the majority Shi'ite population.

There had also been bitter enmity between Saddam and Khomeini since the 1970s. Khomeini, having been exiled from Iran in 1964, took up residence in Iraq, at the Shi'ite holy city of An Najaf. There he involved himself with Iraqi Shi'ites and developed a strong, worldwide religious and political following. Under pressure from the Shah, who had agreed to a rapprochement between Iraq and Iran in 1975, Saddam agreed to expel Khomeini in 1978.

After Khomeini gained power, skirmishes between Iraq and revolutionary Iran occurred for ten months over the sovereignty of the disputed Shatt al-Arab waterway, which divides the two countries. During this period, Saddam Hussein continually maintained that it was in Iraq's interest not to engage with Iran, and that it was in the interests of both nations to maintain peaceful relations. However, in a private meeting with Salah Omar Al-Ali, Iraq's permanent ambassador to the United Nations, he revealed that he intended to invade and occupy a large part of Iran within months. Iraq invaded Iran by attacking Mehrabad Airport of Tehran and entering the oil-rich Iranian land of Khuzestan, which also has a sizeable Arab minority, on 22 September 1980. Saddam declared Khuzestan a new province of Iraq. Thus began the Iran-Iraq War (1980–88).

In the first days of the war, there was heavy ground fighting around strategic ports as Iraq launched an attack on Khuzestan. After making some initial gains, Iraq's troops began to suffer losses from human wave attacks by Iran. By 1982, Iraq was on the defensive and looking for ways to end the war. During the war with Iran, with Iraq in pieces, Saddam, feeling insecure, suggested to his ministers that he might step down. Most took the hint, disagreed and began to flatter him as required. His health minister, Riaz Hussein, foolishly took him at his word and said he would be happy to accept Saddam's resignation. Saddam promptly dragged him into the next room, shot him and had his dismembered body returned to his wife in a carrier bag. As one former official said of Hussein: 'You quickly realize that he trusts absolutely no one. Everyone is a potential enemy. Sometimes you see him with children, and he is smiling and stroking their hair. That's because they are no threat to him.'

Iraq quickly found itself bogged down in one of the longest and most destructive wars of attrition of the twentieth century. During the war, Iraq used chemical weapons against Iranian forces and Kurdish separatists. On 16 March 1988, the Kurdish town of Halabja was attacked with a mix of mustard gas and nerve agents, killing 5,000 civilians, and maiming, disfiguring, or seriously debilitating 10,000 more. His intention was to depopulate Kurdistan, a traditional bastion of resistance, while attention was still on fighting at the front. By mid-1989, he had destroyed 4,000 Kurdish settlements. A British documentary film-maker managed to smuggle out conclusive evidence of the atrocities; bodies lay piled high in desolate villages, a film over their eyes and a horrible slime pouring out of their noses and mouths, their skin peeling and bubbling. An American senator tried to introduce a Prevention of Genocide Act, but Reagan's government quashed it, still thinking its interests lay in keeping Saddam sweet. The attack occurred in conjunction with the 1988 al-Anfal campaign designed to reassert central control of the mostly Kurdish population of areas of northern Iraq and defeat the Kurdish Peshmerga rebel forces. The United States maintains today that Saddam ordered the attack to terrorize the Kurdish population in northern Iraq, but Saddam's regime claimed at the time that Iran was responsible for the attack.

Saddam reached out to other Arab governments for cash and political support during the war, particularly after its oil industry suffered severely at the hands of the Iranian navy in the Gulf. Iraq successfully gained some military and financial aid, as well as diplomatic and moral support, from the United States, the Soviet Union, and France, which together feared the prospects of the expansion of revolutionary Iran's influence in the region. The Iranians, claiming that the international community should force Iraq to pay the casualty of the war to Iran, refused any suggestions for a ceasefire. They continued the war until 1988, hoping to bring down Saddam's secular regime and instigate a Shi'ite rebellion in Iraq.

The bloody eight-year war ended in a stalemate. There were hundreds of thousands of casualties, perhaps upwards of 1.7 million died on both sides. Both economies, previously healthy and expanding, were left in ruins. This didn't stop Saddam declaring himself the victor, and raising monuments and awarding himself an endless string of titles to prove it.

Under Saddam, torture became a customary experience, used not to extract information, but to remodel the very thoughts of the populace. Exacting confessions to non-existent crimes was a means of compelling victims to surrender their individuality, to accept without question the truth as represented by the state. In order to heighten the impression of the Ba'athist organization as omniscient and divine and to accept its leader by cultivating a sense of guilt within the people, the security services were anonymous and selected victims at random. No explanations were offered; the event was efficiently calculated to suggest unimaginable horrors. As Samir al Khali, Iraqi dissident and author wrote: 'The pattern is for agents to pick someone up from work, or at night from his house . . . what one assumes to be the corpse is brought back weeks or maybe months later and delivered to the family in a sealed box. A death certificate is produced for signature to the effect that the person has died of fire, swimming or other such accidents. Someone is allowed to accompany the police and box for a ceremony, but at no time are they allowed to see the corpse. The cost of proceedings is demanded from the family in advance.'

Acid baths were commonly used to make thousands of corpses disappear. Amnesty International detailed thirty methods of torture used in Iraq, from beatings to mutilation, from rape to electrocution, including the gouging out of eyes, the cutting off of noses, breasts, penises and limbs. Heavy metal poisoning was a favoured means of killing off undesirables. Lead and thallium were administered to prisoners in soft drinks during uneventful but deliberately prolonged interrogation. Children were routinely tortured to extract confessions from their parents. In 1985, three hundred children were held at

Fusailyya Prison, where they were whipped, sexually abused and given electric shocks. In order to assist their work, the security forces became master players of the rumour machine. They used it to create the enemy within and then to spread rumours of the horrendous punishments that traitors received. A constant stream of videos showing confessions, trials and executions were released to the public. Ba'ath officials were required to take part in executions and were filmed doing so, thus binding themselves together in responsibility with 'blood cement'.

It was with the application of this Mafia-style ideology of shared guilt that Saddam Hussein opened his account as president. A couple of nights after taking office, he hosted a dinner party for senior Ba'ath officials. After the meal, he casually suggested that they all jot down details of any meetings they might have had with two of their colleagues, Muhie Abdel Hussein and Mohammed Ayesb. He gave no explanation. The following day he informed the Ba'ath Revolutionary Council that the two named officials were the ringleaders of a plot to overthrow the regime. He also added that he was in possession of a complete list of their fellow conspirators. It included several of the highest ranking officials and a quarter of the Revolutionary Council. He read the list with crocodile tears falling down his face. The Ba'ath leadership was subsequently invited to where their former colleagues were now held. There, they were issued with guns, and, along with Saddam, formed the firing squad. The secret police stood behind them, to provide an added spur to their loyalty.

Iraq is potentially a prosperous country. It has vast oil reserves and healthy agricultural resources. Like many Middle Eastern nations its size, borders and very existence are a consequence of colonial influence and the two World Wars. The Ba'ath movement, which never exerted much influence outside Iraq except for a brief time Syria, had its roots in the desire for the collective Arab nation, so long kicked about by the colonial superpowers, to assert themselves as a force on the world stage. Since President Nasser of Egypt, the Arabs have looked for a strong representative and spokesman for all, not just the small, incredibly rich and pro-Western oil states, whose wealth is often bitterly resented among the poorer nations. It was this vacancy that Saddam Hussein had his eye on.

Saddam borrowed a tremendous amount of money from other Arab states during the 1980s to fight Iran and was stuck with a war debt of roughly $75 billion. Faced with rebuilding Iraq's infrastructure, Saddam desperately sought out cash once again, this time for post-war reconstruction. After the costly war with Iran, social unrest began to spread, and with a tide of several million soldiers slopping around the country, Saddam needed another national cause fast to preserve his position. He needed a real victory.

In order to further his plans against Israel, which he openly threatened to burn to destruction, he required money to buy conventional weapons and develop nuclear and biological ones. The need became greater after the Israelis, who have learned to take seriously what other countries dismiss as mere rhetoric, bombed his nuclear facilities. Saddam's theory for removing Israel was indicative of how little he valued human life. Israel's most precious resource is its people. It cannot afford to fight a long, attritional war, such as Saddam was fond of. In the course of such a war Israel would be drained of human life, immigration would dry up and the population would vanish, just as Saddam intended. The bombing of his nuclear facilities made this war too difficult to organize.

Saddam needed money and he had huge debts. To crown Saddam's problems, but also to provide him with the excuse he needed, the price of oil slumped and with it Iraq's income. He rounded on the Gulf oil-producing states, in particular Kuwait.

The end of the war with Iran served to deepen latent tensions between Iraq and its wealthy neighbour Kuwait. Saddam saw his war with Iran as having spared Kuwait from the imminent threat of Iranian domination. Since the struggle with Iran had been fought for the benefit of the other Gulf Arab states as much as for Iraq, he argued, a share of Iraqi debt should be written off. Saddam demanded that Kuwait write off the Iraqi debt accumulated in the war, some $30 billion, but the Kuwaitis refused, claiming that Saddam was responsible to pay off his debts for the war he started.

Also to raise money for post-war reconstruction, Saddam pushed oil-exporting countries to raise oil prices by cutting back oil production. Kuwait refused to cut production. In addition to refusing the request, Kuwait spearheaded the opposition in OPEC to the cuts which Saddam had requested. Kuwait was pumping large amounts of oil, and thus keeping prices low at a time when Iraq needed to sell oil from its own wells at a high price to pay off a huge debt.

Meanwhile, Saddam showed disdain for the Kuwait-Iraq boundary line (imposed on Iraq by British imperial officials in 1922) because it almost completely cut Iraq off from the sea. One of the few articles of faith uniting the political scene in a nation rife with sharp social, ethnic, religious and socio-economic divides was the belief that Kuwait had no right to even exist in the first place. For at least half a century, Iraqi nationalists were espousing emphatically the belief that Kuwait was historically an integral part of Iraq, and that Kuwait had only come into being through the manoeuvrings of British imperialism.

The colossal extent of Kuwaiti oil reserves also intensified tensions in the region. The oil reserves of Kuwait (with a population of a mere two million as opposed to Iraq's twenty-five million) were roughly equal to those of Iraq. Taken together, Iraq and Kuwait sat on top of some 20 per cent of the world's known oil reserves; Saudi Arabia, by comparison, holds 25 per cent.

The Kuwaiti monarchy further angered Saddam by allegedly slant-drilling oil out of wells that Iraq considered to be within its disputed border with Kuwait. Given that at the time Iraq was not regarded as a pariah state, Saddam was able to complain about the alleged slant-drilling to the US State Department. Although this had continued for years, Saddam now needed oil money to stem a looming economic crisis. Saddam still had an experienced and well-equipped army, which he used to influence regional affairs. He later ordered troops to the Iraq-Kuwait border.

As Iraq-Kuwait relations rapidly deteriorated, Saddam was receiving conflicting information about how the US would respond to the prospect of an invasion. For one, Washington had been taking measures to cultivate a constructive relationship with Iraq for roughly a decade. The US also sent billions of dollars to Saddam to keep him from forming a strong alliance with the Soviets. It has recently been revealed that George Bush Senior's administration were still supplying economic aid, intelligence and advanced weapons technology to 'the Butcher of Baghdad' two months before he invaded Kuwait.

US ambassador to Iraq April Glaspie met with Saddam in an emergency meeting on July 25 1990, when the Iraqi leader stated his intention to continue talks. US officials attempted to maintain a conciliatory line with Iraq, indicating that while George Bush Senior and James Baker did not want force used, they would not take any position on the Iraq-Kuwait boundary dispute and did not want to become involved. The transcript, however, does not show any explicit statement of approval of, acceptance of, or foreknowledge of the invasion. Later, Iraq and Kuwait then met for a final negotiation session, which failed.

On 2 August 1990, Saddam invaded and annexed the oil-rich emirate of Kuwait. US President George Bush Senior responded cautiously for the first several days after the invasion. On the one hand, Kuwait, prior to this point, had been a virulent enemy of Israel and was on friendly terms with the Soviets. On the other hand, Iraq controlled 10 per cent of the world's crude oil reserves and with the invasion had doubled the percentage. US interests were heavily invested in the region, and the invasion triggered fears that the price of oil, and therefore the world economy, was at stake. The United Kingdom was also concerned. Britain had a close historical relationship with Kuwait, dating back to British colonialism in the region, and also benefited from billions of dollars in

Kuwaiti investment. British Prime Minister Margaret Thatcher underscored the risk the invasion posed to Western interests to Bush in an in-person meeting one day after the invasion, famously telling him, 'Don't go wobbly on me, George.'

Co-operation between the United States and the Soviet Union made possible the passage of resolutions in the United Nations Security Council giving Iraq a deadline to leave Kuwait and approving the use of force if Saddam did not comply with the timetable. US officials feared that Iraq would retaliate against oil-rich Saudi Arabia, a close ally of Washington since the 1940s, for the Saudis' opposition to the invasion of Kuwait. Accordingly, the USA and a group of allies, including countries as diverse as Egypt, Syria and Czechoslovakia, deployed huge numbers of troops along the Saudi border with Kuwait and Iraq in order to encircle the Iraqi army, the largest in the Middle East.

During the period of negotiations and threats following the invasion, Saddam focused renewed attention on the Palestinian problem by promising to withdraw his forces from Kuwait if Israel would relinquish the occupied territories in the West Bank, the Golan Heights and the Gaza Strip. Saddam's proposal further split the Arab world, pitting US and Western-supported Arab states against the Palestinians. The allies ultimately rejected any connection between the Kuwait crisis and Palestinian issues.

Saddam ignored the Security Council deadline. With unanimous backing from the Security Council, a US-led coalition launched round-the-clock missile and aerial attacks on Iraq, beginning on 16 January 1991. Israel, though subjected to attack by Iraqi missiles, refrained from retaliating in order not to provoke Arab states into leaving the coalition. A ground force comprising largely US and British armoured and infantry divisions ejected Saddam's army from Kuwait in February 1991 and occupied the southern portion of Iraq as far as the Euphrates. Before leaving, Saddam ordered the oil wells across Kuwait to be torched.

On 6 March 1991, referring to the conflict, Bush announced:

'What is at stake is more than one small country. It is a big idea
– a new world order, where diverse nations are drawn together
in common cause to achieve the universal aspirations of
mankind: peace and security, freedom and the rule of law.'

In the end, the overmanned and under-equipped Iraqi army
proved unable to compete on the battlefield with the highly
mobile coalition land forces and their overpowering air
support. Some 175,000 Iraqis were taken prisoner and casualties were estimated at approximately 20,000 according to US
data, with other sources putting the number as high as 100,000.
As part of the ceasefire agreement, Iraq agreed to abandon all
chemical and biological weapons and allow UN observers to
inspect its weapon sites. UN trade sanctions would remain in
effect until Iraq complied with all terms.

The Iraqis were blocked from selling crude oil – their only
export commodity – in the hope that Saddam would be too
broke to reform his shattered army. The result, predictably, was
that he took money from wherever he could to rearm, leaving
his people desperately hungry and devoid of proper amenities
and even basic medicines. Iraq, having once boasted an
excellent medical service, soon had the world's highest
percentage of infant mortality. Not that this seemed to bother
the US or UN too much. Representatives openly admitted that
they hoped the unnecessary misery in Iraq would lead to
'regime change' – a successful revolution. It did not. For over
a decade Saddam remained defiant, sometimes deliberately
breaching the UN sanctions. The US continued to send cruise
missiles into Iraq in retaliation.

Iraq's ethnic and religious divisions, together with the
resulting post-war devastation, laid the groundwork for new
rebellions within the country. In the aftermath of the fighting,
social and ethnic unrest among Shi'a Muslims, Kurds, and
dissident military units threatened the stability of Saddam's
government. Uprisings erupted in the Kurdish north and Shi'a
southern and central parts of Iraq, but were ruthlessly
repressed. In 2005 the BBC reported that as many as 30,000
Iraqis had been killed during the 1991 uprisings.

The USA, which had urged Iraqis to rise up against Saddam, did nothing to assist the rebellions beyond enforcing the 'no fly zones'. US ally Turkey opposed any prospect of Kurdish independence, and the Saudis and other conservative Arab states feared an Iran-style Shi'a revolution. Saddam, having survived the immediate crisis in the wake of defeat, was left firmly in control of Iraq, although the country never recovered either economically or militarily from the First Gulf War. Saddam routinely cited his survival as 'proof' that Iraq had, in fact, won the war against America. This message earned Saddam a great deal of popularity in many sectors of the Arab world.

Saddam increasingly portrayed himself as a devout Muslim, in an effort to co-opt the conservative religious elements of society. Some elements of Sharia law were reintroduced (such as the 2001 edict imposing the death penalty for homo-sexuality, rape and prostitution, the legalization of 'honour killings' and the ritual phrase 'Allahu Akbar' ['God is the greatest'], in Saddam's handwriting, was added to the national flag).

US officials continued to accuse Saddam Hussein of violating the terms of the Gulf War's ceasefire, by developing weapons of mass destruction and other banned weaponry, refusing to provide adequate information on these weapons, and violating the UN-imposed sanctions and 'no fly zones'. Isolated military strikes on Iraq continued to be sporadically carried out by US and British forces, the largest being Operation Desert Fox in 1998. Charges of Iraqi obstruction of UN inspections of sites thought to contain illegal weapons were claimed as the reasons for crises between 1997 and 1998, culminating in intensive US and British missile strikes on Iraq between 16 and 19 December 1998. After two years of inter-mittent activity, US and British warplanes struck harder at sites near Baghdad in February 2001.

Iraqi co-operation with UN weapons inspection teams was questioned on several occasions during the 1990s and UNSCOM chief weapons inspector Richard Butler withdrew his team from Iraq in November 1998 citing Iraqi non-co-operation. He did this without the permission of the UN, although a UN spokesman subsequently stated that 'the bulk of' the Security Council supported the move. After a crisis had ensued and the US had contemplated military action against Iraq, Saddam resumed co-operation. The inspectors returned, but were withdrawn again on 16 December. Butler had given a report the UN Security Council on 15 December in which he expressed dissatisfaction with the level of compliance. Three out of five of the permanent members of the UN Security Council subsequently objected to Butler's withdrawal.

Saddam continued to loom large in American consciousness as a major threat to Western allies such as Israel and oil-rich Saudi Arabia, to Western oil supplies from the Gulf States, and to Middle East stability generally. US President Bill Clinton (1993–2001) maintained economic sanctions, as well as air patrols in the Iraqi 'no fly zones'. In October 1998, President Clinton signed the Iraq Liberation Act. The act called for 'regime change' in Iraq and authorized the funding of opposition groups. Following a UN report detailing Iraq's failure to co-operate with inspections, Clinton authorized Operation Desert Fox, a three-day air strike to hamper Saddam's weapons-production facilities and hit sites related to weapons of mass destruction. Iraq responded by expelling UN inspectors.

After al-Qaeda attacked the USA on 11 September 2001, it was suspected that Iraq had become an important source of support for terrorists and that weapons of mass destruction were being manufactured and stockpiled there. Added to this were rumours of terrorist training camps and this is when the seeds of 'Operation Iraqi Freedom' were sown. Several journalists have reported on Saddam's ties to anti-Israeli and Islamic terrorism prior to 2000. Saddam is also known to have had contacts with militant Palestinian groups. Early in 2002, Saddam told Faroq al-Kaddoumi, head of the Palestinian political office, that he would raise the sum granted to the family of each Palestinian who dies as a suicide bomber in the fight against Israel from $10,000 to $25,000. Some news reports detailed links to terrorists, including Carlos the Jackal, Abu Nidal, Abu Abbas and Osama bin Laden. However, no conclusive evidence whatsoever concerning links between Saddam and bin Laden's al-Qaeda organization has ever been produced by any US government official. The official assessment by the US intelligence community is that friendly contacts between Saddam Hussein and al-Qaeda over the years did not lead to a collaborative relationship, although the issue is still being debated in some circles. Commenting on the Operation Iraqi Freedom documents, the former 9/11 Commission member Bob Kerrey, 'was careful to say that new documents translated last night by ABC News did not prove Saddam Hussein played a role in any way in plotting the attacks of September 11 2001'. As reported by Eli Lake, however, he contended that one of the documents shows that 'Saddam was a significant enemy of the United States'. The document in question, ABC cautioned, 'is hand-written and has no official seal, and does not establish that the two parties did in fact enter into an operational relationship'.

On 4 April 2003, satellite channels worldwide broadcast footage of the besieged Iraqi leader touring the streets of his bombed capital. Smoke was emanating from oil fires in the distance. As US-led ground troops were marching towards the capital, a smiling Saddam Hussein was being greeted by cheering, chanting crowds in the streets of Baghdad.

The domestic political situation changed in the USA after the 11 September 2001 attacks, which bolstered the influence of the neo-conservative faction in the presidential administration and throughout Washington. Bush and his cabinet repeatedly linked the Saddam government to the 11 September attacks on the basis of an alleged meeting in Prague in April 2001 involving an Iraqi intelligence agent and other evidence. Both a Senate select committee and the 9/11 Commission failed to uncover convincing evidence of such a link. In his January 2002 State of the Union address to congress, President George W. Bush spoke of an 'axis of evil' comprising Iran, North

Korea and Iraq. Moreover, Bush announced that he would possibly take action to topple the Iraqi government. Bush stated, 'The Iraqi regime has plotted to develop anthrax, and nerve gas, and nuclear weapons for over a decade.' 'Iraq continues to flaunt its hostility toward America and to support terror,' he added.

As the war was looming on 24 February 2003, Saddam Hussein talked with CBS News anchor Dan Rather for more than three hours – his first interview with any US reporter in over a decade. CBS aired the taped interview later that week.

The Iraqi government and military collapsed within three weeks of the beginning of the US-led invasion of Iraq on 20 March 2003. The United States made at least two attempts to kill Saddam with targeted air strikes, but both failed to hit their target, killing civilians instead. By the beginning of April, coalition forces had occupied much of Iraq. The resistance of the much-weakened Iraqi army either crumbled or shifted to guerrilla tactics, and it appeared that Saddam had lost control of Iraq. He was last seen in a video that purported to show him in the Baghdad suburbs surrounded by supporters. When Baghdad fell to the coalition on 9 April, Saddam was still preparing to leave.

As the US forces were occupying the Republican Palace and other central landmarks and ministries on 9 April, Saddam Hussein had emerged from his command bunker beneath the Al A'Zamiyah district of northern Baghdad and greeted excited members of the local public. In the BBC *Panorama* programme 'Saddam on the Run' witnesses were found for these and other later events. This impromptu walkabout was probably his last and his reasons for doing what was certainly extremely dangerous and almost cost him his freedom, if not his life, are unclear. It is possible that he wished to take what he thought might be his last opportunity to greet his people as their president. The walkabout was captured on film and broadcast several days after the event on Al-Arabiya Television and was also witnessed by ordinary people who corroborated the date afterwards. Bodyguards and other loyal supporters including at least one of his sons and his personal secretary accompanied him.

After the walkabout Saddam returned to his bunker and made preparations for his family. According to his eldest daughter, Raghad Hussein, he was by this point aware of the 'betrayal' of a number of key figures involved in the defence of Baghdad. It appears there was a lot of confusion between Iraqi commanders in different sectors of the capital and communication between them and Saddam and between Saddam and his family were becoming increasingly difficult. This version of events is supported by the former information minister Muhammad Saeed al-Sahhaf. At the time, he was referred to by the West as 'Baghdad Bob' and 'Comical Ali' due to his consistent denials that US and British forces had made any progress towards Baghdad, even when they were actually there. Even the former information minister struggled to know what was actually happening after the US captured Baghdad International Airport.

The Americans had meanwhile started receiving rumours that Saddam was in Al A'Zamiyah and at dawn on 10 April they dispatched 300 US marines to capture or kill him. As the Americans closed in, and realizing that Baghdad was lost, Saddam arranged for cars to collect his eldest daughters Raghad and Rana and drive them to Syria. His wife Sajida Talfah and youngest daughter Hala had already left Iraq several weeks beforehand. Raghad Hussein stated in an interview for *Panorama*: 'After about midday my dad sent cars from his private collection for us. We were told to get in. We had almost lost contact with my father and brothers because things had got out of hand. I saw with my own eyes the [Iraqi] army withdrawing and the terrified faces of the Iraqi soldiers who, unfortunately, were running away and looking around them. Missiles were falling on my left and my right – they were not more than fifty or one hundred metres away. We moved in small cars. I had a gun between my feet just in case.'

Then according to the testimony of a former bodyguard, Saddam Hussein dismissed almost his entire staff: 'The last time I saw him he said: "My sons, each of you go to your homes." We said, "Sir, we want to stay with you. Why should we go?" But he insisted. Even his son, Qusay, was crying a little. He [Saddam] was trying not to show his feelings. He was stressed but he didn't want to destroy the morale of the people who were watching him, but inside, he was definitely broken.' After this Saddam changed out of his uniform and with only two bodyguards to protect him, he left Baghdad in a plain white Oldsmobile and made his way to a specially prepared bunker in Dialah on the northern outskirts of the city.

Ayad Allawi in interview stated that Saddam stayed in the Dialah bunker for three weeks as Baghdad and US forces occupied the rest of Iraq. Initially he and his entourage used satellite telephones to communicate with each other. As this became more risky they resorted to sending couriers with written messages. One of these couriers was reported to have been his nephew. However, their cover was given away when one of the couriers was captured and Saddam was forced to evacuate the Dialah bunker and resorted to changing location every few hours. There were numerous sightings of him in Beiji, Baquba and Tikrit to the north of Baghdad over the next few months as he shuttled between safe houses disguised as a shepherd in a plain taxi. How close he came to being captured during this period may never be made public. Sometime in the middle of May he moved to the countryside around his home town of Tikrit.

A series of audio tapes claiming to be from Saddam were released at various times, although the authenticity of these tapes remains uncertain.

Saddam Hussein was at the top of the 'most-wanted list', and many of the other leaders of the Iraqi government were arrested, but extensive efforts to find him had little effect. In June a joint raid by special operations forces and the 1st Battalion, 22nd Infantry Regiment of 1st Brigade and the 4th Infantry Division captured the former president's personal secretary Abid Hamid Mahmud, the Ace of Diamonds and number four on the most wanted list after Saddam and his sons

Uday and Qusay. Documents discovered with him enabled intelligence officers to work out who was who in Saddam's circle. The cooks, the bodyguards, the drivers, and photographs proved a goldmine. One photograph, taken just two years beforehand, showed a row of bodyguards lined up with Saddam, who is looking every inch the Mafia don. One by one the Americans put names to faces, found their homes, then they planned to catch them. Manhunts were launched nightly throughout the Sunni triangle. Safe houses and family homes were raided as soon as any tip came in that someone in Saddam's circle might be in the area.

In July 2003, in an engagement with US forces after a tip-off from an Iraqi informant, Saddam's sons were cornered in a house in Mosul and killed.

According to one of Saddam's bodyguards, the former president actually went to the grave himself on the evening of the funeral: 'After the funeral people saw Saddam Hussein visiting the graves with a group of his protectors. No one recognized him and even the car they came in wasn't spotted. At the grave Saddam read a verse from the Koran and cried. There were flags on the graves. After he finished reading, he took the flags and left. He cried for his sons.'

This story, however unlikely, at least provides an explanation for the missing flags, which did, indeed, disappear after the burial. The commander of the 1st Battalion, 22nd Infantry Regiment, in Tikrit and Auja, where the sons were buried, had the cemetery heavily guarded. According to the American military, US forces removed the flags to prevent Saddam's sons being honoured as martyrs. These flags are now to be found at the National Infantry Museum at Fort Benning, Georgia.

The raids and arrests of people known to be close to the former president drove him deeper underground. Once more the trail was growing cold. In August the US military released photofits of how Saddam might be disguising himself in traditional garb, with grey hair, and even without his signature moustache. By the early autumn the Pentagon had also formed a secret unit – Taskforce 121. Using electronic surveillance and undercover agents, the CIA and Special Forces scoured Iraq for clues. Their orders were clear, to capture or kill high value target number one, Saddam Hussein.

By the beginning of November, Saddam was under siege. His hometown and powerbase were surrounded and his faithful bodyguards targeted and then arrested one by one by the Americans. The noose was tightening day by day. Protests erupted in several towns in the Sunni triangle. Meanwhile some Sunni Muslims showed their support for Saddam.

On 12 December, Mohamed Ibrahim Omar al-Musslit was unexpectedly captured in Baghdad. Mohamed had been a key figure in the president's special security organization. The 1st Battalion, 22nd Infantry Regiment, in Tikrit, had captured his cousin Adnan in July. It appears Mohamed had taken control of Saddam on the run; he was the only person who knew where he was from hour to hour and who was with him. According to US sources it took just a few hours 'interrogation' for him to crack and betray Saddam.

Within hours Colonel James Hickey (1st Brigade, 4th Infantry Division) together with US Special Operations Forces launched Operation Red Dawn and under cover of darkness made for the village of ad-Dawr on the outskirts of Tikrit. The informer had told US forces the former president would be in one of two groups of buildings on a farm codenamed Wolverine 1 and Wolverine 2.

On 14 December 2003, the Islamic Republic News Agency (IRNA) of Iran first reported that Saddam Hussein had been arrested, citing Kurdish leader Jalal Talabani. Other members of the Governing Council, US military sources and UK Prime Minister Tony Blair soon confirmed these reports. In a press conference in Baghdad, shortly afterwards, the US civil administrator in Iraq, Paul Bremer, formally announced the capture of Saddam Hussein by saying, 'Ladies and gentlemen, we got him.' Bremer reported that Saddam had been captured at approximately 8.30 p.m. Iraqi time on 13 December, in an underground 'spider hole' bunker at a farmhouse in ad-Dawr near his home town Tikrit, in what was called Operation Red Dawn. Bremer presented video footage of Saddam in custody.

Saddam Hussein was shown with a full beard and hair longer and curlier than his familiar appearance, which a barber later restored. His identity was later reportedly confirmed by DNA testing. He was described as being in good health and as 'talkative and co-operative'. Bremer said that Saddam would be tried, but that the details of his trial had not yet been determined. Members of the Governing Council who spoke with Saddam after his capture reported that he was unrepentant, claiming to have been a 'firm but just ruler'. Later it emerged that the tip-off that had led to his capture had come from a detainee under interrogation.

Shortly after his capture, Saddam Hussein was shown on a Department of Defence video on Al-Jazeera receiving a medical examination.

According to US military sources, immediately after his capture on 13 December Saddam was hooded and his hands were bound. He was taken by a military vehicle to a waiting helicopter and then flown to the US base located in and adjacent to one of his former palaces in Tikrit. At this base he was paraded before jubilant US soldiers and a series of photographs were taken. After a brief pause he was loaded onto another helicopter and flown to the main US base at Baghdad International Airport and transferred to the Camp Cropper facility. Here he was photographed officially and had his long beard shaved. The next day members of the Iraqi Governing Council, including Ahmed Chalabi and Adnan Pachachi, visited him in his cell. It is believed that he has been kept at this high security location for most of the time since his capture. Details of his interrogation are unknown.

During his first appearance before the Iraqi Special Tribunal, on 30 June 2004, Saddam Hussein (held in custody by US forces at Camp Cropper in Baghdad) and eleven senior Ba'athist officials were handed over to the interim Iraqi government. The purpose of this was for Saddam to stand trial for war crimes, crimes against humanity and genocide.

Particular attention has been paid in the trial to his activities in violent campaigns against the Kurds in the north during the Iran-Iraq War, and against the Shi'ites in the south during the revolts of 1991 and 1999.

The aftermath of this war was, and still is, terrible. Even though Saddam Hussein was finally captured, the seemingly endless killing of Iraqi civilians, caught in the crossfire between occupation troops and Islamic militants, who have also turned on their fellow Iraqis, has horrified the world.

The Butcher of Baghdad may have gone, but the agonies of Iraq's 'regime change' have spawned countless new butchers.

Up to the time of going to press there have been the following developments in the trial of Saddam Hussein's trial.

On 1 July 2004, the first legal hearing in Saddam's case was held before the Iraqi Special Tribunal. Broadcast later on Arabic and Western television networks, it was his first appearance in footage aired around the world since his capture by US forces the previous December.

On 17 June 2005, the former Malaysian prime minister, Mahathir Mohamad, announced the formation, under his joint chairmanship, of an international Emergency Committee for Iraq, with the main objective of ensuring fair trials for Saddam Hussein and the other former Ba'ath Party officials being tried with him.

On 18 July 2005, Saddam was charged by the Special Tribunal with the first of the expected series of charges, relating to the mass killings of the inhabitants of the village of Dujail in 1982 after a failed assassination attempt against him.

On 8 August 2005, the family announced that the legal team had been dissolved and that the only Iraq-based member, Khalil al-Duleimi, had been made sole legal counsel.

On 19 October 2005, Iraqi authorities put Saddam Hussein back on trial – four days after the 15 October referendum on the new constitution. The trial was adjourned until 28 November.

On 8 November 2005, Adel al-Zubeidi, a defence attorney during the Saddam Hussein trials on the legal team representing Taha Yassin Ramadan, was killed.

On 28 November 2005, Chief Judge Rizgar Mohammed Amin adjourned the trial until 5 December to allow time to find replacements for two defence lawyers who were slain and another who fled Iraq after he was wounded.

On 5 December 2005, Saddam's legal defence team stormed out of the court after questioning its legitimacy and asking about security issues regarding the protection of the defence. Saddam along with his co-defendants railed against Chief Judge Amin and the tribunal.

On 6 December 2005, Saddam Hussein shouted that he would not return 'to an unjust court' when it convenes for a fifth session the following day. At the end of the session, when the judges decided to resume the trial the next day, Saddam suddenly shouted as the judges left: 'I will not attend an unfair trial' and added, 'Go to hell!'

On December 21 2005, Saddam Hussein claimed in court that Americans had tortured him during his detention 'everywhere on [his] body' and that he had bruises as proof. None were seen, however.

On 23 January 2006, Rauf Rashid Abd al-Rahman was nominated interim chief judge of the tribunal. He replaced former chief judge Rizgar Amin, also a Kurd, who resigned after complaining of government interference.

On 15 March 2006, Saddam was called by the prosecution as a witness. On the stand, he made several political statements, saying he was still the president of Iraq and calling on Iraqis to stop fighting each other and to fight American troops instead. The judge turned off Saddam's microphone and closed the trial to the public in response.

Iraqi prosecutors recommended on 19 June 2006 that Saddam receive the death penalty together with his brother Barzan al-Tikriti and former Vice-President Taha Yassin Ramadan.

On 21 June 2006, Khamis al-Obeidi was found shot to death, after ten men wearing Iraqi police uniforms kidnapped him and drove him off in Iraqi police vehicles. He was the chief defence attorney for Saddam Hussein and his brother Barzan Ibrahim al-Tikriti.

228

Also on 21 June, it was reported that Hussein had begun a hunger strike in protest at the assassination of his lawyer Khamis al-Obeidi.

On 23 June, a US official reported that Saddam had ended his hunger strike after missing only one meal.

On 25 June 2006, Khalil al-Dulaimi, Saddam's chief lawyer, gave an interview with the Associated Press in which he quoted Saddam as saying the following: 'These puppets in the Iraqi government that the Americans brought to power are helpless. They can't protect themselves or the Iraqi people. The Americans will certainly come to me, to Saddam Hussein's legitimate leadership and to the Iraqi Ba'ath Party, to rescue them from their huge quandary.' According to the Associated Press, al-Dulaimi indicated that Saddam may wish to negotiate a role in ending the Iraq insurgency by making the verdict in his trial a bargaining chip. There are no indications, however, that the US or the Iraqi government is seeking help from Saddam to end the insurgency.

On 27 June 2006, two of Saddam Hussein's lawyers, Ramsey Clark, a former US Attorney-General, and Curtis Doebbler, held a press conference at the National Press Club in Washington DC, to call for immediate security for all the Iraqi defence lawyers. They also made a lengthy complaining and documented statement of the unfair trial being conducted by the American authorities, using Iraqis as a front. The two lawyers claimed that the United States had refused to provide adequate protection for the defence lawyers despite repeated requests that were made and that the United States was intentionally ensuring an unfair trial.

On 13 July 2006, it was reported that Saddam and 'other former regime members' had begun another hunger strike on 7 July to protest the lack of fairness in their trial including the murder of defence lawyer Khamis al-Obeidi.

On 21 July 2006, an open letter to the American people from Saddam Hussein was released by his lawyers to the media. The letter dated 7 July urged Americans to 'Save your country and leave Iraq'.

On 23 July 2006, it was reported that Saddam had been taken to hospital where he was being fed by a tube as a result of his hunger strike.

Robert Mugabe

In recent years, Mugabe has emerged as one of Africa's most controversial leaders. His critics accuse him of being a 'corrupt dictator', and an 'extremely poor role model' for the continent. In 1980, when Robert Mugabe became Prime Minister of the former British colony of Rhodesia, now called Zimbabwe, approximately 70 per cent of the country's arable land was owned by approximately 4,000 descendants of white settlers. However, he reassured white landowners that they had nothing to fear from black majority rule. This was not exactly the truth. Mugabe accepted a 'willing buyer, willing seller' plan as part of the Lancaster House Agreement of 1979, among other concessions to the white minority. As part of this agreement, land redistribution was locked up for a period of ten years. In order not to hamper the South African ANC in its negotiations with the apartheid regime, land reform was to remain an issue on the backburner until the ANC came to power in 1994. By then, Robert Mugabe had become Executive President of Zimbabwe and declared that he intended to govern until he was one hundred years old.

British occupation of the area began in the 1890s, under the leadership of Cecil Rhodes, after whom the area was renamed Rhodesia. Britain granted Rhodesia self-governing colony status with responsible government in 1923. What this meant was that there was a local parliament, but that London retained some powers (notably relating to African political

231

advancement). Southern Rhodesia (as it was called then) was ruled via the Dominions Office rather than the Colonial Office, although, strictly speaking, the country was not a Dominion (like Canada, Australia, South Africa, etc.), because London still had a large say in its future. However, like many African 'colonies' at the time, the country was originally split more along tribal lines, than national ones. There are two main tribes in Zimbabwe: the dominant Shona, to which Mugabe belongs, and the Ndebele. Other tribes, such as the Lemba and the Karanga Bantu, also lay claim to what was once the ancient kingdom of Great Zimbabwe.

Robert Mugabe was raised at Kutama Mission, Zvimba District, north-west of Harare (then called Salisbury), in what was then British-controlled Southern Rhodesia. He was raised as a Roman Catholic and was educated in Jesuit schools. He qualified as a teacher at the age of seventeen, but left to study for a BA in English and History at Fort Hare University in South Africa, graduating in 1951, where he met contemporaries such as Julius Nyerere, Herbert Chitepo, Robert Sobukwe and Kenneth Kaunda. Mugabe holds several honorary degrees and doctorates from various universities around the world, although many of them are in the process of being rescinded. From 1958 to 1960, Mugabe taught in Ghana, where he became interested in Marxism and African nationalism. It was there that he met Sally Hayfron, who later became his first wife.

Sally Mugabe was well respected and died in 1992 from a chronic kidney ailment (their only son died aged four, while Mugabe was in prison). In 1962, she was active in mobilizing African women to challenge Ian Smith's Rhodesian constitution, which resulted in her own imprisonment. When she became Zimbabwe's First Lady in 1980, she served as deputy secretary and later as secretary of the ZANU Women's League. She also founded the Zimbabwe Child Survival Movement. Sally Mugabe launched the Zimbabwe Women's Co-operative in the UK in 1986 and supported Akina Mama wa Africa, a London-based African women's organization focusing on development and women's issues in Africa and the UK. On her death she was buried in the National Heroes Acre in Harare, Zimbabwe.

From 1953 to 1963, Southern Rhodesia was part of the Federation of Rhodesia and Nyasaland. The federation fell apart in 1963 when Northern Rhodesia gained independence from the UK as Zambia and Nyasaland gained independence as Malawi. Southern Rhodesia reverted to its status as a crown colony in Britain, but was now known as Rhodesia.

In Rhodesia, from the 1960s onwards, the formation of a number of political parties along with sporadic acts of sabotage came about as a result of African impatience with the pace of reforms and then in opposition to increased repression. Mugabe returned to Southern Rhodesia in 1960, where he became publicity secretary for the National Democratic Party (NDP). Led by Joshua Nkomo, the NDP was a nationalist political party that opposed white rule in the colony. After the NDP was banned in 1961, Mugabe became secretary general of Nkomo's new party, the Zimbabwe African People's Union (ZAPU), which was also soon banned due to its opposition to white rule. Mugabe broke with Nkomo and ZAPU in 1963 and helped form the more radical Zimbabwe African National Union (ZANU) with Ndabaningi Sithole. He soon became the secretary general of the banned ZANU. In 1964, he was arrested for his political activities and detained by the Rhodesian authorities along with other nationalist leaders, Joshua Nkomo and Edson Zvobgo, for ten years. Mugabe studied law during his time in prison, receiving degrees from the University of South Africa and the University of London by correspondence. While imprisoned Mugabe remained an extremely popular nationalist figure, and many ZANU members came to support him as leader of the party instead of Sithole.

ZANU was influenced by the Africanist ideas of the Pan Africanist Congress in South Africa and by Maoism, while ZAPU was an ally of the African National Congress and was a supporter of a more orthodox pro-Soviet line on national liberation. On his release, Mugabe left Rhodesia for Mozambique in 1974 and led the Chinese-financed military ZANU army, the Zimbabwe African National Liberation Army (ZANLA), in the war against Ian Smith's government.

On 18 March 1975, Chitepo (the leader of the Zimbabwe African National Union) was killed by a car bomb in Zambia. Kenneth Kaunda's government blamed ZANLA commander Josiah Tongogara. He was arrested and Mugabe unilaterally assumed control of ZANU from Mozambique. Later that year, after squabbling with Ndabaningi Sithole, Mugabe formed a militant ZANU faction, leaving Sithole to lead the moderate Zanu (Ndonga) Party, which renounced violent struggle, unlike Mugabe's more militant faction.

In the late 1970s, South African prime minister B. J. Vorster, under pressure from Henry Kissinger, forced Ian Smith to accept in principle that white minority rule could not continue indefinitely. On 3 March 1978, Bishop Abel Muzorewa, Ndabaningi Sithole and other moderate leaders signed an agreement at Governor's Lodge in Salisbury. The United African National Council won the elections under Bishop Abel Muzorewa, but international recognition did not follow and sanctions were not lifted. The two 'Patriotic Front' groups under Mugabe and Joshua Nkomo refused to participate and continued the war.

The incoming government did accept an invitation to talks at Lancaster House in September 1979. A ceasefire was negotiated for the talks, which were attended by Smith, Mugabe, Nkomo, Edson Zvobgo and others. The Lancaster House Agreement was the independence agreement for Rhodesia, now known as Zimbabwe. It was signed on 21 December 1979. The agreement effectively ended the white rule in Rhodesia under Ian Smith; it was signed between the Patriotic Front (PF), consisting of ZAPU (Zimbabwe African Peoples Union) and ZANU (Zimbabwe African National Union) and the Zimbabwe Rhodesia government, represented at that time by Bishop Abel Muzorewa and Smith.

Eventually the parties to the talks agreed on a new

constitution for a new Republic of Zimbabwe with elections to be held in February 1980. Mugabe had to concede to accepting twenty seats reserved for whites in the new parliament and to the inability of the new government to alter the constitution for ten years. His return to Zimbabwe in December 1979 was greeted with jubilation by enormous crowds.

After a campaign marked by intimidation from all sides, but especially from the white minority at the time, the Shona majority was decisive in electing Mugabe to head the first government as prime minister on 4 March 1980. ZANU won fifty-seven out of eighty Common Roll seats in the new parliament, with the twenty white seats all going to the Rhodesian Front. An observer at the time wrote: 'the harassment and intimidation practised by the security forces, the police and auxiliaries against ZANU-PF and to a lesser extent against Nkomo's Patriotic Front (PF) did not work as expected. We were told again and again by local ZANU-PF leaders that the strong-arm methods of the military forces of the government would turn the people against the party favoured by the white minority, the UANC. Of course, this is, in fact, what happened.'

Mugabe, whose political support came from his Shona-speaking homeland in the north, attempted, initially, to build Zimbabwe on a basis of an uneasy coalition with his Zimbabwe African People's Union (ZAPU) rivals, whose support came from the Ndebele-speaking south, and with the white minority. Mugabe sought to incorporate ZAPU into his ZANU-led government and ZAPU's military wing into the army. ZAPU's leader, Joshua Nkomo, was given a series of cabinet positions in Mugabe's government. Mugabe then improved health and education for the black majority as agreed under the Lancaster House Agreement. However, Mugabe was torn between this objective and pressures to meet the expectations of his own ZANU followers for a faster pace of social change. Zimbabwe was a seriously divided country at independence in 1980. Ten years of war had not only served to liberate Zimbabwe, but had created divisions within it. Mugabe knew he had to find a way of keeping order.

In October 1980, Prime Minister Mugabe signed an agreement with the North Korean President, Kim Il Sung, that they would train a brigade for the Zimbabwean army. This was soon after Mugabe had announced the need for a militia to 'combat malcontents'. However, there was very little civil unrest in Zimbabwe at this time. In August 1981, 106 Koreans arrived to train the new brigade, which Mugabe said was to be used to 'deal with dissidents and any other trouble in the country'. Even by August 1981, there had been very little internal unrest. Joshua Nkomo, leader of the mostly Ndebele-led PF Party, asked why this brigade was necessary, when the country already had a police force to handle internal problems. He suggested, in a way that was eerily prophetic, that Mugabe would use it to build a one-party state.

Mugabe replied by saying that dissidents should 'watch out', and further announced that the brigade would be called 'Gukurahundi', a Shona word meaning 'the early rain which washes away the chaff before the spring rains'. The chaff (hundi) remains after the corn has been removed during the process of threshing. In post-independent Zimbabwe, the term 'gukurahundi' is a euphemism used for the actions of Robert Mugabe's Fifth Brigade in the Ndebele provinces of Matabeleland and the Midlands during the early to late 1980s. Between 1982 and 1985 the Fifth Brigade brutally crushed any resistance in Matabeleland, fought by Ndebele groups. Over 20,000 civilians died and were buried in mass graves.

The members of the Fifth Brigade were drawn from 3,500 ex-ZANLA troops at Tongogara Assembly Point, named after Josiah Tongogara, the general of Zanla, the militant wing of Mugabe's ZANU during the revolutionary war. There were a few ZIPRA troops in the unit for a start, but they were withdrawn before the end of the training. It seems there were also some foreigners in the unit, possibly Tanzanians. The training of the Fifth Brigade lasted until September 1982, when Minister Sekeramayi announced training was complete. The first commander of the Fifth Brigade was Colonel Perence Shiri (who currently commands the air force). The Fifth Brigade was different from all other army units in that it was not integrated into the army. It was answerable only to the Prime Minister (then Robert Mugabe), and not to the normal army command structures. Their codes, uniforms, radios and equipment were not compatible with other army units. Their most distinguishing feature in the field was their red berets, although many reports note that Fifth Brigade soldiers would sometimes operate in civilian clothes. The Fifth Brigade seemed to be a law unto themselves once in the field.

By early 1982 there were groups of bandits in Matabeleland. Armed men were killing, robbing and damaging property. The government responded by launching a double attack in Matabeleland. The first attack was on the dissidents, and the army units used were the Fourth Brigade, the Sixth Brigade, the Paratroopers, the CIO and the Police Support Unit. The second attack was on ZAPU and its unarmed civilian supporters, mainly in rural areas and at times in the cities. The units used for this second, undeclared conflict, were the Fifth Brigade, the CIO, the PISI and the ZANU-PF Youth Brigades. The government's attitude was that the two conflicts were one and the same, and that to support ZAPU meant to support the dissidents. ZAPU denied that it was supporting dissidents. Whatever the truth of this, it is clear that thousands of innocent civilians in Matabeleland were killed or beaten and had their houses burned during these years, mostly by government forces. Skeletons have been taken out of mine shafts at Antelope Mine in Matobo, and at Old Hat Mine in Silobela in the Midlands, together with coins showing that the victims had been killed after independence. In 1983, bodies were also taken from a mass grave at Cyrene Mission in Matobo. These bodies at Cyrene showed clear evidence of gunshot wounds.

It is not surprising, therefore, that when many Zimbabweans think about the Zimbabwean Defence Forces, they are more likely to associate soldiers and their leaders with corruption and violence against Zimbabwean citizens than they are with the maintenence of peace and the defence of Zimbabwe's borders.

An abortive ZAPU rebellion headed by Nkomo, and discontent in Matabeleland, spelled the end of this uneasy coalition. In 1983, Mugabe dismissed Nkomo from his cabinet, which triggered bitter fighting between ZAPU supporters in the Ndebele-speaking region of the country and the ruling ZANU. Between 1982 and 1985, the military brutally crushed armed resistance from Ndebele groups in the provinces of Matabeleland and the Midlands, leaving Mugabe's rule secure. Mugabe has been accused of committing mass murder during this period of his rule, killing any opposition to his government, with the UK government turning a blind eye. A peace accord was negotiated in 1987, resulting in ZAPU's merger (1988) into the Zimbabwe African National Union-Patriotic Front (ZANU-PF). Mugabe brought Nkomo into the government once again as vice-president.

In 1987, the position of prime minister was abolished, and Mugabe assumed the new office of executive president of Zimbabwe, gaining additional powers in the process. He was re-elected in 1990 and 1996, and, amid claims of widespread vote-rigging and intimidation, in 2002. Today, he operates with dictatorial powers, and has stated that he intends to govern until he is one hundred years old. He is the Chancellor of the 'flagship' University of Zimbabwe and all the other state universities.

In 1991, amid international pressure and short on hard currency, Zimbabwe embarked on a neo-liberal austerity programme, but the International Monetary Fund suspended aid, claiming that the reforms were 'not on track'. The international world had begun to worry about the policies and behaviour of this 'self-elected' executive president, and had begun to deny any funds to Mugabe because his 'reforms' had long since stopped being on humanitarian terms.

At the same time he was pursuing a 'moral campaign' against homosexuals. According to Mugabe homosexuals are 'less than pigs and dogs'. He also calls homosexuality a 'white disease'. This made what he deemed 'unnatural sex acts' illegal with a penalty of up to ten years in prison. The seriousness of this offence was made public with several high-profile arrests including his predecessor as president of Zimbabwe, Canaan Banana, who was convicted of gay sex offences, and sentenced to a ten-year prison term.

Mugabe was also criticized for Zimbabwe's poorly justified participation in the Second Congo War in the Democratic Republic of the Congo at a time when the Zimbabwean economy was struggling. The Democratic Republic of the Congo had been invaded by Rwanda, who were seeking to institute a change of government, and Uganda claimed that its civilians, and regional stability, were under constant threat of attack by various Congo-based terrorist groups. Mugabe threw his support behind the existing Kabila government in Congo. The war raised accusations of corruption, with officials alleged to be plundering the Congo's mineral resources. President Robert Mugabe was the most ardent supporter of intervention on Kabila's behalf, lured by Congo's rich natural resources and a desire to increase his own power and prestige in Africa. Kabila and Mugabe had signed a US$200 million contract involving corporations owned by Mugabe and his family, and there were several reports in 1998 of numerous mining contracts being negotiated with companies under the control of the Mugabe family.

During Mugabe's rule, social policies enacted by the regime can be seen to have had a negative impact on the population. According to the latest statistics from the World Health Organization (WHO), Zimbabweans have the shortest life expectancy in the world: thirty-seven years for men and thirty-four years for women. Zimbabwe also has the highest rate of year-on-year inflation in the world, estimated in late May 2006 by Imara Asset Management Group to be approaching 2,000 per cent. One example of a large price rise occurred on 24 April 2006, when public hospital fees rose by more than 2,700 per cent.

By 1997, the 'willing buyer, willing seller' land reform programme broke down after the new British government, led by Tony Blair, decided unilaterally to stop funding it. With the Labour Party gaining power and old imperial values being set aside, members of his government felt themselves under no obligation to continue paying white farmers compensation. Or, in minister Clare Short's words, 'I should make it clear that we do not accept that Britain has a special responsibility to meet the costs of land purchase in Zimbabwe. We are a new government from diverse backgrounds without links to former colonial interests. My own origins are Irish and as you know we were colonised not colonisers.'

On 11 February 2000, a referendum was held on a new constitution. The proposed change would have limited future presidents to two terms, but as it was not retroactive, Mugabe could have stood for another two terms. It would also have made his government and military officials immune from prosecution for any illegal acts committed while in office. In addition, it allowed the government to confiscate white-owned land for redistribution to black farmers without compensation. It was defeated, after a low 20 per cent turnout, by a strong urban vote, fuelled by an effective text message campaign.

Mugabe declared that he would 'abide by the will of the people'. The vote was a surprise to ZANU-PF, and an embarrassment before parliamentary elections due in mid-April. Ignoring the referendum results, almost immediately self-styled 'war veterans', led by Chenjerai 'Hitler' Hunzvi, began invading white-owned farms. On 6 April 2000, parliament pushed through an amendment, taken word for word from the draft constitution that was rejected by voters, allowing the seizure of white-owned farmlands without due reimbursement or payment. Also, now Mugabe could rule for as long as he wished.

Within this context, it is clear that the Zimbabwean government decided to move forward unilaterally with land reform outside of the 'willing buyer, willing seller' framework. As of September 2006, Mugabe's family owns three farms: Highfield Estate in Norton, 45km west of Harare, Iron Mask Estate in Mazowe, about 40km from Harare, and Foyle Farm in

Mazowe, formerly owned by Ian Webster and adjacent to Iron Mask Farm, renamed Gushungo Farm after Mugabe's own clan name. Since Mugabe began to redistribute white-owned landholdings, he has faced harsh attacks, externally mostly from Western countries including Zimbabwe's former colonial power the United Kingdom, the USA and Australia, and internally from trade unions and urban Zimbabweans, who overwhelmingly supported the opposition Movement for Democratic Change.

Mugabe faced Morgan Tsvangirai of the Movement for Democratic Change (MDC) in presidential elections in March 2002. Amid accusations of violence and claims that large numbers of citizens in anti-Mugabe strongholds had been prevented from voting, Mugabe defeated Tsvangirai by 56 per cent to 42 per cent. The Zimbabwean registrar-general Tobaiwa Mudede declared that Mr Mugabe had won a fifth term in office after the results from all 120 constituencies were returned. He said that Mr Mugabe had won 1,685,212 votes against 1,258,401 for challenger Morgan Tsvangirai, leader of the Movement for Democratic Change (MDC).

Mugabe was helped by an unprecedented turnout of 90 per cent in his rural stronghold of Mashonaland (55 per cent of the population voted overall), although there were credible claims that the turnout may have been rigged. When election observers from South Africa claimed at a press conference that they had found no evidence of vote rigging, the assembled press burst out with laughter.

After the election result on 4 march 2002, the European Union planned to extend the range of sanctions against Zimbabwe, targeting more members of the leadership. Earlier in the year, the EU imposed a travel ban on Mr Mugabe and nineteen members of his regime and froze their overseas assets. Two years before his first wife Sarah Mugabe's death, Mugabe had married his former secretary Grace Marufu. She was forty years his junior. Grace Marufu Mugabe gave birth to three children: Bona, Robert Peter Jr and Bellarmine Chatunga. As first lady, she has been the subject of much criticism, both nationally and internationally, for her luxurious lifestyle. When she was included in the 2002 European Union travel sanctions on her husband, one EU parliamentarian was quoted as saying that the ban 'will stop Grace Mugabe going on her shopping trips in the face of catastrophic poverty blighting the people of Zimbabwe'.

When the 2002 election results were announced, Mugabe's opponent Mr Tsvangirai is reported to have said: 'We foresaw electoral fraud but not daylight robbery. We find ourselves unable to endorse the purported election of President Robert Mugabe as Zimbabwe's president in this election. It's the biggest election fraud I've witnessed in my life . . . the people need to lead the way, whether passively or not. We seek no confrontation with the state because that's what they want. But the people themselves have to decide what action to take.'

In Harare's townships people stood in line for two days to vote in the belief that they were consigning Mr Mugabe to history. Angry Zimbabweans looked to Mr Tsvangirai to confront the government.

One young voter from Harare who was an MDC supporter is reported to have said, 'We need Tsvangirai to tell Mugabe he cannot steal this election. The soldiers have guns so we cannot fight him but we can make sure he cannot rule us. We must strike, we must march, we must show that we are not goats.'

The government, sensing murmurs of revolt, put the army on full alert, deployed troops in key townships and the police set up roadblocks on the main roads into Harare to stop and search vehicles for weapons. Around 5.8 million people, out of Zimbabwe's population of almost 12 million, are registered to vote. However, up to 3.4 million Zimbabweans who live overseas – many of whom are believed to be opposition supporters – are barred from voting.

On 9 March 2003, US President George W. Bush approved measures for economic sanctions to be levelled against Mugabe and numerous other high-ranking Zimbabwean politicians, freezing their assets and barring Americans from engaging in any transactions or dealings with them. Justifying the move, Bush's spokesman stated that the president and congress believe that 'the situation in Zimbabwe endangers the southern African region and threatens to undermine efforts to foster good governance and respect for the rule of law throughout the continent'. The bill was known as the Zimbabwe Democracy Act and was deemed 'racist' by Mugabe.

On 3 July 2004, a report adopted by the African Union (AU) executive council, which comprises foreign ministers of the fifty-three member states, criticized the government. The AU had sent a mission to Zimbabwe from 24 to 28 June 2002, shortly after the presidential elections.

Zimbabwe was criticized for the arrest and torture of opposition members of parliament and human rights lawyers, the arrests of journalists, the stifling of freedom of expression and clampdowns on other civil liberties. The African Union congress accepted the report.

More parliamentary elections were held in Zimbabwe on 31 March 2005. The elections were said to 'reflect the free will of the people of Zimbabwe' by the South African observers, despite accusations of widespread fraud from the MDC.

By now the fraud was visible to the entire world. All of the 120 elected seats in the 150-seat parliament were up for election. The ruling Zimbabwe African National Union-Patriotic Front Party (ZANU-PF) of President Robert Mugabe won the elections with an increased majority against the opposing Movement for Democratic Change (MDC). ZANU-PF won seventy-eight seats to the MDC's forty-one, with one independent. (At the 2000 elections, ZANU-PF had won sixty-two seats to the MDC's fifty-seven.) According to the Zimbabwe Election Commission, ZANU-PF polled nearly 60 per cent of the vote, an increase of 11 per cent over the 2000 results. The MDC's vote fell 9 per cent to 39 per cent. ZANU-PF now has a two-thirds majority in the legislature, allowing the government to change the constitution.

Pius Ncube, the Roman Catholic Archbishop of Bulawayo,

led a consortium of Christian faiths opposed to Mugabe. Ncube has won human rights awards for opposing the alleged torture and starvation used as a political weapon by the Mugabe government. In 2005, Ncube has called for a 'popular mass uprising' in the style of the Orange Revolution or Tulip Revolution to remove Mugabe from power.

On 8 April 2005, Mugabe defied the European Union travel ban, because it does not apply to Vatican City, by attending the funeral of Pope John Paul II. He was granted a transit visa by the Italian authorities, as they are obliged to under the Concordat.

In May 2005, Mugabe and his government attracted unprecedented international criticism, including greater Church condemnation than ever before, when over two hundred thousand people from urban areas were left homeless due to their homes being bulldozed as part of Operation Murambatsvina. While Mugabe's government has translated this to mean 'Operation Clean-up', the more literal translation, in Shona, of 'murambatsvina' is 'getting rid of the filth'. It covered the entire country of Zimbabwe. Every day, in every urban part of the nation, the people awoke to find more buildings fallen around them and more families displaced. Families had their homes and possessions ruthlessly burned to the ground, or were given a few hours to remove what they could save before bulldozers came in to demolish entire structures. Estimates, to date, of the displaced vary from 300,000 to over a million, and hundreds of thousands more have lost their sources of income in the informal sector.

The government, under the auspices of the Ministry of Small and Medium Enterprises Development, began by arresting 20,000 vendors countrywide, destroying their vending sites, and confiscating their wares. Thousands more escaped arrest, but have lost their livelihoods. Harare, the capital, was among the worst affected cities: police action was brutal and unannounced. Sculpture parks along the main roads, which have been there for decades, were smashed. Beautiful works of art on roadside display, created out of stone, wood and metal, some standing up to two metres high, were smashed. Within days, bulldozers had moved in to take away the remains of these works of art. Vendors, who had been operating in the same places without complaint or interference for their entire working lives, were confronted with riot squads without any warning, rounded up, arrested, and had to watched helplessly while their source of livelihood was destroyed. Their wares were taken by the police, and were sold off through 'auctions' in which the police bought goods worth hundreds of thousands of dollars for a few dollars. These auctions were not open to the general public, and there was no process of highest bidder, any minor offer was accepted. No records or receipts were kept during this process. Police were also reported to be selling goods stolen by them from vendors directly to the public.

In the city of Bulawayo, over 3,000 licensed vendors had their stalls and wares totally demolished by police riot squads. In the same city, Fort Street Market, developed earlier by Minister John Nkomo, was also forcibly closed and people selling there were arrested and had their goods, including imported electrical goods and clothing, taken.

As well as outlawing all forms of vending, the government also pursued other small and medium enterprises. Blocks of apartments housing tailors, hairdressers, plumbers and so on were raided, tenants thrown out and their enterprises shut down as illegal.

It was the destruction of housing that caused the most immediate and unrelenting hardship. Literally thousands of dwellings were bulldozed, displacing people on a massive scale. Not even in apartheid South Africa were close to half a million people ever forcibly relocated in the space of a few weeks. It is difficult to estimate how many houses have been knocked down, but in Harare, entire suburbs have disappeared. In addition, in every street of every suburb, cottages and structures in back yards were taken down, leaving lodgers without accommodation.

In Victoria Falls, 3,368 houses were knocked down, and photographs and interviews by independent observers show that in most cases these were not casual dwellings but proper houses built out of concrete blocks with corrugated iron roofs. Six kilometres of vending stands that had been used to sell carvings to tourists for the last three decades were also torched to the ground. It is estimated that more than 20,000 people were displaced, in a tiny town with fewer than a 100,000 residents. In Beit Bridge, more than a hundred dwellings were knocked down, and, again, vending stands destroyed.

Across the length and breadth of Zimbabwe, families were seen sleeping under trees or on pavements, trying to protect small children, the elderly and the ill, from winter weather and thieves, with no access to sanitary facilities, and nowhere to cook or store food properly. From tiny babies, only days old, to old people on their deathbeds, thousands were left homeless and forced to sleep outside. In the bus stations families sat hopelessly next to furniture and building materials salvaged from the onslaught, waiting in vain for buses prepared to carry the loads to rural areas. Those with trucks struggled to access scarce diesel, which at that time cost up to Z$50,000 per litre, when the official price was Z$4,000 per litre; those with fuel charged extortionate rates to move desperate families short distances. People were sent to remote, rural areas without jobs, without food, without furniture and without houses where they would be at the mercy of a ZANU-PF-dominated rural leadership to whom they would have to appeal for a space to live.

The government made no contingency plans whatsoever to move people, or to create new housing for them. The deliberate destruction of homes in a nation that already faced unemployment, hunger and collapsing resources, was nothing short of wicked. Zimbabwe had become a nation of internally displaced people, with its own citizens becoming refugees within their own country's borders.

Observers have speculated that this policy was retributive. Most of the MDC's forty-one parliamentary seats were in urban constituencies. Mugabe's aim was to displace MDC supporters from urban centres into rural areas where they would be forced to toe the line by a powerful ZANU-PF-supporting traditional leadership, which controls access to communal resources. The prospect for democracy in Zimbabwe seems increasingly grim.

Some African leaders have condemned Mugabe: Archbishop Pius Ncube, the Roman Catholic Archbishop of Bulawayo in Zimbabwe; Archbishop Desmond Tutu, who has called Mugabe 'a caricature of an African dictator'; writer Wole Soyinka who has called Mugabe's regime 'a disgrace to the continent'; and Botswana's president, Festus Mogae, who distanced himself from the SADC statement opposing the commonwealth suspension of Zimbabwe. Mugabe has also been condemned by Western non-governmental organizations such as Amnesty International, who charge him with committing human rights abuses against minority Ndebeles, the opposition MDC, white landowners and homosexuals.

Yet, although President Mugabe encounters considerable opposition from the West, he has some supporters in the developing world. Mugabe retains considerable popularity throughout Africa. For example, in 2004 the monthly magazine *New African* had its readers vote for the '100 Greatest Africans'. Mugabe came third, behind only Nelson Mandela and Ghanaian independence hero Kwame Nkrumah. In addition, in December 2005, Kenneth Kaunda, Zambia's former long-time leader, voiced support for Mugabe, stating that the Zimbabwean president 'would pull through because he enjoyed the support of ordinary Zimbabweans who were punished for claiming back their land'. Mugabe's supporters tend to dismiss much of the criticism as being racially motivated, and characterize it as being little more than the bitter remarks of those who have been disadvantaged by his policies.

Still, those 'disadvantaged' by Mugabe's policies run into the hundreds of thousands, and most are not white, and if the recent election results, and their aftermath, are anything to go by, he is not that popular in his own country. Yet, he is still in power – and will perhaps remain there until he is one hundred years old – for he is able to remake the constitution as he wishes and his hundred-year mark is only thirteen years away.